THE
THE MAN OF GOD

THE PRIEST
THE MAN OF GOD
HIS DIGNITY AND HIS DUTIES

By
St. Joseph Cafasso

Translated from the Italian by
Rev. Patrick O'Connell, B.D.

"The Lord hath sworn, and he will not repent: Thou art a priest for ever according to the order of Melchisedech."
—Psalm 109:4

TAN Books
Charlotte, North Carolina

DEDICATED BY THE TRANSLATOR AND HIS BROTHER
TO THE MEMORY
OF THEIR DEAR PARENTS.

Nihil Obstat: Jacobus Mitchell
                  Censor Deputatus

Imprimatur: ✠ Michael Browne
                  Episcopus Galviensis

TAN Books
Charlotte, North Carolina
1979

TABLE OF CONTENTS

———

                                                                    PAGE

FOREWORD : vii

PREFACE BY : Canon Allamono, nephew of the Saint ix

INTRODUCTION : Short Life of the Saint xi

FIRST CONFERENCE : The Nature of the Office of the
    Priesthood 1

SECOND CONFERENCE : The Dispositions necessary to
    become a Good Priest 19

THIRD CONFERENCE : Modesty 36

FOURTH CONFERENCE : Flight from the World 52

FIFTH CONFERENCE : The Priest must be a man of Prayer 67

SIXTH CONFERENCE : Delicacy of Conscience 82

SEVENTH CONFERENCE : The Spirit of Religion 98

EIGHTH CONFERENCE : (1) The Priest's Recreations 114

    (2) Concerning Games and Public Spectacles 130

NINTH CONFERENCE : The Zeal of a Priest 141

TENTH CONFERENCE : Good Example 152

ELEVENTH CONFERENCE : Preaching 164

TWELFTH CONFERENCE : The Ministry of Confession 180

THIRTEENTH CONFERENCE : The Qualities of a Confessor . . 194

FOURTEENTH CONFERENCE : The Way to Hear Confessions . . 209

FIFTEENTH CONFERENCE : The Priest Devoted to Mary . . . 224

SIXTEENTH CONFERENCE : The Comforts and Consolations
    of a Priest 238

CONCLUSION 255

FOREWORD

The English translation of this work by S. Joseph Cafasso, *The Priest the Man of God : His Dignity and His Duties,* which we now present to the public is intended as a companion volume to *The Sacred Heart and the Priesthood* published by us in 1947. Both books treat of the same subject: The dignity of the priest, his duties and the virtues with which he should be adorned, and each book throws light on the other.

The two panegyrics of St. Joseph Cafasso by St. John Bosco under the title, *A Saint speaks for another Saint,* recently published by us are intended as an introduction to the present volume.

Readers who may wish to have a fuller account in English of the life and work of St. Joseph Cafasso will find it in *Walk while you have Light: The story of St. Joseph Cafasso, the Priests' Priest,* published by the Grail last year. Two other volumes of the Saint's sermons remain for publication: the first is *The Spiritual Exercises for Priests,* the second, *The Spiritual Exercises for the Laity.* English translation of these two volumes are in preparation and will be published as soon as possible.

Our thanks are due to the Consolata Fathers of Fatima who kindly lent us the 1925, 1947 and 1955 Italian editions of this book, all of which have been consulted. They also lent us the two volume life of the Saint by Fr. Luigi Nicholis de Robilant from which the short account of the Saint given as introduction to this volume was complied.

PATRICK O'CONNELL
8th September, 1958

PREFACE

Preface to the first edition of the Conferences of St. Joseph Cafasso to the clergy by his nephew Canon Allamano, Founder of the Missionary Institute of Consolata.

On the 23rd June 1860, Don Joseph Cafasso, Rector of the Ecclesiastical College for Priests and Prefect of Conference on Moral Theology, died in the odor of sanctity. Taken away at the early age of forty-nine, his sacerdotal career, judged by earthly standards, was of short duration, but, judged by the amount of work accomplished, it was long and fertile. By his prodigious activity, in a short time, he accomplished such a vast amount of work, and the luminous example of the virtues of his sacerdotal ministry has left such a profound impression, that even today all who have known him are filled with wonder, and his name resounds and is blessed not only in Turin but in all Piedmont.

More precise information about his heroic labors and eminent virtues will be found in a book now in preparation and soon to be published (The work in two vols. by Fr. Luigi Nicholis de Robilant). In this book will be found a detailed account of his many-sided labors: of his work as professor of moral and pastoral theology to the young priests; of his frequent courses of spiritual exercises to the clergy; of the exercise of the priestly ministry in the confessional, by the bedside of the dying, in the prisons and even on the scaffold for those condemned to death. An account also will be found in the beneficent and salutary influence he exercised over the Piedmont clergy in most difficult times; of the part he played in the foundation of the many charitable institutions of Turin of his time; and above all of his eminent virtues and supernatural gifts which merited for him from his contemporaries the title of Model of Priests.

Not the least proof of the extraordinary activity, thanks to which in a few years he did so much good, are the numerous manuscripts of moral theology and sermons. Among the latter are several courses of Meditations and Instructions for the Spiritual Exercises of the Clergy which he preached for many consecutive years in the Sanctuary of St. Ignatius at Lanzo.

These conferences, being now deprived of the heat and life which they received from the voice and gestures of the sacred orator, appear but a pallid image of those memorable Meditations which, according to our celebrated Canon Giordano, moved profoundly the coldest hearts and left an indelible impression on those who heard them even once. Nevertheless, as they are the fruit of long meditation and display an accurate and profound judgment, they will always remain remarkable for their wealth of ideas and fullness of treatment, for the soundness and precision of moral teaching and, much more, for the practical observations and applications, so original and appropriate that they penetrate to the very depths of the heart and touch its most intimate fibers.

All this is expressed with a simplicity, warmth and unction that reveal a most pious soul and heart inflamed with zeal for the sanctification of souls. But although in literary form they may be somewhat deficient and would require retouching and correction, I did not think that such should be done lest the charm that was proper to the servant of God in both speaking and writing should be obscured.

I am confident that the presentation of this course of Meditations, which will be followed by the corresponding Instructions to my venerable colleagues in the priesthood, will be both pleasing and useful ; and that it will be able to cooperate in some way in the good done by my venerable uncle and predecessor in his providential and beneficial Mission to the Clergy.

Turin, 20th June 1892.
Canon Joseph Allamano,
Rector of the Ecclesiastical College
of Consolata.

Introduction

The little book recently published by us entitled "*A Saint speaks for another Saint*" giving an account of the life and work of St. Joseph Cafasso by St. John Bosco was intended as an introduction to the volumes we are now publishing. We recommend that this little book or the larger life of our Saint entitled "*Walk while you have Light,*" published by the Grail, be procured and read to make the reader acquainted with the author of these conferences.

For the benefit of those who may not be able to procure either of these books, we give here the following brief account of the life and work of the Saint.

He was born on the 15th January, 1811 at Castelnuovo d'Asti, now Castelnuovo Don Bosco, in the Province of Piedmont about twenty miles from Turin. He had as contemporaries two other Saints who, like him, exercised their apostolate in the city of Turin: St. Joseph Cotelengo, who was twenty-five years his senior, and St. John Bosco, who was only a little more than three years his junior. St. Joseph Cotelengo was the founder of the famous hospital at Turin, which has now ten thousand inmates and has existed for over a century, without bank account or funds, depending on Divine Providence alone.

Joseph Cafasso was the third child of a family of four. His parents, who were remarkable for their charity to the poor, were small farmers who had to supplement their scanty income by working on neighboring farms. Joseph was a saint from his infancy; his sanctity was the result of victories gained over himself and it increased with his years. Even in his childhood he had certain days set apart for mortification, and he fasted every Saturday in honor of Our Blessed Lady. From childhood he attended daily Mass which he served with joy when permitted, and was a model of devotion. He was gifted with a keen intellect and a good memory, and was first in his class at school. He never lost a moment, he even took a short cut to the school and studied his lessons on the way. He appeared to be aware that his life was to be a short one, and that it would not be long enough for the work for God he hoped to accomplish. By his strong character based on humility, and his determination never to offend God, no matter what humiliation it might cost him, he gained an ascendancy over the other pupils and even over people older than himself.

As soon as he came to the age of reason, his mother accustomed him to give alms to the poor, which he gladly did, and even added the best of his own meals to what his mother gave him. When scracely ten, he began his spiritual apostolate. He loved to teach catechism to the poor children of the district, and on Sunday evenings he would gather the neighbors and, standing on a chair because he was of small stature, he would repeat for them the sermon he had heard that morning in Church.

Seeing such evident signs of a vocation, his parents decided to educate him for the priesthood. They sent him to a school in the neighboring town of Chieri, where he studied Latin and afterwards Philosophy. As there was no vacancy in the major seminary of Turin, he began the study of Theology under the Pastor of his native parish, and completed it at Chieri, when a major Seminary was opened there.

He was a model student, humble and always ready to help other students. His companions gave him the name of "the new Aloysius" on account of his modesty, gentleness and angelic disposition.

He was ordained priest in 1833 at the age of twenty-two, having got a dispensation for defect of age. After ordination, he went to Turin to attend one of the post-graduate courses there. There were three such courses in Turin at the time. Having attended the lectures of the three in succession, he selected the one presided over by a very learned and virtuous priest named Don Guala. The course consisted of moral and dogmatic theology, Sacred Scripture, Patrology, Liturgy and Sacred Eloquence. He was easily the first amont the young priests who attended the course, and when his three years' studies were completed he was selected by Don Guala as assistant professor. He was a brilliant lecturer. His fame soon spread over all Piedmont and even beyond it, and attracted students not only from Turin but from the surrounding dioceses. He aimed at making the young priests not only learned in theology but saintly men and efficient ministers of the Gospel.

Jansenism was rampant at the time. A large number of the clergy were tainted with it; they held rigorous views and deterred people from approaching the Sacraments, but their lives were far from virtuous. Don Cafasso was the apostle of hope and confidence and advocated frequent and even daily Communion. By correct explanation of the principles of Moral Theology, by preaching the mercy of God in season and out of season and by training the young priests to work with him in the prisons among men considered by the Jansenists as unworthy of the Sacraments, he fortified them against the errors of that pernicious heresy.

When Don Guala, the Rector of the Institute became old and infirm, Don Cafasso took charge and was appointed as his successor when he died.

There was a church dedicated to St. Francis of Assisi attached to the College, of which the Rector was Pastor. Don Cafasso had charge of the Church and spent long hours each day, usually from 7 a.m. till 9:30 or even 11 a.m. hearing Confessions in it. His fame for learning and sanctity attracted great numbers of penitents there. He gave preference to working men and after them to servant girls, and if there was not time to hear the wealthy and the titled folk before his classes began, he asked them to return.

Besides performing all his duties as Professor and Pastor, never missing a class or being a minute late, he found time for other forms of apostolate in Turin, the chief of which were teaching catechism to poor children, visiting the sick and the various prisons of the city, and giving missions and retreats.

Don Cafasso and Don Bosco

Though Don Cafasso and Don Bosco were neighbors, they did not become acquainted till Don Cafasso had become a clerical student and was already sixteen years old. Don Bosco was then but a boy who loved games and fun, and Don Cafasso had already acquired the wisdom of a man of experience. He became Don Bosco's adviser, helped him in his difficulties, and when he was ordained Don Cafasso received him

into the College of which he was now professor. Don Cafasso was accustomed to bring some of the young priests with him to help in teaching catechism; having found Don Bosco by far the most suited for this
work, he advised him to devote himself to it when his three years course
was finished. He procured a house for him, and when he was driven out
of it on account of the noise the boys made, Don Cafasso got another
for him and supplied him with funds for the work. He continued to
help him and advise him until the time of his death, and Don Bosco,
though only a few years younger than he, would do nothing without
consulting him.

His work among the Poor

He sought out the poor in their homes and trained the young priests
under his charge to visit them and help them. He never refused an alms.
He gave away all that he owned himself, and generous people, knowing
his great charity, gave him large sums of money, being persuaded that
it was the best way to help the poor. He was particularly kind to those
who, as the result of some calamity, had fallen into poverty. He did not,
however, allow himself to be imposed on, and when he had prudent
reason for suspicion, he sent a servant to visit the houses of people who
appealed for help, to see what they had for meals. The servant often
found that some of the people who said that they were in want had
well-supplied tables.

Visiting the Prisoners

The prisons in Don Cafasso's time were gloomy places infested with
vermin. There was communication between the prisoners, and of the
inmates of the prisons, the wicked had the greatest influence. It was
among these outcasts of society that Don Cafasso spent most of his
free time. He visited each prison at least once a week, and some of them
once a day, and spent long hours there, usually four or five hours at a
time. He returned home each night bringing with him on his person,
the vermin of the prison, which he jocularly called "living silver and
moving riches."

He prepared the way for his spiritual ministrations by corporal benefits, but when actually hearing Confession he never gave anything, even a medal. His distributed various kinds of gifts among the prisoners: tobacco, money, fruit, clothes, religious objects.

He instructed the prisoners in the truths of religion, and not being in any hurry to leave, he did that work thoroughly. He prepared them for the Sacraments and heard their Confessions. There is no case on record in which he failed to convert even the hardened sinners among them. He brought some of the young priests under him to visit the prisons and made it part of their training to help the poor and needy and visit those in prison. He helped to get employment for those among the prisoners who from time to time were liberated.

Those condemned to Death

Don Cafasso singled out for special kindness criminals condemned to death. He visited all these frequently, instructed them and prepared them for death. He accompanied them all to the scaffold—fifty-seven from Turin prisons and seven others from other towns. He succeeded in getting all these to go to the Sacraments. He was not satisfied with merely converting them but endeavored to make them saints. He exhorted them to accept capital punishment with resignation and told them that if they did so with perfect dispositions, they were in a state to go directly to Heaven without passing through Purgatory, for by dying a violent and dishonorable death they were performing the heaviest penance that could be imposed on anyone in this world. He even gave them a commission for him to execute when they went to Heaven, which was to kneel before the throne of Mary and intercede for him.

Adviser to Bishops and Priests

People of all classes not only from Turin but from distant places came to him for advice: bishops, priests, lawyers, titled folk, simple people and even non-Catholics. He solved difficult cases of conscience with marvellous facility. He was a very learned man and was hardly equalled by anyone of his time for practical knowledge of Moral Theology and then, he was a Saint and got special light in prayer. He was never known to give a wrong solution or wrong advice.

Don Cafasso as a Preacher

During the twenty-four years that he spent at the College of St. Francis, he was Professor of Sacred Eloquence as well as of Moral Theology. In the volume of his conferences to priests that we are now publishing one conference is devoted to preaching. In it we find the principles that he inculcated and the directions that he gave to young priests. His knowledge of the art of preaching was not acquired by merely reading books but from life-long practice which began when he was a boy. He became one of the most effective preachers not only of his own time but in the history of the Church. He was both learned and eloquent, and had a beautiful delivery. However, he trusted in none of these things, but rather in prayer and penance. In each sermon he made it his aim that not one person would leave the church without being converted. He preached every Sunday at the Church of St. Francis and he frequently gave retreats to both clergy and laity. His favorite place for giving retreats was at the Sanctuary of St. Ignatius where there was a church and residence on a mountain 2,800 feet high. It was there that the Conferences in this volume were first delivered. The Conferences which he gave on these occasions were always written and his manuscripts are still preserved. There are about sixty sermons in all, including those to the laity, covering about 1060 pages. These were published in Italy and have gone through several editions. It is these sermons that are now being published in English for the first time.

His Saintly life

Don Cafasso was truly a man of God, a holy priest. All his words and acts breathed forth the delicious odor of celestial virtue. Some saw in him a resemblance to St. Philip Neri on account of his humility, others to St. Alphonsus Liguori for his learning, others to St. Vincent de Paul for his devotion to the poor and those in prison, others to St. Aloysius Gonzaga for the innocence and purity of his life, others to St. Francis de Sales for his burning love for God and his gentleness of manner, others to the Cure of Ars for the austerity of his life and his work in the confessional.

His Austerities

In the matter of food, he mortified himself from his very infancy. One would imagine that he had no sense of taste for he preferred unsavory to tasty food. He fasted every Saturday even as a child, and from the time of his Ordination, every day was for him a fast day. For breakfast he took only a little bread without coffee or milk; for mid-day meal he took a plate of soup and a little bread but no fruit or sweets of any kind. When he became Rector, he began by waiting until dinner was nearly finished before he came; after some time, he did not come until dinner was over, and then he took a little bread and wine as he passed through the Refectory on his way to visit in the College Chapel.

He was a man of prayer; the views that he expresses in his Conference on Prayer were exemplified in his life. In spite of his many duties, he was able to find long hours for prayer. The secret of how he was able to do the work of several men and to do it well, and at the same time to find long hours for prayer lay in the fact that he spent little time eating, and little time sleeping. He was always last in the church each night and was first up in the morning. After a long preparation, he began his Mass each morning at 4.30 a.m. He spent no time idly. He had taken two vows: one to do what was most perfect, the second to waste no time. St. John Bosco stated in his panegyric that in the thirty years that he had known him, he had never known him to waste time. Besides his fasting he practiced other rigorous austerities; he used instruments of penance: the hair-shirt, chains, the discipline. His undergarment was found each week by the woman who washed it to be stained with blood. Whenever a criminal was to be executed he watched the whole night before the Blessed Sacrament and often scourged himself to blood.

His Devotions

His great devotions were: to the Passion, to the Sacred Heart, to the Mass, to the Stations of the Cross, to the Blessed Sacrament, to our Blessed Lady, to St. Joseph, to many of the Saints, to the Souls in Purgatory in whose favor he recommended the heroic act.

His Holy Death

When he was completing his forty-ninth year his health was still good, and to judge by appearances one would say that he had many years still to live. He himself was aware that such was not the case. St. John Bosco was convinced that the day and the hour of his death had been revealed to him, and in his panegyric of him gives several reasons for this belief.

Judged by the amount of work he had accomplished, and the small amount of time he spent at meals and in bed he had lived a very long life. *"For venerable old age is not that of a long time, nor counted by the number of years. A spotless life is venerable old age. Being made perfect in a short time, he fulfilled a long time."*

He made his preparation for death on the first Sunday of the month and devoted the whole day to it. He made his Confession as if it were to be his last, received Holy Communion at Mass as Viaticum, and received Extreme Unction in spirit as if he were a dying man. He recited the prayers for the dying and kissed the Crucifix as if it were the moment of expiring, and then imagined that Our Lady obtained for him another month to prepare for death.

His last illness began on June 9 as he was hearing Confessions. He was obliged to go to bed and, on the third day of his illness, finding that he had still a little strength left, he got up and spent a few hours in the Confessional until he became quite exhausted. He had great devotion to Our Blessed Lady and it was his constant prayer that he should die on a day dedicated by the Church to her. His prayer was granted, for he died on a Saturday, a day consecrated by the Church to Our Lady. It was a Saturday within the Octave of the Feast of Mary Consolatrix, and was on the vigil of St. John, who is the principal patron of pious works of mercy for those condemned to death, to whose benefit he had devoted so much care. St. John Bosco believes that Our Lady appeared to him at the moment of death and conducted him to Heaven.

PATRICK O'CONNELL
8th September, 1958

The Nature of the Office of the Priesthood

"WHO ART THOU?" This was the question put by the messengers from the Sanhedrim to St. John the Baptist, the Precursor of our Divine Lord. The prophets from all Judea had begun to talk about him, extraordinary things were related about him, and his fame was increasing every day. The chief priests assembled in council said: We must know who this man is; we must see with whom we have to deal. It was for this purpose, as you know, that they sent a delegation to find out. In like manner, but not through others, I myself wish to put the question to you, venerable brethren, at this our first meeting: Who is this man who in the world is called an ecclesiastic, a priest? Who is this personage whom some bless and others curse? Who is he whom the whole world talks about and criticizes, and who is the subject of discussion by all pens and all tongues? What is the significance of that name which resounds in every corner of the world? If we have left our homes and are gathered here on retreat, it is precisely for the purpose of occupying ourselves with this man, of meditating on him during these days that we have done so. It now behooves us more than anyone else to find out and know who this man is.

✦ THE PRIEST AS THE WORLD JUDGES HIM

Who then is the priest? If I ask the people of the world, some will exalt him to the skies, others will seek to lower his prestige to the dust. Each one defines him according to his outlook. Some regard him as a happy, fortunate man, others look upon him as a useless lazy individual without any occupation. Some say that he is a harsh, obstinate man, insensible to the troubles and needs of his people. Others, on the contrary, say that he is a man devoted to the public good, although misunderstood and ill-treated by the world.

✢ THE PRIEST AS PRIESTS JUDGE HIM

I attach no importance to this gossip of those who have neither the competence nor the right to pass judgment on the clergy, but I turn to you, priests, and I ask you what is a priest? From you, at least, I shall receive a just, exact, complete reply. And do not imagine that it is so easy even for us who have the name and character of priests to give the reply.

We shall study this man, the priest, for eight consecutive days. We shall study him alone to the exclusion of every other subject that might interfere with our considerations, and after our eight days of continuous study, we shall have, perhaps, an imperfect idea of this mysterious individual, of this man who unites in himself what is most sublime in Heaven with the baseness of earth, who forms in himself that complex being, that mixture of the human and the divine which makes him such a hidden mystery that we do not know what to call him, whether a god or a man. I shall not here give my opinion on that point, for each of you will have time during the days of retreat to clarify his ideas about what a priest is and about the nature of his office.

During these days we shall in the first place, investigate what a priest is, what are the dangers to which he is exposed, what virtues are required in him and what are the means to attain them. We shall then consider what is his office, how sublime it is, and how important; we shall examine the way in which the priest should discharge the duties of that office and the motives that should urge him to do it properly.

✢ WHAT IS A PRIEST?

What is a priest? In order to define clearly what he is, I shall avail myself of the distinctions that St. Bernard made concerning ecclesiastics and shall consider him in his nature, in his person, and in his habits. *Quid in natura, quis in persona, qualis in moribus!* In his nature he is a man like others. In his person, his dignity is above that of all other men in the world. In his conduct and habits, he should be a man totally different from all others as he is by his dignity and office. These are the three points which I propose for your consideration in this our first meditation during which we shall begin the work of studying this man with whom we shall try to get acquainted during these days.

✣   Priest, Know Thyself!

"Man, know thyself,"[1] is an ancient maxim inculcated by the pagans; study and investigate yourself until you arrive at knowing yourself! This knowledge alone would suffice to reform the world. All the disorders and scandals of the clergy would disappear immediately if they knew themselves. It is because he lacks this knowledge that the priest becomes neglectful of his duties. Although clothed as a priest and bearing the priestly name and priestly character, he lives the profane life of a man of the world simply because he does not realize who he is. It is because he fails to know himself that he demeans himself and, instead of fleeing from dangers, rashly exposes himself to them and falls. But this is not all; the worst is, that while such a priest is lacking in this fundamental knowledge, he foolishly thinks that he possesses it and will take no care to acquire it. Just try the experiment of saying to such a priest that he should be a little more circumspect, that he should not go to such a place, that he should recollect who he is, and you will immediately get the answer from him that he knows his dignity better than you do, that he knows his duties and does not need anyone to tell him. Poor priest! He does not know himself and, what is worse, he is persuaded that he knows himself sufficiently well, and therefore there are no means of making him enter into himself and acquire at least some idea of himself and his exalted dignity.

The priest, on the contrary, who begins to doubt about himself, who fixes his eyes a little on the lofty dignity of that state in which God has placed him, who considers the wickedness of the world in which he lives and its many dangers, will be seen to fix his attention upon himself, to study now one aspect, now another of his needs and of his duties. He will be always happy when he can get enlightenment on his state and his duties either from a friend, or from a book or from a spiritual conference. He never stops or wearies in the pursuit of that knowledge, for according as he acquires it he perceives the importance and the need of making still further progress. And just as no one neglects the pursuit of that knowledge more than he who is lacking it, so no one is more eager and takes greater care in its pursuit than he who has begun to possess it. Let us, venerable brethren, put ourselves among the number of those latter and, beginning by having at least a doubt about ourselves, let us give ourselves wholeheartedly to the study of ourselves during these days; let us study ourselves, thread by thread, so to speak, so that when our retreat is finished and we are departing from here, each one may be able to say to himself: I think I have succeeded in some measure at least in knowing myself, in knowing my state. It seems to me that now I am able to say: I know who I am, I know what it means to be a priest.

I   THE PRIEST IN HIS NATURE

Who then is a priest considered in his nature? Note that when I say a priest I do not mean someone far away from here, I mean myself and, in like manner, each of you means yourself. The priest is a man like other men. God might have selected that personage, so extraordinary in his destiny, from among His noblest creatures but He did not do so; having actually selected him from among men, He might have endowed him with some external prerogatives. He might have exempted him from some of the common miseries of humanity and thus make him at least singular and, in some respects, naturally eminent among other men; but no, the priest is a man like other men: "Every high priest taken from among men is ordained for men in the things that appertain to God."[2] He is born, he lives, he dies like any other. He has need of repose, of food, of comfort, like others, and he is subject to the same miseries of body and soul: now he is sad, now joyful, now he weeps, now he laughs, now he fears, now he hopes. Yes, he is a man and very much so, and the miseries of others are the same as those of the priest. From this funda-mental truth which is clear and evident, and which it is not necessary for me to discuss further, each one deduces consequences according to his outlook. The world and evil-minded people deduce their own, those ecclesiastics who do not know themselves or their dignity deduce theirs, and finally good priests deduce consequences for their own betterment.

✤ Conclusions Drawn By the Wicked World

The world and those who do not practice their religion reason thus: What is a priest and what claims is he making because he wears a particular kind of dress, adopts a certain name, has a certain position? What has he to do with us? He is a man as we are. He has his profession, as we have ours; for the rest, he is a man like others, neither more nor less. Why should I allow myself to be impressed by him; why should I be dictated to by him; live under his directions and even disclose to him the most secret thoughts of my heart, when I know that he is a man the same as myself? Let him follow his trade, I will follow mine. The time is past when the name of priest sounded imperiously in the ears of simpletons. Poor blind people! They do not know what they are saying. Such reasoning results in want of respect for the person of the priest, of docility to his exhortations, and God grant that it does not lead to the loss of faith and religion! I will say no more about the people who reason thus because they are not here, and this retreat is not for them. Let us turn to what concerns ourselves; for it will be truly beneficial for us.

✤ Conclusions Drawn By Tepid Priest

I am a man like others, why wonder then if I fall into certain miseries common to all men? Note, venerable brethren, that it is a priest who speaks thus, and that the human weaknesses to which he refers are not merely distractions in prayer or impatience, but unseemly conduct that causes one to shudder. I am a man like other men, he says, and why cannot I have a good time, why cannot I have certain consolations and take part in certain pastimes? If the layman can do so, I have the same right; even though I am a priest, I have not ceased to be a man like him. Why then all this wondering and gossiping because I frequent a certain house, because I attend a certain party, because I go to a certain place, because I speak and jest like men of the world? How many laymen act in that way, and who reprimands them? Continue therefore, and don't be deterred by gossip! Ah, if there is one here with such sentiments— and indeed there are, alas, such among the clergy—I would like to say to him: "you are more deserving of compassion than of reprimand, you are more an object for pity than for scolding; you belittle your position, because you are ignorant of what it is, and you wish to make your low estimate of it an excuse for your dissipated, worldly life. I will tell you in a few moments that what you say is not true; that you are, on the contrary, a man different from others, and therefore your conduct should be different also." For the present, venerable brethren, let us give a passing glance at the conclusions which the good and prudent among the clergy will draw to their own advantage.

✥ CONCLUSIONS DRAWN BY GOOD PRIESTS

We are men like others, therefore we are, like others, liable to make mistakes, to err, to slip, to fall; therefore we must be alert and on our guard. We are men in our speech, in our conversation, in our judgments. We are men even in the exercise of our ministry—at the altar, in the confessional, in the performance of our most sacred duties—therefore we must have vigilance, reserve, gravity, modesty, if we do not wish to have other more baneful proofs that we are men. Although clad in the livery of the priest, anointed and consecrated with holy chrism, we are however composed of flesh and blood, and our character, however holy and venerable it may be, does not guarantee us against the assaults and snares of our enemy. We are men like others, therefore, we should not be dismayed or disheartened if the Lord permits certain humiliating, obstinate, tenacious temptations. It is no dishonor to the priest to be assaulted, whatever be the assault; it is rather an honor. The wrong will be in yielding or in wavering. We are men, therefore let us learn from ourselves and our human weaknesses how to treat other men, how to handle them with tact and gain them over. The study and knowledge of oneself is a great school for the priest who has to cure the defects of others. We shall be able to find out from the study of ourselves what it is that most attracts men, the force of such attractions and the obstacles that have to be overcome. But if any priest wishes to do good and not merely beat the air, he must first adopt for himself the means that he suggests to others, he must use those weapons that he wishes to put in the hands of others in order to be able to measure their force and consequence. He should, for example, ask himself: what effect would this word, this advice, this correction, this threat, this invective have on myself if it were made to me at that time and in that manner? This is a great school in which I can train myself, and if I apply to others the knowledge gained it will seldom fail to produce a good effect, because I am a man just as they are and I can confidently expect that effects produced in myself will be produced in others as well. Finally, we are men and, as such, we are subject to real defects and imperfections, not to mention anything more serious. If therefore anyone eager for our good and anxious for our improvement has the charity to warn us about some defect, instead of getting indignant and thus repaying this act of charity with bad humor—which however is the usual coin with which such friendly warnings are repaid—let us recognize our misery and our weakness, and thank whoever has the goodness to correct us for his charitable act, and let us profit by our faults and humiliations to exercise greater vigilance over ourselves and our behavior. This is what the priest does habitually who knows, and lives intimately persuaded that he is a man like other men. However great his dignity, exalted his position, high the esteem in which he is held, even if he were to be regarded as a saint, he must always remember that he is a man, and as such he must restrain his senses, moderate his appetite, guard his eyes, avoid places of dissipation, shun dangerous company, make use of the only means that can render him victorious in temptations and dangers—prayer and flight. This is good for him, for it is enough for a priest to forget that he is a man just for a moment to bring some misfortune on himself.

Let us take these reflections to heart, venerable brethren, and whatever be our state, dignity, or the solid virtue that we believe we possess, we are all the time men and, as such, we should always have a low opinion of ourselves, distrust our own strength and walk cautiously, vigilantly, and watchfully.

II THE PRIEST IN HIS PERSON

Who is the priest in his person? The wicked world that Christ condemned will say that he is a man like other men, but the world does not stop to consider who he is and only seeks to lower him and despise him. I will not delay to discuss the opinion of the world, for we here all know who the priest is, considered in his person, in his vocation and in his dignity. "*The word priest*" says Denis the Areopagite, "*connotes the most august person in the world, a person truly divine.*"[3] The great Pontiff, Innocent III, speaking of the priest and of the dignity to which he is raised because of his office, says that he is placed between God and man, beneath God, but above man: *Inter Deum et hominem medius constituitur; citra Deum sed ultra hominem minor Deo, sed major homine.*[4] He cannot be called God, but neither can he be called a mere man. He is like a middle person between God and man, but nearer and more closely belonging to God than to man, as the Apostle, St. Paul called Timothy: "*But thou, O man of God.*"[5] And here, observes a commentator, it would appear at first sight that St. Paul should have called his disciple by a different name, for—the priesthood having been established on earth for men, "*every high priest is ordained for* men"[6]—he should have rather called him a man for other men, than a man for God; but no, he calls him "a man of God," and with reason, for the ambassador belongs rather to him who sends him than to those to whom he is sent. The priest is indeed ordained for men, but that does not make him one of them or cause him to belong to them. He belongs to Him who sent him and is "a man of God." Just as in the natural order, observed Hugo of St. Victor, it has pleased God to choose one star from among the others and make it regulate the world by its light and influence, so in the moral order too, He has been pleased to choose a man among others, to raise him up to a sublime dignity and surround him with splendor, in order that he might be the leader and director of all others. St. Ignatius Martyr, speaking of the priesthood, calls it "the apex of all things."[7] The priest excels all men and is the summit of all things, whether honors, dignities, titles or degrees. I shall not delay here to quote for you the remarkable eulogies on the grandeur and dignity of the priesthood by the two great doctors of the Church, St. Ambrose and St. John Chrysostom. The passages that I have quoted suffice to give an idea of who the priest is in person and dignity.

✤   THE PRIEST SHOULD KNOW HIS OWN DIGNITY

Let us come now to the consideration of how necessary and important it is that the priest should realize fully and in a practical way the greatness of his dignity, because if he does not know it and esteem it, it would be impossible for him to avoid lowering it and degrading it, for he cannot esteem it if he does not know it. We see this exemplified every day in ordinary, familiar affairs. If a person puts on a precious garment without knowing it has any special value, he will take no care of it, and it will not be long before it is stained and covered with mud. Therefore, St. Ambrose has well said that the first thing a priest should learn is his own sacerdotal dignity in order that he may be able to preserve it—*Dignum est ut dignitas sacerdotalis prius noscatur a nobis et deinde servetur a nobis.*[8] Do you believe, venerable brethren, that so many priests would debase their own greatness with worldly, profane, unseemly actions; would it be possible that so many ecclesiastics should expose their dignity to ridicule and laughter in places of profane amusement and take part in vulgar jokes and games if they had a proper idea of the dignity of their office? To such priests may be fitly applied the words of the Psalmist: "*Man when he was in honour did not understand.*"[9] They have studied for the priesthood, they have been ordained priests and they have been performing the duties of a priest for many years, yet they do not know either what they are, or what they are doing, or where they are. In dignity they are raised up to Heaven—"*Quasi jam in coelum translati*"[10] but they are blind and ignorant, and do not know who they are. They regard themselves as ordinary men, and associate with other men just as a man of the world; in trafficking, in money-making, in amusements, on the streets, in houses with people of every sort, as if there were not much distinction between the priest and the idler, the vagabond, the worldly or even the irreligious: "*Man when he was in honour did not understand: he is compared to senseless beasts, and is become like to them.*"[11] Poor ecclesiastics! They make others weep at seeing how they misuse and humiliate the dignity of the priesthood and expose it to ridicule. A day will come when they themselves will lament that they missed their dignity and brought it into contempt, and God grant that it may not happen to them to have to lament it for all eternity!

✢ THE PRIEST'S DIGNITY MUST BE UPHELD BY A VIRTUOUS LIFE

But you will ask how can the great dignity of us priests be upheld? Worldly greatness is maintained by the authority to command, by luxurious trappings and by external pomp. Our dignity, however, is maintained by much more precious means; by being equipped with true and solid virtue. Give me a virtuous priest and I will show you a man who is always truly great, august, venerable, even though he may have no revenue or titles or important employment. Even though he may be misunderstood and humiliated by the world, you will always have in him a man who towers over the world and, what is more important, you will have true, honorable greatness enhanced by all its decorum; a greatness that makes itself respected by the good and even by the bad. No, to be truly great in our profession it is not sufficient to be raised up to exalted positions, to have honorable titles. These things are only miseries which have nothing whatever to do with true greatness in a priest; we must keep our attention fixed on facts, we must be provided with, and consolidated in virtue. "What we are by profession" says St. Ambrose, "we must show by deeds rather than by mere names" —*Quod sumus professione, actione potius quam nomine demonstremus.*[12] And here we have come to the most important of our considerations, which is to see what a priest is or what he should be in his external actions.

III   THE PRIEST IN HIS HABITS

III Qualis in moribus. The ecclesiastic is a man like other men considered in his nature. He is greater than other men if we consider him in his person, and he is different from other men if we look at him in his actions. We shall see the reasons why he should be a different man, what it is that will make him different from others and what will happen when he is not.

✢ THE PRIEST SHOULD BE DIFFERENT FROM OTHERS

That a priest should be different from others in his habits, or that he ought to live differently, I shall show by two simple, clear reasons.

(1) *By His Vocation*

A man ought to adapt himself in his manner of living to his state, to his condition, to his degree; the gentleman lives as a gentleman, the artist as an artist, the citizen as a citizen, and so on; this is the most natural thing in the world. Therefore that an ecclesiastic should live as an ecclesiastic is a legitimate conclusion. In addition, the ecclesiastic by virtue of his vocation has been separated from others, raised up and transformed into a different man; therefore the life of others cannot be adapted or suitable for him; therefore in his habits he must be a different man and live differently.

(2) *The Priest Should Be the Light of the World*

A further reason; we priests know that we ought to be the light of the world, the salt of the earth, the teachers of the people, and that these offices are not just mere titles or empty names, but that they involve real obligations and duties which none of us can neglect. Now give me a priest who in his habits is like other men, whose conduct and life are like those of other men, I ask, where is the light which should illuminate the world, where is that salt that should preserve it from corruption, where are those lessons for others, if a layman is in a position to say with regard to a priest: I have everything and I do everything that the priest has and does, my life is like his, in his actions he is in no way superior to me. What a fine master in Israel such a priest would make if he allows himself to be equalled, if not surpassed, by the layman! Someone might here object and say: even though the priest be not different from other men, he can carry out the duties assigned to him by means of learning and sound doctrine, he can illuminate, preserve, teach. It would appear therefore that the reasons given why the priest should be different from other men have not great weight. This, brethren, is not so, as I will show you. Whoever has a duty to fulfill is obliged to make use of all the means necessary to fulfill it; he is bound by this consideration, if for no other reason, to apply himself to those means which are most useful and efficacious; and this obligation is undeniable; it follows from what we have said. Now among the means that have weight with the people to obtain the ends that we have mentioned, the example of an edifying, virtuous life is certainly the most powerful. All the knowledge of a priest will be sterile if his sermons and exhortations and advice is not supported and sustained by the force of his example. What I have said therefore stands. A common life like the layman's is not sufficient for a priest who wishes to discharge the duties of his office. I shall not dwell further on this point, for it is evident. I pass on to consider what things are required to make a priest a man different in habits from other men.

✤ IN ORDER TO BE DIFFERENT FROM OTHERS THE PRIEST MUST

(1) *Abstain from Evil More Than Others*

Two things are required in our case. There are many vices among men and sin abounds; the priest should not only be free from these but he should keep far away from them. Among men there are also the good and virtuous and these are not few; the priest should endeavor to surpass these in virtue and goodness. Thus ordering his life, he becomes a man different from others, and although the priest without this differentiating quality might become a great man, even if he does, he will be a man like others since he lacks that quality of excellence which consists in living differently from others. This is easily said, but it is not so easy to put it into practice. In order to clarify our ideas on this important point, let us go in spirit round the world to see among the various ways of living that we shall find, what becomes a priest, in order that we may adopt it into our lives. I shall not speak of those who live habitually in sin and who show themselves publicly given to certain vices such as licentiousness, impiety, excesses in eating and drinking; it is evident at once that such a kind of life is not suitable for a priest. Let us examine other failings which do not strike the eye so much, but which nonetheless are reprehensible or at least dangerous. That layman, for example, does not appear to do anything very bad, but yet does nothing good. One day after another is passed in sleep and laziness and idleness, and the years of his life are spent the same way. That is not right, it is a sin. It does not therefore suit a priest who should be a man different from others. That other man does nothing bad, but he frequents a certain house, is unduly familiar with certain persons, which gives rise to suspicion and gossip. This kind of life gives scandal and is sinful. A priest in these circumstances could not avoid giving rise to a little suspicion although his life and conduct may be innocent and holy. He should regulate his life in a different way, since he is a man different from others. That other person goes to Sunday Mass but he is so distracted, restless, and bored that his presence is certainly not edifying; this is sinful, because it is not sufficient to do something in itself good, it must be done in a fitting manner. An ecclesiastic should behave quite differently from that; his bearing should be distinguished by gravity, modesty, attention, composure, so that just to look at him one would say immediately, that is a man different from others.

We might go on discussing various other faults and failings found among men: this man says that he has pardoned his enemy and harbors no ill feeling, however, he adopts an air of aloofness and haughtiness towards him; if he can avoid saluting him he does so, if he is forced to salute him, everyone notices that it is done through courtesy and not out of affection. In order not to find himself in that person's company, he invents a thousand pretexts; this is not proper, it gives bad example and causes people to say that there is still bitterness in his heart. Woe to the ecclesiastic who is not on his guard about this point! Very often it comes from pride and self-love. Once the ecclesiastic allows himself to be dominated by such failings, he becomes a man like others, punctilious, obstinate, tenacious.

(2) *The Priest Must Practice Virtue More Than Others*

In the world there are many good and virtuous people; if the ecclesiastic wishes to keep his position, to preserve his dignity, and show by his conduct that he is the singular person he really is, he must excel, otherwise he puts himself on the same level with others by his conduct. "The ecclesiastic," says St. Gregory the Great, "is wanting in what he owes to his position, not only when he puts himself among the number of those who live badly, but also when he does not excel good and pious laity in living virtuously. His virtue should not be of the common sort, it should be singular: *Ejus operatio debet esse singularis, nec inter malos, tantummodo quae recta sunt faciat, sed bene quoque operantes subditos sicut honore ordines superat, ita etiam morum virtute transcendat.*"[13] But a good life without grave defects suffices for the laity, why should it not suffice for an ecclesiastic? Would a work by a grammarian that is considered well done be considered to be equally well done, if the author had been a rhetorician? It would be sufficient for a grammarian to avoid errors and add that little ornament and elegance which are inseparable from the subject, but that would not be sufficient for a rhetorician. The work of each profession has its own standard. The comparison is taken from profane occupations, but it throws light on our subject.

What a great thought this is, my dear Fathers, and how it ought to stimulate us! In the world, there are people who pray much, well, we priests should pray more. There are others who frequent the Sacraments and gain great fruit from doing so: we should surpass them. There are people who, when offended, humiliated, blamed, show no resentment; they suffer in silence, they pardon; but the priest should go still further, he should pray for his enemies, he should do good to them as far as it is in his power. There are people with such delicate consciences that they not only abstain from committing all mortal sins, but they would not deliberately commit a venial sin for all that is in the world. The ecclesiastic should not be inferior to them. On the contrary, he should try to surpass them since otherwise the disciple would be seen to be above the master, which cannot and ought not to be, for Our Lord says: "The disciple is not above the master."[14] Therefore the ecclesiastic should look around him from time to time and see whether anyone is trying to surpass him, or has surpassed him, and if he finds that he has, he should not allow that supremacy to stand. If in the house in which I live, there is a virtue, I also should have that virtue and in a higher degree. If in that position in which I happen to be, in that countryside, in that town, in my neighborhood, I perceive people who are making progress in virtue, who from day to day go on increasing in humility, mortification, patience, detachment from the world, I should regard it as a challenge to me to take part in the race, and to look to it that I shall always be first, because that is my place. Otherwise, I, a priest, would cease to be that man, distinct and different, that I am, and in which state I have the right and duty to keep myself.

But perhaps some of you may think that I am going too far; that I want to transform a man into an angel, and that a priest should be sinless. My dear brothers in Christ, there is no question of destroying the nature of man in the priest. It has been made clear at the very beginning that the priest is a man, but it is claimed, and the claim is fully justified, that he should be a man different from others in his habits since he is different and distinct in his dignity.

If other men's defects are many and notable, those of the priest should be few and light. If other men commit them, with full advertence, in the case of the priest, they should be the result of surprise more than of will; and if unfortunately he happens to fall, he should make sure to surpass other sinners in his amendment. Instead of remaining in sin he should rise more promptly than others, have a more noble repentance, a more intense and profound horror for sin, and should learn from that fall to walk more cautiously for the future, and to put more zeal into the service of God.

I say that the priest should always and in every case be superior to any of the laity. And this is not an exaggeration on my part; it is a consequence that follows necessarily from the consideration of what the priest is, and is the common opinion of the Fathers of the Church. St. Ambrose says: "*God requires that there be nothing plebeian, nothing characteristic of the common herd in the priest; that in his pursuits, manners and customs there should be nothing in common with the disorderly multitude.*"[15] Origen applies to the priest the test given by Jeremias: "*I sat not in the assembly of jesters .... I sat alone.*"[16] and he adds: "*When our life is such that no one is equal to us, then we can say: I sat alone, as the Prophet Jeremias has said.*"[17] And the Council of Trent repeated the same thing clearly in these words: "*Clerics should surpass laymen in conduct as they do in office.*"[18]

✧ IF THE PRIEST IS NOT BETTER THAN OTHERS:

But it is needless to prolong the discussion by quoting further authorities, since the matter is clear. And what will happen when the priest does not succeed in being the person who "sits alone," as Origen says; when he differs in nothing in his habits from other men, in contradiction to what St. Ambrose requires of him; when he does not stand out above all other men, as the Council of Trent says he should? This is the last point that remains to be discussed.

(1) *The Laity Will Be a Cause of Confusion For Him*

The first of many fatal consequences, the first loss, will be for ourselves. The laity will be for us a cause of confusion, humiliation, reproof and perhaps also of condemnation one day: "Let the priests be ashamed if the laity are found to be holier in their lives."[19] "What a great shame," repeats St. Jerome, "for a priest to allow himself to be equalled in virtue by a layman"; *Magna cunfusio esse pares.*[20] "And what could be more unseemly," exclaims St. Peter Damian, "than that an ecclesiastic should not distinguish himself from a layman in his conduct? He would be like the great lord whose manners differ in no way from an unlettered peasant." *Turpe est, quem a laicorum turbis separat professionis conditio si vel domestica conversatio laicum esse convincat.*[21] And really, speaking among ourselves, would it not be a great shame, an insult in fact, if some lay person were to come to any of us and say to our face: "Look, you are an ecclesiastic, I am an ordinary person of the world, you are a most exalted personage, and I, one of the most wretched. You are gifted and learned, I ignorant, you are a master and I a scholar, nevertheless I do as much as you do, in fact, I do more than you, my life is like your life but it is better than yours. I deprive myself of various amusements and pastimes, but you do not do so, in fact one would think that you would die if you had to go without them. I am not punctilious, I don't quarrel about every word; I let things pass and pretend not to see them, I keep silent and suffer, but you! Woe to the person who touches you! He will never hear the end of it. I keep a guard over my eyes, I restrain my appetite and my tongue more than you; in church, during Mass and Benediction, I am more devout and adopt a more reverent attitude than you. I am a mere lay person, you are a priest, and yet I feel that I am making more progress than you in the virtues; in humility, patience, meekness, charity, purity, in fact, in everything." Tell me, my dear brethren in Christ, would we not regard it as a most shameful and humiliating situation if only one person among the laity was able to address such language to us? However, it is not one but many who are in a position to do so, and if they do not, it is their virtue, not our merit that prevents them. Let us then be ashamed, my dear Fathers, for we have every reason to be, and let us make our ashamedness serve to spare us something more terrible at the end of our days.

(2) *The Laity Will Be Scandalized*

The second evil, still more baneful than the first, that will happen when the priest is not a man different from others in his life and habits, is the scandal and confusion of the people. We have said that the priest in the moral world is like the sun in the physical; if the material sun were to become dark or if its light became inferior to that of the other stars, the result would be dismay and confusion over our whole earth. The same may be said of the priest who should shine like the sun in his life and example among the people. If he loses his light or if his light becomes dim, you will see what disorder will result. And what greater evil can happen to a people than that they should be deprived of light to see, of a master to teach and guide them, as would happen in the case I make?

"*The people shall rush one upon another, and every man against his neighbor: the child shall make a tumult against the ancient, and the base against the honourable.*"[22] This is the sad picture that the Prophet Isaias draws of a country or a city in which the priest is not better than others. Who will obey such a priest? Who will listen to his preaching, go to Confession to him, or accept his correction, if he is the same as the rest of them? "What edification will the disciple receive if he sees that he is better than his master?"[23] asks St. Jerome. If I do not shine some one else will do so, therefore there will not be all that evil, someone will say. The virtue of others does not diminish my wrong. The evil that a priest does causes harm to other good priests, because the whole body becomes infected with it, at least in the opinion of the people. Woe to that place where the people can say: the priest is just the same as I am; our chaplain, our parish priest, our confessor, our pastor is the same as the rest of us. St. Jerome says that this is sufficient to ruin the Church.[24] It undermines and destroys the Church of Christ when the laity are better than the clergy; this is the third fatal consequence that results from the clergy sinking to the level of the laity.

Religion and the Church have not need of human support in order to survive; but if there is a sensible, a tremendous shock, it is always when the clergy lower the Church in the eyes of the multitude by the lives they lead; when they make themselves like the laity, bad like them, or not better than them. Pope Gregory the Great, speaking to the Roman clergy said: "God sustains no greater injury from anyone than from priests, when He perceives those whom He has appointed to guide and correct the people give the example of an evil life."[25] I do not intend to dwell further on this matter at present, for perhaps I shall have occasion to speak of it again later on, but it is sufficient to have referred to it, because each one can form for himself an idea of the confusion and harm that will result when the priest is not different from others in his life and habits.

Let us conclude therefore with the memorable words of the Council of Trent: *Sic decet omnino clericos* (the word *decet* is sometimes used in the sense of fitness, but here it has the meaning of strict duty); *decet omnino clericos vitam moresque suos omnes componere, ut . . . . nihil nisi grave, moderatum ac religione plenum praesferant* (and note the reason given): *ut eorum actiones cunctis afferant venerationem.*[26] Let each one of us therefore, beginning from today put his hand to the work of reforming himself. Let us run over the whole day and examine all our actions. Everything that is not grave, religious, worthy of respect should be removed. That manner of dressing, of speaking, of celebrating Mass, those conversations, those pastimes should be reformed. Frequentation of those places which are not worthy of a priest should cease. Each one of us in going out from here should be a man different from others, a man who in everything gains for himself and merits veneration and respect; *ut eorum actiones cunctis a afferant venerationem.*

1 De Consid. lib. 2. cap. 4.
2 Hebr. 5:1.
3 De Hier. cap. 1.
4 Serm. 2. In cons. pont.
5 1 Tim. 6:11.
6 Hebr. 5:1.
7 Epist. 10 ad Smyrn.
8 De dign. Sac. I.
9 Psalm. 48:13.
10 De Sacerd. lib. 3, cap. 5.
11 Psalm. 48:13.
12 De dign. Sac. lib. I.
13 De Cura Past. P. cap. 3. II.
14 Matt. 10:24.
15 Lib. I. Epist. 6 ad Iren.
16 Jer. 15:17.
17 Hom. 2 in Ierem. 15.
18 Sess. XIV, in tit.
19 Petr. Blesens. Serm. ad Sac. 59.
20 Epist. ad Tit cap. 2.
21 Opusc. de Vita Can.
22 Isai. 3:5.
23 Epist. ad Tit. cap. 2.
24 Ibid.
25 Hom. 17 in Evang.
26 Sess. XXII, De Reform. cap. I.

The Dispositions Necessary to Become a Good Priest

*T*HE PRIEST, as we have seen this morning, is a man like other men in his nature, in his tendencies, in his inclinations, also in the human weaknesses to which he is subject, in the defects into which he may fall, in the dangers that threaten him and in the obstacles and difficulties that he has to surmount. Yes, in all these things a priest does not differ from other men, except it be in having a heavier cross to bear. Nevertheless, he must be a man different from others, not so much by the dignity to which he has been raised, the character with which he has been clothed, the powers which he exercises, the titles that he bears, as by everything that regards each one of his actions. He must be different in his manner of perceiving, speaking, working, different in all his habits, so that the life of a layman however good will not equal that of the priest.

It cannot be denied that the accomplishment of such a work, of such a marvellous undertaking, must cost much labor and require special study. Be that as it may, the work must be done, and we are gathered here together to study how it is to be done and to set ourselves with good will to succeed in accomplishing it. For this, certain dispositions are indispensable, without which it would be useless to attempt, and our efforts would be in vain. We must therefore apply ourselves and be firm and constant in the use of those means that conduce to the desired end. But notwithstanding our best efforts we shall find obstacles, perplexities, hindrances, and dangers of every kind which cross our path and seem determined to prevent us from becoming those men that we ought to be. We must therefore do violence to ourselves and adopt the proper helps to overcome them. Cost what it may, whether little or much, I must absolutely become that distinct man since I am a priest. This is in broad outline the object of our conferences; to indicate the way to make an ecclesiastic a man different from the general run of men. The end of this man, singular, special and unique in his kind, and the means to attain that end, will form the subject of the rest of my talks during this retreat.

✣   The Priest Should Have a Just Idea of His State

Coming then to the subject of this evening's conference, there are two principal dispositions necessary in order to become men different from the rest of the men in the world. The first is to conceive a just idea of our state and of its supreme excellence; the second, to set ourselves to the task of attaining true success in becoming good priests with a firm, decisive will and at whatever cost may be necessary. Take the first of these two dispositions: suppose the priest does not know his state, or that he has only a weak, limited idea of it; efforts based on such an idea would achieve nothing. The question we are dealing with is, as you see, of the utmost importance. There are precious graces available during these days of retreat; these and the greatness of the work on hand demand of us that we give our full cooperation in order to win the fruit required.

✣   What the World Thinks of the Priesthood

What idea reigns in the world about the priestly state? What do people think of it? The priesthood is regarded as a comfortable career, a state of quiet repose in which the priest does not know how to spend his days or in which he passes them engaged in trifles and useless pursuits; a state in which there are more amusements than labors. It is regarded as a state, if not of luxury, great fortune and riches, at least as an easy and secure means of livelihood. Finally, it is regarded as a state in which the priest has full, total liberty to live according to his inclination and to do whatever his whims may suggest to him. Thus people think, and they even say it to our face without any shame, to make fun of us or to insult us. Look at those lazy priests, they say, from morning to night they don't know what to do with themselves, they live and die in idleness. Many good people think much the same thing, and some through ignorance, and others through good nature say that there is no other state of life so fortunate as ours because we have almost nothing to do. The worst part of the evil is that not a few priests say, if not by words, at least by their actions, that our state is really one of inactivity and idleness. All these people are very much mistaken and, by such talk and such conduct, they do a great wrong not only to our persons but to our state, which is very different from what they think it is. St. Augustine says: "To a person who considers the question lightly, nothing appears more comfortable, but in reality nothing is more laborious and burdensome. The world considers it a state of repose and enjoyment, but it is on the contrary a state of hardship, labor and fatigue. The world considers it a state of ease, pleasure and luxury, on the contrary, it is one continuous chain of sacrifices and mortifications. Finally, the world considers it a life of liberty in which the priest is free to act according to his good pleasure, while on the contrary it imposes a continuous and absolute subjection, complete reserve and a thousand restrictions." Let us stop for a moment to examine the case.

⁜ What the Priesthood Really Is

(1) A State of Labor.

The priesthood is a state of exhausting labor. Everything in the priest shows us an active, hard-working man, given to laborious occupations. The nature of his mission, the number and variety of the offices laid upon him, the exactness with which they must be fulfilled, the account which he must one day render to the Lord, the rewards which are promised, the chastisements which are threatened, all show clearly and palpably that the intention of Him who has entrusted us with this office certainly was not to allow us to remain lazy and unoccupied. We need not cite in proof of the above mere words and sentences; we have but to look and see what was the life of the first Priest, our Divine Redeemer. During His abode at Nazareth, far from leading an idle life, He came to be called the workman, because He was always seen to be engaged in labor. During His public mission, we know what hardships and labors He endured, and how He sacrificed even the time necessary to take food and to sleep. Let us look at His Apostles who modeled their lives on that of the first Priest and imitated His life more by deeds than by words in order to hand down the pattern of it to us their successors. They were so much surrounded with various occupations and oppressed by the weight of business, that they were soon obliged to seek the help of others in order that they might be able to carry out all their duties.

Let us look at all those ecclesiastics who have left after them a good name for their own persons and for their state. What exertions and labors they endured during the long years of their ministry! Look at all those good priests who live in our own time always engaged in labor, occupied from morning to night; they certainly have no time to lose. If there had been another more convenient way, if one could be a good priest without labor and fatigue, these men would have known where to find it, but it is not possible to be a good priest without labor and fatigue. God wants only laborers for His vineyard, the Church wants only ministers who work and exhaust themselves for the needs and the benefit of the faithful. She expressly forbids that anyone be ordained unless the needs or the utility of the Church requires it. How then can anyone boast or think that he is a good priest if he does not occupy himself, if he does not work? Man is born to work; he is condemned to eat his bread in the sweat of his brow. Is it possible that the priest, because he is called to the sanctuary, should be the only one to eat his bread without earning it? It can't be denied that some priests do very little, and perhaps spend days, if not months and years without being able to say what they have done. However, even though this may be true of many ecclesiastics, I state clearly and I will have to repeat it several times, that what many priests do is one thing, and what they ought to do is another. Woe to the priest who, in the discharge of his duties or in what regards his state of life, begins to look around him and to say: other priests do so; such a priest and such another who are men of reputation do so; there can't therefore be so much harm, we may go ahead and perhaps improve a little, but the obligations can't really be so grave as some people say; when others do so, I can do so as well. Woe to the priest, I say again, who begins to sooth his conscience with such reflections and thus make for himself a new gospel! We tell the people that they are not to mind what others do, that each one must think of himself, and we often repeat that each one will have to render an account of his own soul, and that the example of others will not excuse him and cannot save him. Yes, these are truths which we know how to tell others and to repeat again and again, but how many times should we not apply them to our own case? Such a priest might go and hear Confessions, he might get up a little earlier, he might teach catechism and visit his people, but he does none of these things and yet nothing is said to him. Why should I have to get up earlier? Why cannot I do the same thing? This is the line of argument adopted very often. And by whom? By priests! I shall not stop to refute it, because you can all see that the argument is hollow; I shall merely repeat—because the matter is of such great importance— that whoever wishes to become a good priest and live as such must not look at what others do, he must look at himself and his duties, and so regulate himself; each one must think for himself.

(2) *The Priesthood Is a State of Sacrifice and Self-Denial*

The state of the priest is a state of sacrifice and self-denial. If we take the inactive, indolent priest who does nothing, the priest with the name and the habit only, his life in certain respects can be a life of comfort and ease and pleasure, because ordinarily he has no worries about his livelihood, and can therefore live free from care. Being free from business worries and the entanglements of the world, he can, more than any other, lead a life according to his tastes and good pleasure, and can amuse himself or repose without nausea if, putting aside the great duties of his state, he wishes to think of, and attend to purely corporal satisfaction. But suppose this priest wishes to develop his ecclesiastical character, to live the life of a true priest, and to carry out the duties of the state to which he has been called, then I say that his days cannot be anything else but a continuous series, an uninterrupted chain of privations, sacrifices and mortifications, whether from the part of himself, or from the world, or from the nature and character of his ministry.

❖ SACRIFICES WHICH THE PRIEST'S LIFE DEMANDS

With regard to privations and sacrifices on the part of himself, I shall treat of two kinds only. Both the blameless character which the priest should show forth so as to avoid even the appearance, the very shadow of evil, and the spirit of detachment from everything in the world, united with the spirit of recollection, of prayer and of union with God in which the true priest must live, demand privations and sacrifices. If you go over the day of a priest who wishes to live that life and be animated with that spirit you will see how many times in the day he must go against his inclinations and deny himself.

Begin with the morning; other priests, and perhaps many of them, spend the early hours in quiet tranquil sleep. When they rise, perhaps they spend the day in some pleasant, restful occupation; in walks in the country, in visits. The good priest does not spend his day in that manner; he remembers that he is a priest, and the thought of his duties, of the glory of God rouses him out of bed, calls him, draws him to the church, to the confessional, to his priestly duties. How many times in the course of the day, occasions will present themselves to the priest as well as to the layman to take part in profane occupations, in business, in news-mongering, in amusements, in meetings, in useless conversation. He is a man like others, he feels himself violently attracted to these things, all the more so because to his own inclinations and human weakness there are added the excitement and the temptation of companions, of relatives and friends. But he must not; woe to him if he begins to yield! He can in a very short time become imbued with the spirit of the world, and if he does, he will become, by rapid stages, empty, dissipated and worldly. And how could some priests have become so absolutely worldly as to occupy themselves more with the world than with God except through ceasing to live a life of privations and through forming for themselves a false idea of the priesthood as a state in which a priest may enjoy all the pleasures that come his way and even go in search of comforts and pleasures?

This consideration alone should be sufficient to keep a priest in a continuous state of self-denial, for he is continually surrounded and allured by objects which, if not bad in themselves, are at least worldly and profane, and of which, without exception, he should deprive himself altogether. If, however, necessity or some good reason demand, he should use them prudently so as to keep the heart free and keep complete control of his inclinations in every case. This cannot be obtained without continuous sacrifices.

✢ Privations And Sacrifices Imposed By the World

As to the acts of self-denial and sacrifices of the second kind, those which concern the world, it is not necessary to dwell on them at great length, because we know what bitter morsels that cruel master gives his votaries to swallow. And what will not the world do to us priests whom it regards as its first and greatest enemies, as indeed we are? It it not satisfied with obstructing our works, criticizing them, slandering us in our persons and in our ministry, it claims to be able to discover our very thoughts and intentions, and it interprets them according to its own standards. This is what we may expect from the world. The Holy Spirit warns those who wish to give themselves to the service of the Lord that they must prepare themselves for trials and sacrifices and battles: "*Son, when thou comest to the service of God, stand in justice and in fear: and prepare thy soul for temptation.*"[1] If this is true of the ordinary faithful, what can a priest expect who is a captain in God's army and a leader of the servants of the Lord? From the moment in which he has entered on the ecclesiastical career, a young man will not be able to take a single step without the world with its ally, the devil, seeking to obstruct him according to the times and circumstances; now by open persecution and violence, now by reproach and censure, now by raillery and sarcasm, now by assuming the appearance of piety and religion.

✢ Sacrifices Imposed By Our Ministry

Finally, our ministry itself demands sacrifices of us, sacrifices at all times. At every hour the good priest must be ready; by day and by night, early in the morning and late at night, even when he is tired, no time is excepted. Then there are sacrifices which result from the various classes of people: from the tedious, the coarse, the uncouth, the boorish, and from enemies and adversaries. Finally, our spiritual duties of every kind demand sacrifices. Of these, I shall confine myself to one branch only; the administration of the Sacrament of Penance. What exercise of patience and self-denial does not the administration of this Sacrament demand of the priest! And what deep and varied knowledge is required to deal with so many people, so different in opinion, in disposition, in character, and in occupation! What efforts and application to study are required to obtain the knowledge necessary to carry out properly these formidable obligations! The study required is, in a sense, infinite because a priest can never be said to have got to the end of it; it must be renewed repeatedly, so that it becomes each time practically a new labor. Does not all this tend to make the life of the priest a life of continual sacrifice and self-denial?

From the few points that we have touched on, each one can easily become convinced that our lives are very different from what the world judges them to be, and perhaps also from what some of ourselves imagined them to be. For, are not good, virtuous priests sometimes heard to lament and exclaim: "we never thought that we would have so many crosses, contradictions and vexations, and that we would have to encounter so many and so varied difficulties!" And why this lamenting and useless complaining? These difficulties were to be expected, for on entering the priesthood we had good intentions, although in the depth of our hearts we may have imagined it to be a comfortable, easy life, whereas on the contrary it is, or it ought to be, a life of self-denial and sacrifice.

Finally, it is a life of subjection requiring constant reserve and circumspection. Some people are accustomed to make a great difference between the state of a religious and that of a secular priest. Leaving aside other considerations, I will merely observe here that the state of the religious is regarded as a state of complete subjection and continuous dependence, and that of the secular, as a state of total and complete liberty. I admit that there is a difference under certain aspects; that there are special laws and regulations for religious; but we should be careful not to allow ourselves to be deceived, for the difference is more in name than in fact, it is more apparent than real. I therefore say, and you will agree with me, that the secular priest living in the world should live in greater subjection, he should use greater reserve and more circumspection, so that in reality his life is more bound and restricted than that of the religious living in the cloister. I know that the religious has many rules and regulations which the priest in the world has not; it is true that the priest has not renounced his own will by a formal vow of perpetual obedience, but is not the obligation assumed by him at Ordination by an implicit vow, inherent in and inseparable from his state, and is it not that which matters? From the day on which he entered the ranks of the ecclesiastics and became one of them, he contracted all the obligations and bonds of that state; obligations and bonds which do not leave the poor priest a moment of liberty. Take all the rules of the monk, all the statutes of his community, all the vows that he has made, and interpret them with all the rigor you wish, they don't equal that great volume of rules and precepts and bonds and canons which regulate the life of the priest in the world. I do not speak of the numerous duties which his office and ministry lay upon him, nor do I wish to quote for you the various prescriptions and canons of the Church regarding him, and by which he is, as it were, bound and chained, nor do I think that there are any among you who regard these ecclesiastical rules and regulations as mere counsels or disciplinary prescriptions to save appearance or to prevent the most flagrant abuses.

I do not believe that there are any among you who entertain that false opinion, that gross error; and it is not my intention to speak of it at present. I shall confine myself to the consideration of the continuous and uninterrupted series of bonds and restrictions which are real precepts and obligations imposed upon us by our life as priests on earth and the part we have to play in the world. There are cautions to be observed when we are in our houses, when we go abroad, when we are in the streets, when we are in church, when we are engaged in the discharge of our sacred duties. There are restrictions in our speech, in our looks, in taking our meals, in our recreations, and even in taking our repose; so that one might say that there are as many rules and canons binding us as there are eyes watching us. Our every movement, our every look, every step we make, every word we say, the most insignificant of our actions is observed, weighed and interpreted. And who would call that a free independent life? Is that a life of full liberty and free from control, as some people would give us to understand? Tell me therefore: Is not the priest who is living in the world and is pointed out and watched from morning to night without being able to hide himself, and without hope that people would make allowance for him or pardon him whether in small or great, a thousand times more bound and restricted than the monk shut up in the cloister? Add to this: of the many eyes that are constantly watching him some are good, but severe and delicate, and take note of our smallest faults and are scandalized by them, but most are hostile, prejudiced, malignant, and are therefore quick to see anything wrong, to magnify, to misinterpret, to exaggerate. Therefore, greater caution, greater reserve are necessary in order not to scandalize the one, and not to give an opportunity for slander to the other.

But, you will say, at least in his own house away from the eyes of the world, the priest can enjoy a little more liberty. Even there we must be constantly on our guard and not be too confident. At first sight it would seem that the priest has not need of so much caution in his own house, and I agree that he requires less than in public, but not so little as to dispense altogether with watchfulness. The priest is in his own house, but there are people who enter it and leave, and when leaving, believe me, they always take away something about us; we do not perceive it, we are not aware of it, perhaps, but it is so. The priest is in his own house, but there is someone else also in the house, and even if it be only one person, that one person is sufficient; for sooner or later, by one way or another, people will come to know the life of the priest, to know not merely his principal actions but his most trivial; how long he sleeps, what he says, what he eats, even to a joke or a smile.

If there is question of a layman, no one pays much attention, but since there is question of a priest, such is the idea that people have about him that everything assumes a value whether for good or for bad, according to its nature. The houses of priests, being placed in the midst of the world, may be said to be made—as a Roman of ancient times wished his house to be made—with transparent walls, so that everyone outside can see what is being done inside. So it happens in the case of our houses; in some way that we cannot explain, the people outside can see in just as if the walls were transparent. For that reason, St. Jerome addressed the following advice to the clergy of his time: "Do not imagine that in your house you are sheltered from the world, for as it is placed in the middle of it, it is like a mirror, and should be like a pulpit preaching virtue; all eyes are directed towards you and the people believe that they have the right to do whatever they see you doing."[2] Let each one regard the warning of this great Doctor of the Church as directed to himself, and be firmly convinced that the life of the priest is a life of subjection and restraint when outside his own house; and that it is a life of subjection and reserve while inside it, and therefore that it is a life of subjection that demands continuous circumspection.

If that is the way the case stands, someone may say, who would be able to live such a life? Priests make their lives a little simpler than that, they are not so restricted; each one says and thinks what he pleases. That is not so; however, I do not intend at the present stage to discuss the question of what a priest must do or omit in order not to give occasion for scandal, I hope to be able to deal with that question another time. Here I will speak only in general of the virtue with which the priest should be furnished: "*That the man of God may be perfect, furnished to every good work*"[3]*;* of the good example which he should give in everything without any exception: "*In all things show thyself an example of good works*"[4]*;* of the unblemished reputation which St. Paul insists that the priest should preserve: "*Let them minister, having no crime.*"[5] "*Holy, unspotted and blameless before Him.*"[6] All these obligations, I say, necessarily require the greatest caution and reserve in everything and at all times. And woe to the priest who thinks he can dispense himself from this caution and reserve! It is impossible for him to avoid falling or stumbling or sinking, all the more so, as I have said, because it does not require either a long time or a great occasion; a want of caution in his looks or his speech or his jests might suffice, for he would then no longer be the perfect man, the edifying man, the blameless man that St. Paul insists that he should be.

However, all do not speak in this manner: there are many good priests who do not take matters in this sense or interpret them so strictly; there must be prudence and reserve, they admit, but not that subjection or those restrictions of which I have spoken. I do not want to decide what the custom should be but merely to say that the priest who is penetrated with a lofty idea of his state should live watchful over himself, that he should always be as if in an assembly, that he should keep a tribunal sitting constantly over his daily conduct, and that he should not be satisfied with a general daily checkup upon himself, but that as far as possible he should weigh each action, each word, each glance; judge them, condemn them, and do some penance for them if they deserve it. Besides, recall to mind that I have said that I was speaking of the ecclesiastical state, not of individuals; the state is one thing, the way in which people behave in that state is another; the duties of that state is one thing, the carrying out of these duties is another. I have already stated, and I repeat it, our state is a state of labor, a state of sacrifice, a state of continual restrictions and continual subjection. Whether you believe it or do not believe it, whether you carry out these duties or do not carry them out, whether you wish it or do not wish it, that is how the case stands for me and for you, and let the priest who thinks it is otherwise be persuaded that he does not know his state sufficiently well, that he does not know his duties and not knowing them, it will be impossible for him to carry them out, and not carrying them out, how will he finish up?

But someone may object: this system of things, this continuous and rigorous austerity is not made for me, it does not appeal to me, it is impossible for me to adapt myself to it. Ah, my friend, is that what you think at this time of retreat? Why did you not reflect on this question formerly? Why embrace a way of life, a state without knowing it? Now there is no remedy. The state is the same for all, there is no exception for anyone. We are priests, and whoever wishes to be so, whoever wishes to work out his salvation in this state has no other rule of life to observe, no other road to follow; and when a priest has come to the point of say-ing, as indeed, too many think: "Let who likes follow that rule of life, let who likes spend his life in study, self-denial, continuous watching over himself and subjection, I say frankly: That is not for me, I don't want even to hear about it; if I thought I would have to live in that manner I would never have become a priest." To such a priest one might reply without hesitation: "It would have been better for you, better for the Church, and better for the interests of God also if you had adopted a different career." But seriously what reply can be given to a priest who speaks in that manner? As long as he makes excuses and tells of his difficulties, there is hope that he may be persuaded and a way out may be found, but when he gives a definite refusal the case is finished, it is useless to speak to speak to him, and all that we can do for him is to pray for him.

II The Priest Must Have a Resolute Will to Succeed

The second disposition that we must have in order to become good priests is an honest, sincere, and resolute will to succeed. It seems to be almost needless to speak of this disposition to one who is already a priest, since as he has embraced this state of his own free choice, for certainly no one has forced him, and as he has voluntarily adopted this career, he must have had the intention to be a priest and to take on himself the duties and obligations of a priest. However, I believe that it is of the greatest importance to subject this intention to an examination and analyze it, to see what it is worth and to know what we have to hope from it; for even the best exhortations will have no effect on us unless we are animated with the generous determination of which I have spoken.

❖ THREE KINDS OF WILLS

Now with reference to this question of our own sanctification, I distinguish three kinds of wills or intentions in those who have become priests. Some have embraced this state without any definite determination about their sanctification; others have had a vague limited intention but only up to a certain point. When I become a priest, they say, I shall think of the life I shall have to lead and of what will suit me best. The third class consists of those who advance to the priesthood resolute and determined to succeed fully and entirely, at any cost, in becoming true and holy priests. Of the first and second class I can tell you at once that you may hope for nothing.

❖ THE FIRST CLASS: INTRUDERS

Let us begin with the first class. How can it happen that a person should embrace the ecclesiastical state without the will to be an ecclesiastic? No one has forced him, probably no one has even suggested it to him, he came to the decision of his own free will. How then could it have happened? The explanation of the mystery is this: among those of the first class I place all those who have embraced the ecclesiastical state for human motives; as a means of subsistence, either because they were in a quandary about what career they should adopt, or to what art they should apply themselves, or because they failed in an attempt to gain a livelihood, or for family reasons, because their parents wished it in the hope of material gain. For these or other similar motives they embraced the ecclesiastical state without taking the trouble to study the spirit and the duties of the state, being content with the ecclesiastical dress and the character of priesthood to gain their end. A certain young man who was about to be ordained showed himself very contented and why? Because, he had made his daily bread secure; because he had found an employment and would no longer have to trouble about a livelihood. That is the case of those who wish to become ecclesiastics for worldly reasons but who give no thought to becoming so in spirit and in deed. If you ask them what they intend to do as priests, they will tell you that they intend to recite the Divine Office, to celebrate Mass and to do what other priests do. But that is not enough, the mere carrying out of these works materially is not that which forms the true priest. These are worth just as much as the spirit which animates them, and when that is absent, it will happen in the course of time that either they will neglect these duties, or they will do something worse. And indeed they will prove it to you if you say to any of them that they should apply themselves more to the duties of their ministry, that they should think more about study, give themselves more to recollection and retirement, in a word, live more the life of an ecclesiastic. They will reply frankly that these things do not concern them; let other priests act according to their beliefs, they have all that they desire and have no need of more; and with this the question is closed for them. There is nothing to be surprised at in all this; they have become priests for mere material ends, they have reached their objective and they are not going to give themselves further trouble. This is the cause of the lamentations of the Fathers which you all know: *There are many priests but few true priests, many priests in name, but few priests in deed; the world is alive with priests, but there are few laborers in the vineyard of the Lord.* Some have taken upon themselves the priestly office because it is necessary for success in their objective but they do not carry out the duties of the office, and if they cannot help carrying them out materially, they give no thought to them.

✧ THE SECOND CLASS

The second class is composed of those who have entered the priestly state with intentions good in themselves, but what were these intentions? Not being fully persuaded of the importance and high dignity of their state, they propose to themselves a certain limited idea of priestly conduct and goodness, and if they do not say it with words, they make it known by facts that they are content to remain as they are and that they do not consider it necessary to rise any higher. In fact, if you exhort them to advance, to become more filled with the ecclesiastical spirit, to give themselves more resolutely to the practice of virtue and mortification, to detachment from the things of the world, to recollection, they will say immediately: "Oh! I do not feel myself disposed to rise any higher, I have always been satisfied to remain as I am; let those who wish advance higher. A person might indeed say of them they become priests by halves, a little of God, and a little of the world; now occupied with the affairs of the Church, now, with the affairs of the world. One day they labor, the next they do not. One day they spend in the works of the ministry, the next in parties and buffoonery. One day they are inclined to pray, the next, their heads are full of dissipation and distractions, so that their life is a medley of things sacred and profane, of ecclesiastical and worldly. They might truly be called amphibious beings as a pious author has called them. If you observe them, if you listen to them at a given moment they seem to be zealous priests, if you watch them at another time they are no longer so. And what have we to hope for from such a class of priests? I have already told you only too truly that there is not much to be hoped for from them, in fact nothing at all; and why? The reason is that we are in a state which permits of no mediocrity. The priest may be compared to the rod of Moses; raised aloft in the air, it works miracles, thrown on the ground it becomes a serpent that kills, that poisons. Therefore, either we are true priests, and then we will do immense good, or we are not, and then we will be instruments of great evil. It is not possible for us, I repeat, to maintain ourselves in a state of mediocrity.

What is said of a person who has a great enterprise on hands, who is engaged in a great lawsuit, or who is charged with the conduct of an affair of great importance can be strictly applied to us. If that person succeeds, he becomes a man distinguished by his riches, by his fame or by his genius; if he fails, he is a man lost and ruined. Thus it is with the priest, who has to deal with the most important affairs in this world; for he has to engage in a lawsuit, to carry on a struggle of the highest import with the world and the devil. If he is victorious, he is an outstanding man and cannot fail to be distinguished among his fellowmen. If, on the contrary, he deals with the great affair weakly and incompetently, then he is the vilest, most abject and most useless of men. The explanation is this: if the priest, even though he be a man of little ability, is truly good and recollected, a man who avoids places of dissipation and is given to study, the pursuit of virtue and mortification, and occupied with the affairs of the Church, you can say that he is an eminent man, distinct from the crowd and truly great, for he is so indeed. Even though he be of poor ability, without titles or high office and almost unknown, he is a pearl of great price, a treasure of great value by reason of the virtue with which he is adorned, of the good that he does by his word and example, and of the blessings that he obtains by his prayers.

Suppose on the contrary that the priest falls short by half of the standard of his calling; then you have a ruined man, a man who should be among the greatest of the world but who has become useless, harmful, wicked, not merely on account of the failure to produce good works, but much more on account of the evil which in course of time he will cause.

✣   THE THIRD CLASS

What conclusion then are we to draw from what has been said? It is that whoever wishes to be a priest should make up his mind decidedly and determinedly to be a priest truly, completely, and entirely. "*If you seek, seek,*"[7] said the Prophet Isaias. Some one will ask: Should not the Prophet have said: "If you do not seek, seek?" But no, what the Prophet said is right, for he had to deal with a people who wished and did not wish, a people who were hesitating. He called on them to make up their minds and said to them: If you wish to seek the Lord and serve Him, seek Him and serve Him truly and not merely in appearance: "If you seek, seek."

Let us priests repeat the same thing; let us resolve once for all to be true priests, if we wish to be priests at all. For what is the use of having the character of the priesthood, of wearing the habit, and of performing some of the duties of a priest, if at the same time we are worldly, dissipated, idle and devoted rather to secular affairs than to the pursuit of virtue and the works of our ministry? Let us confront ourselves with this challenge of the Prophet and, since we are priests, let us make ourselves priests in the full sense of the word. Let us add what is to be added, and take away what is to be taken away; let us reform whatever needs reform in our manner of life, be it much or little, whether the cost be small or great in order that we may succeed in being true priests. Away then with idleness and inactivity that make us lose so much time. Let those places, houses, companions be avoided, those excessive amusements, those appearances at theatres, fairs and markets cease; for what business has a priest in such places and with such people? Let the priest give himself to study, to prayer and to labor, and by adopting such a rule of life, it will not require a long time to make him a true priest, a man distinct from others and eminent, if not in the eyes of the world, at least in the eyes of God, which is the thing that matters, a man who will do immense good among ourselves and among others.

Let us then take a generous resolution to become true priests during these days of retreat, and we will see the giant strides that we will make in virtue along the road to Heaven. See what a man is capable of doing who sets before himself an aim to be accomplished and says to himself: At all costs I am determined on doing it, I am firmly resolved to succeed. People commonly say that such a resolution works miracles. And why cannot a priest do that? Why cannot we here do it? Well then, let each of us say, I am a priest, I wish to become one in deed and fact, I wish to succeed at all costs: I shall study, I shall pray, I shall leave aside everything else, I shall make every effort until I reach the goal; I am determined to become a priest, not a priest in name and appearance merely, but in deed, in spirit, in heart, a priest in fine furnished with all the virtues of my state, all the more so, because for us there is no turning back, for we are priests for ever. If we are true and real priests our crown is certain, but if we continue in our listlessness and inactivity—priests and not priests; laymen and not laymen—then our crown will be in jeopardy; there will be danger for us in life, there will be danger for us at death, and there will be much more danger for us in eternity.

---

1 Ecclus. 2:1.
2 Hyeron. ad Eliodor.
3 2 Tim. 3:17.
4 Titus 2:7.
5 Titus 1:6.
6 Coloss. 1:22.
7 Isai. 21:12.

Modesty

W E HAVE SEEN yesterday that although the priest is by nature a man like other men, he should make himself a special man, distinct from others by his virtue, as he is by his office and character. We have considered the dispositions which are necessary as a basis and foundation, in order to succeed in forming in ourselves that special man. Now coming to the means to be employed in erecting this great edifice, in accomplishing this great work, which is to become a perfect priest, it is necessary to study him separately in his external relations with other men, and in his interior life, which it is that characterizes him before God and forms the basis and foundation of that exterior which he must show to men: *The first solicitude of the priest should be the formation of the interior man.*[1]

✢ EXTERIOR DEPORTMENT

To commence then with the exterior, we ask: what should the external character of the priest be and what does the formation of it demand? It should be a ray from the Divinity or rather a mirror that reflects it. God, who is invisible to the human eye on this earth, has willed to give the consolation of His presence in a certain manner to men in order that they may be able to contemplate Him, approach Him and speak to Him, and in order to accomplish this what has He done? He has selected a man, separated him from other men, invested him with His powers and elevated him so high as to constitute him His minister and representative upon earth, so that the believer who sees him should say within himself: "Behold my God," that is to say, "Behold a person who reminds me of God, who represents God for me, who resembles God, and in a certain manner makes me see God with my eyes." Ah! what a great and lofty thought is this! And what nobility of rank for a priest! And at the same time what immense weight of responsibility sufficient to strike a priest with terror who reflects even a little upon it! What disillusionment for a priest who is reluctant to believe that our state is one of reserve, of subjection, of restraint when he thinks that he must everywhere and always represent in his person a God who lives and takes up His abode on earth! And what is it, you will ask me, that is necessary for the formation of the exterior of the priest which must be so regulated as to make him like a God upon earth? One virtue alone, I reply, or rather, one virtue which includes in itself all the other virtues. When we have acquired this virtue we shall have accomplished in ourselves in miniature a work truly great; but if this virtue is absent the work is spoiled, and the priest, far from being a ray of the Divinity or a mirror that reflects it, will be only a spectre showing more or less deformed and repellant the idea of his Lord. This virtue, my brethren, is modesty, a virtue little known and esteemed, and therefore little practiced by us priests. It will be the subject of our conference today; we shall consider what is this virtue, what is its importance and how it is to be practiced.

I   WHAT IS MODESTY?

St. Thomas, speaking about modesty, observes that the word is derived from the Latin word *modus*. In this sense it would appear that modesty is only a property common to all the virtues, for there is no virtue that does not observe measure, but that is not what we mean when we speak of modesty. "It is a special virtue, and it consists in moderating the movements and actions of our bodies so that they may be becoming and seemly both in what is done seriously and what is done in play." You are not to understand by this that it is a gift or quality purely external and mechanical; it is a true virtue which has its foundation and principle and root in the interior of the soul, that is to say, in the perfect disposition and moderation of the passions and affections of the soul, and it is manifested by those external signs by which it adjusts, moderates and disposes the exterior of the man, in the same way as it keeps the interior actions of the soul adjusted and disposed.

From this we can see that modesty is not a virtue merely in ap-
pearence, of little importance and characteristic only of certain persons
and certain states, such as women, or religious or novices. It is a true
virtue, a great virtue, a virtue common to all, a virtue rich and precious
above all others, as St. Ambrose says: *Modesty is riches; it is riches in the
eyes of God before whom no one is rich, it is riches because it is a portion of
God.*[2] This is great praise of the virtue of modesty, and it merits to be
well pondered over. *How is modesty riches? It is riches in the eyes of God
before whom no one is rich.* How can a virtue have such magic force as
to be able to transform a wretched man to such an extent as to make
him become rich and great even in the eyes of God before whom all are
poor? And let us not think that a Doctor of the Church of such keen
judgment has spoken without reflection; *Modesty is riches,* he said, relying on solid authority and supported by good reasons. In fact the Apostle St. Peter, speaking of the vanity of external ornament, recommended
the faithful of his time not to go in pursuit of such frivolity but to pay
attention to and esteem the interior man which manifests itself in a
quiet, modest spirit, and is rich in the sight of the Lord; "Whose adorning, let it not be in the wearing of gold, or the putting on of apparel;
but the hidden man of the heart, in the incorruptibility of a quiet and
meek spirit which is rich in the sight of the Lord."[3] The reasons which
determined our Saint to call modesty riches must have been very strong.

✥ Modesty Is Precious:

(1) Because It Supposes Many Other Virtues

I have already stated that this virtue, although external, has, according to the Angelic Doctor, its roots in the interior. And just as health,
although it consists in the perfect equilibrium and good disposition of
the internal organs, nevertheless manifests itself by external signs of
vigor, vivacity, and warmth; just as the excellence of a clock, which consists in the perfect accord of its internal mechanism, manifests itself by
the exact indication that it gives externally, so it is with modesty. That
which we see in the modest ecclesiastic, that which we read, from head
to foot, in the well-ordered and composed priest is but the indication
of a treasure which is hidden and buried within. I mean to say that it is

nothing less than the effect of the virtue, the strength of character, the mastery with which that priest commands in the interior of his house; of the wonderful and almost divine manner in which he regulates, adjusts and disposes his whole self.

It is impossible to conceive a man who is well-ordered, composed and modest, who has not at the same time all his passions in perfect control. Ask yourselves how could a priest be modest in his deportment, in his words, his gestures, his looks, if he has not humility, patience, meekness, charity, chastity and prudence? How could a priest possess these virtues, if he has not the habit and practice and the continuous prompt and absolute exercise of that general virtue which is called the mortification of his humor, his character and all his senses? Some time and in some cases he might be able to feign, to force himself to pretend, but to do it habitually without even thinking of it, to do it with facility and promptitude, is impossible without complete mastery over himself, which is not obtained without a very long and vigorous exercise of the virtues, especially of mortification. And in all this what a store of virtues, what an accumulation of merits, to make him rich in the eyes of God!

(2) *Because It Increases the Other Virtues*

But there is still more. Modesty not only presupposes and has as basis and foundation many other virtues, but it increases them and strengthens them because it keeps them always active and exercised, and that is another source of merit and riches before God. Indeed, modesty, if it is properly considered, is like a cross on which the whole man is nailed, day and night, both when he is alone and when he is in the company of others, whether he is engaged in labor or whether he is reposing. On this cross is nailed not only his hands and feet, but every part of his exterior being; his eyes, his ears, his tongue, and even the hairs of his head may be said to be nailed to it without interruption, without rest and without truce. Tell me then, is not this form of living in the continual exercise of virtue a perennial source of great riches and merit? Modesty is therefore riches, riches in the eyes of God with whom the lowering of the eyes does not pass without merit, and the mortification of a look may profit more than the acquisition of a kingdom.

(3) *Because Modesty Is a Portion of God*

Modesty is riches in the eyes of God, and is riches because it is a portion of God. What is the meaning of those great words; "A portion of God?" I cannot give you the exact meaning, but they certainly signify something very great. Some would explain them by saying that the virtue of modesty is a great gift from God, others, that in as much as modesty contains in itself great wealth of merits, it will obtain in Heaven a special reward in the possession of the Lord; but most authorities explain them by saying that the virtue of modesty has this special effect, that if communicates to man in external appearance and form a certain air of divinity. This last explanation would accord marvelously with what we read about our Divine Redeemer; that His modesty was of such kind and to such a degree that it made him an object of admiration before men and angels, and that even amidst all the humiliations He suffered, it caused Him to be recognized as a God of sovereign majesty. *The God of majesty appeared modest among men,*[4] says St. Ireneus, and St. Ambrose writes that such was the composure and the splendor of His person that it was sufficient to look at Him in the face to know Who He was: *The majesty of the Divinity hidden within shone in His face.* Dionysius the Areopagite makes a similar statement about the Blessed Virgin, that a person looking at her would be moved to rapture, that he would have adored her as God, if faith did not forbid him.

Let us conclude therefore in eulogy of this great virtue that *modesty is riches; riches* because of the store of merits that is included in it; *riches* by reason of so many merits gained by the continual exercise of self-denial and mortification; *riches;* finally, on account of the form that it imprints and stamps on the person who possesses it, so much so as to give him a portion, a share of God Himself.

II IMPORTANCE OF MODESTY

Having seen the nature and recognized the inestimable value of modesty, it only remains for us to consider its importance in order to spur us on to acquire it. There are three principal motives that should urge us to cultivate this great virtue: our own credit and reputation, the edification of our neighbor, and the honor and glory of our God.

(1) *For the Honor of God*

Let us commence with the last because it is the most noble, the most sublime, and that should always be the first consideration for a priest who is a man of God. Is it not our wish that God be esteemed, honored and served with respect, reverence and love? Let us, by the modesty of our exterior conduct, cause the people to have a great and worthy opinion of Him. The common people, generally speaking, form their idea of God, of religion and of all pious practices and functions from the idea and judgment that they form of His ministers. Modesty, as we have seen, is that virtue which causes the priest to be venerated like a divinity; and the respect and veneration which the faithful conceive for him they extend at the same time to his ministry, to his functions, to religion, and to God Himself, because they know that these things constitute a unity. If they think of them, if they speak of them, if they approach them, each of them is measured with the same esteem and the same regard. Suppose the priest appears unworthy in their eyes on account of his lack of gravity and composure, everything appears vile and contemptible to them: despicable is his ministry, despicable is the religion he preaches, despicable are the religious practices and functions, and this contempt, a person might say, extends even to God. St. Ambrose says: *It is fitting that our actions should bear public testimony to and proclaim the truth and divinity of our religion so that those who see the minister adorned with congruous virtues may confess the Lord and venerate Him who has such servants.*[5] What admirable force is that virtue which teaches the people in a masterful way the idea and concept of God Himself and of His religion! And we need not be surprised, for it is a thing that is seen everywhere in the world and we ourselves have experienced it. If we enter a house about whose inhabitants and owners we know nothing, by merely seeing and considering the people in the house—the servants and family—we immediately, in spite of ourselves, form an idea of, pronounce a judgment on the owners. If we find the occupants grave and composed, the house suitably equipped, in good order and gracefully adorned, there arises in us naturally a certain respect and reverence for the servants, and with it a high opinion of the house and a veneration for its owners, and we go on repeating in our minds: "Oh! how fine these people must be who have servants and a family in such good order! On the other hand, if, as soon as we put our foot into the house, we meet with people of quite a different sort, puerile, frivolous, dissipated, without order or method, we come to have a low idea of servants, house and masters, even though we force ourselves to think otherwise, so true is it that the goodness of the servants and ministers redounds to the honor and glory of their master. I therefore repeat with St. Ambrose that the conduct of the minister should be such that those who see him should praise and venerate the Lord who has such servants.

On an occasion when a solemn religious function was celebrated in public there were clergy of various grades and also ecclesiastical students, and among a group of laymen who were present, there was one who asked which were the priests, and which the students, because he could not distinguish between them. A man gave him a sign by which he could distinguish between them, and do you know what was the sign? Perhaps it was that the priests were those who were better dressed, who appeared to be older, and who were placed in a more dignified position. No: it was just the sign that we have been discussing. "Look," he said, in a voice loud enough to be heard by many; "Look at those who have their eyes modestly cast down, those are the priests." This is the line of reasoning, and the method of identification according to which the common people recognize us and judge us, and it brings me to consider the second motive we have to cherish this virtue, which is the edification of our neighbor.

(2) *Importance of Modesty for the Edification of*
Our Neighbor

And on this question it is not necessary to give many reasons because the matter is too clear. Example, it is, according to the opinion of all, which most efficaciously and almost infallibly touches, moves and influences others. Preaching, almsgiving and persuasion edify, instruct and move people to do good, but not with the force of example. What the Fathers of the Council of Trent have said on this question is well known: *There is nothing which more efficaciously draws others to piety and to the assiduous worship of God than the life and example of those who have dedicated themselves to the Divine ministry.*[6] *The Life:* this refers to the virtue which makes the priest good and holy, but it is not sufficient to edify. Even though a priest were an oracle of learning, a Seraph of love, so long as he gives no external sign, so long as he does not make his virtue known, he does not fulfill that other duty, which is, besides being good, to edify others and draw them on to virtue and holiness. *Example:* This does not consist in learning or dignities or titles or dress, but in the composed and modest exterior, and that it is which is necessary for the edification of our neighbor. Virtue makes the priest good in himself and for himself; example makes him good for others. And this example, which is nothing else than modesty, gives just that which shows forth the goodness and virtue of the priest and is that which, properly speaking, edifies, but why? The same Council gives the answer; *Because it is an unending form of preaching.*[7] It is a continuous sermon, a manner of preaching that makes the priest all tongue from head to foot. He preaches with his eyes, with his hands, with his feet, and even with his hair, and this manner of preaching is so strong and efficacious that it never goes without fruit, because it either gains the person who sees it or condemns him. It either spurs him on to do good or it confounds him and puts him to shame for his evil conduct. And it was this very line of reasoning that a holy Father used in order to persuade an ecclesiastic to adopt the constant practice of this virtue. He said to him: Whoever looks at you with the eyes of an interior man—that is whoever looks at you with reflection—will have received instruction by merely looking at you even though you do not open your mouth. For when you show a modest exterior you will reprove delinquents even while you keep silent.

Let us keep this well in mind: a quiet and tranquil countenance, eyes cast down, a pleasing and candid appearance, the head firm and quiet, a dignified deportment, a grave and natural walk, clean but simple dress will all have the effect of a sharp reproof for frivolous, inconstant, worldly men given to the pleasures of life. St. Chrysostom had already expressed the same sentiments for the ecclesiastics of his time: "*The outward bearing* (of the priest), *his walk, his words and acts will all have a beneficial effect on those who hear him and those who see him.*" Everything in the modest ecclesiastic will help to make the people conceive a high and worthy idea of God and of His religion, as I have already said; it will help to edify our neighbor and draw him on to the practice of that virtue which makes him who practices it so lovable and which clothes him with so many attractions; it helps, in fine, to make the world conceive a high esteem of us, which is the third motive.

(3) *Importance of Modesty for Our Own Reputation Necessity of Having a Good Name*

First of all, you must not think that the care of the priest's own reputation and of the esteem in which he is held is the result of pride and that it must be displeasing to the Lord. No, that cannot be when you work from a proper motive; then it is prudence, it is the rule of good government, it is the practice of charity, and it is a debt to justice. "For what concerns yourself in particular, you are not to care about having honor and esteem," says St. John Chrysostom, "on the contrary, you should seek rather humiliation and contempt, for that is material for and practice of the most beautiful virtues, and will serve to gain an abundant store of most precious merits." But the same does not hold for what concerns the salvation of others, for if a priest loses his good name, his ministry would be useless and might even be harmful. *The preaching of the priest whose life is despised, is held in contempt,* says St. Gregory.[8] And what use could you make of a priest who enjoys little credit or esteem? To such a priest the words of Our Lord may be applied: "And the unprofitable servant cast ye out into the exterior darkness."[9] A person who takes no care of his reputation, and thus becomes good for nothing, allows himself to be reckoned among the most obscure and wretched. Indeed, what good could a priest do who has not the esteem, the respect and confidence of the people? If you put him at the altar, what edification will his Mass give? If he ascends the pulpit, what attention will be paid to his exhortations even though he be a gifted preacher, full of energy and zeal, and his doctrine sound? If he sits in the tribunal of penance I would like to know how many true penitents he can count to whom he will be really useful. As for me, I do not know who would be willing to put his soul in the hands of one whom all know to be incapable of directing and regulating his own. In fact, no matter what functions you entrust to him, even the most sacred and the most tremendous, they will enjoy no more respect among the people than the priest who fulfills them.

Therefore the Apostles, when seeking for companions to help them in their ministry, rightly insisted that these should be above all men of credit and reputation. "Wherefore, look ye out among you seven men of good reputation, full of the Holy Ghost and wisdom"[10] St. Paul among the many grave precepts which he gave to those two great ecclesiastics, Timothy and Titus, gave as one of the principal, that they should so conduct themselves that none of their flock would dare to be wanting in esteem for them.

III   Modesty Helps Us to Acquire a Good Name

I shall not dwell further on this point. What I have said should suffice to make it clear. I rather go on to the question; what is it that will gain for the priest the esteem and reputation so necessary for him in order to do good to his neighbor? Above all, it is modesty. It is true that esteem for a person is based on internal virtue, but it is modesty that manifests this virtue exteriorly, gives a becoming appearance to the exterior man and bears witness to the virtue within which cannot be seen: "*A man is known by his look: and a wise man . . . is known by his countenance. The attire of the body . . . . and the gait of man, show what he is.*"[11] The value of gold is indeed in its substance; but that which certifies its value, which cannot be seen, is that which can be seen and touched, such as the color, the sound, the weight and the other qualities that can be apprehended by the senses: "*Who is a wise man and endued with knowledge, among you?*"—that is the internal virtue. "*Let him shew by a good conversation, his work in the meekness of wisdom.*"[12] that is, according to St. James, the exterior deportment.

IV   Practice of Modesty

Sufficient has been said about the importance of modesty. Let us pass on to determine the material for and the practice of this virtue. You know that the material is ample. Look at the priest from head to foot, there is not a part of his person that is excepted; modesty should cover and clothe him completely. Consider the priest anywhere you wish—in the church or outside the church, in his home or on the street, at labor or at rest—everywhere you should find in him this virtue, if he is a true priest. No circumstance of place or time or business can dispense him from it.

We have already seen at the beginning of this conference the views of the Angelic Doctor; that modesty has for the primary and direct scope and material all the movements and actions of the body, and so arranges them that they may be becoming and worthy of respect, both those concerning his serious work and those concerning his recreation. Whether the priest is engaged in serious work, or jests, or takes part in some amusing pastime, modesty should regulate all, not merely his actions, but the things that belong to the use, convenience or adornment of his person, *so that all may be becoming and worthy of respect*. This is what the Fathers of the Council of Trent meant when they laid down rules for the whole body of the clergy in such grave form: *Therefore it is most fitting that clerics called to the service of the Lord should all so arrange their life and conduct that they show nothing in their dress, their carriage, their walk, and in all other things, but what is grave and moderate, and befitting for their calling.*[13] They prescribed modesty in dress, modesty of the hands, the manner of holding them, moving them, when to keep them at rest, with what moderation, regard and measure. They laid down rules about how he should deport himself on the street and how he should walk in church; they laid down rules for his speaking which directed him how to speak well, how he should moderate the tone of his voice, his gestures, how he should choose his words, because the wrong use of a single word is capable of seriously injuring a priest's reputation. They added the phrase: *in all other things,* thus laying down rules for all his conduct, because they did not wish that the priest should appear defective in anything, but that he should show forth gravity, moderation and *religion* in everything. But what did they mean by *religion?* They meant that he has to make known to everyone and in everything—whether he eats, or sleeps, or laughs, or jests, or walks, or amuses himself—that he is a man of religion, a man of God.

Let those who ask why so many rules, why such rigor that admits of no excuse—*sic decet omnino*—listen to the reason given by the same Council: *in order that their actions may gain for them the veneration of all*[14]*;* in order that all may have respect for the priest, may trust him and venerate him. To gain this object there is no more efficacious means than modesty, as St. John Chrysostom observes.[15] And do not imagine that such a spirit, and such delicate solicitude for the conduct of the clergy began in the Church only at the time of the Council of Trent. St. Augustine had already recommended in almost the same terms to the clergy of his time: *In walk, in posture, in dress and in all your movements, let there be nothing that will give offense to anyone who sees you.*

✣ MODESTY IN CHURCH

Now although the scope of this virtue is so vast and extensive, I shall stop to recommend it especially in church during the sacred functions in what regards the exterior of our persons but particularly, the custody of our eyes. We are witnesses daily of irreverences, of scandals, of dissipation, of which many lay people are guilty in the sacred edifices and during the sacred functions, and we are accustomed to rebuke them for the wickedness of their conduct and the lack of faith. This indeed is only our duty; but I do not hesitate to say that our own lack of modesty, the want of composure and the carelessness of our outward appearance in these same places and at these same functions must be held to be in great measure the cause of these abuses. Do we not see priests who, in church, at the altar, in the confessional, and even when vested for Mass, not only raise their eyes, but turn them round in all directions and fix them on people as if they wished to study them, and who are so uneasy and restless, craning their necks and moving hands and feet, that they show plainly that they cannot control themselves? How is it possible for the people to be edified at such a sight and learn to respect the house of God, and stand with reverence and composure? On one occasion it happened that a layman came into a church looking for a priest to hear his Confession. As soon as he entered he saw a confessor who, having despatched a penitent from one side of the confessional before turning to the other, had a good look round the church, and, not content with that, leaned out straining his eyes in order to get a better view of everything. At such a sight the man took his hat and went out saying that such a confessor would hardly suit him.

But some priest will say: I do it without thinking of it, and without hardly being aware of it. What difference does that make? The harm is done all the same, and do not think that you can be excused because there is not actual advertance; antecedent advertance is sufficient. You know that you have that habit, and why do you not strive to mend it? But in my country, in the place where I am, I have always done so, and no one has ever said anything, no one has ever been scandalized, so far as I know. No one has been scandalized! But the way in which so many people behave in church—in fact almost all in some places—shows only too plainly whether they have been scandalized or not. Therefore, I repeat that if we priests were all that we should be in church while sacred ceremonies are going on, and above all when we are vested; if we were mirrors of the Divinity by our modesty, if we were recollected, grave, dignified with our eyes fixed and cast down, I think that more than one scandal, more than one irreverence would be prevented in the house of the Lord. The layman, however rude and ignorant or hostile he may be, will not have the audacity to show himself irreverent if he has before him habitually a priest who, by his composure and modesty, reminds him of the place in which he is, or who makes him desist quickly if he is guilty of irreverence.

But what are the means that will help the priest to acquire this virtue? Do not think that in order to be modest one must be sad and melancholic, for a serene, tranquil and joyous appearance is the effect of this virtue: *Vultus serenus,* says St. Bernard, *quamdam in facie hilaritatem praetendit.*[16]

✢   MEANS TO ACQUIRE MODESTY:

(1) *Reflection*

The means that I suggest to acquire this virtue are two: one is of the mind, reflection, the other is a work of the hands. The reflection that I mean is the thought that we are always under the eyes of God. If the sight and presence of a great personage of the world so overawes us and makes us so cautious that we measure every word in order to avoid anything unbecoming or impolite, what force should not the thought of the presence of God have for a person of lively faith? God hears me, God sees me, God is looking at me; at this moment He is looking at how I stand, how I walk, He sees me laughing, He is listening to the joke I make. But for the priest there is still more; this God who sees me, who is looking at me is the same God who has charged me with the office of representing Him. If I speak, it is as if God speaks, if I look, it is as if God looks; if I sit or walk or amuse myself, it is as if God did these things: I am His representative, His instrument, all my acts are rather His than mine, because I do them through Him and on His account, and this is so in every case even in the least of my actions. He gains from them or He loses by them. Everything I do can augment or diminish His honor, since the figure, the appearance that God makes here below in this world depends on me. Ah! what courage, what stimulus will not this consideration give to a priest of lively faith to content and please God, and to so act that he will not have to see His honor and glory diminished!

(2) *Mortification*

However, along with this consideration we require a work of the hands; it will be the same as that employed with a plant that can be kept in order only with difficulty. Let us take the vine, which among all plants may be said to be the most disorderly, the most lawless and the most wanting in method. What do we do to keep it in order? We cut it, we prune it, we clip off superfluous leaves, we bind it, until we make it one of the most docile of plants, and we arrange it so as to present the best appearance. This is the work of the hands to be employed with ourselves in order to make ourselves composed, well-ordered and modest. Those eyes of ours, that tongue, those hands, indeed, our whole body, is more disordered and lawless than any plant. The eyes wander, the tongue wags, now it is a look of curiosity, now an uncontrolled gesture, now a manner of acting a little too free, a word too many, an uneasy, fidgety, dissipated manner of acting, speaking or deporting ourselves, so that our whole being looks like a tissue or mass of confusion and disorder, like a vine that is abandoned to itself. What then is to be done? I am the master and it lies with me to command. Let those looks be controlled, those eyes cast down, that word remain unspoken, those hands kept steady, our walk be more grave and our manner of sitting more becoming. I make a pact not only with my eyes, my tongue, my hands, my feet, even with my hair, but also with my whole person, with my whole self, so that nothing is done, no movement is made without my thinking of it, wishing it and agreeing to it. You will see how in a short time this body, however uncontrolled it may be, will be put in order and will appear quite different from what it used to be formerly; and the faithful, astonished, surprised, edified will all ask who is this priest so devout, so recollected, so modest? Who is he? You do not know him, but he has been here so long, you have seen him so often, and do you not recognize him? Indeed no, it appears that he is not the same man; the man we knew could not stand steady, his eyes were always wandering, now he appears to be really a different man. He is a different man, and the same man, as you wish. He is the same in person but different in way of acting, in deportment, in manners, just as the vine after being well pruned is still the same vine, although it appears completely different.

You will tell me that this work will be difficult, all the more so because you are not accustomed to it. I reply that the priest of good will who, as we have said yesterday, seriously wishes to make himself a worthy ecclesiastic will find the means and the strength to do it. It will be difficult, but very many laymen who have neither the motives nor the obligations that we have, do it. It will be difficult, but the difficulty will go on diminishing every day, and a time will come, and will come soon, when it will cost us more to omit that mortification than to practice it; it will be difficult, but even though it is, it should be done, because the unmortified priest will by it become more modest, and consequently, a more worthy representative of God upon earth; it will be difficult, but let us recollect that God will keep an account of even our smallest effort: every act of control that we exercise over our senses, were it even only over the movement of an eyebrow, will be written down and recompensed. Oh, what store of merits a priest can lay up who gives himself to this practice! Suppose he only performs ten of those acts of control over the senses each day—and indeed it will be almost impossible for the priest to limit himself to that number when he is a mortified man, for he will make many more, even hundreds each day—but suppose he makes only ten, multiply that by the weeks, the months, the years—what a store, what a weight, what a crown of merits he will have on his bed of death to bring with him into eternity! And all this will be accomplished without great labor, without noise, unknown to the world and almost to himself. Even ourselves will be amazed when surrounded with these works, we will hear them one day like a choir of so many voices saying to us: these are your works. The world too, more amazed still, will be compelled in spite of itself on that great day of the General Judgment to see, recognize and acknowledge this obscure and hidden but truly great and heroic virtue of the good priest. Amen.

1 Conc. Hild. de Can. cap. XIII.
2 Summa 2. 2.ae, q. 160. a. 1. et 2.
3 De Offic. lib. I. cap. 18.
4 1. Petr. 3:4.
5 De Offic. lib. I, cap. ult.
6 Sess. XXII. De Reform. cap. I.
7 Sess. XXV. De Reform. cap. I.
8 Hom. XII, in Evang.
9 Matt. 25:30.
10 Acts 6:3.
11 Ecclus. 19:26-27.
12 James 3:13.
13 Sess. XXII. De Reform. cap. I.
14 Ibid.
15 Hom. I de Dei nat.
16 Form. hon. vit. cap. 6.

Flight from the World

<hr />

✣ FORMATION OF THE INTERIOR

*T*HE PRIEST, as we have seen, must first form his exterior by means of mortification and modesty and, having become a mirror of virtue so as to be able to represent with the least degree of unworthiness possible the Divinity upon earth, his next step must be to enter within in order to examine, reform and perfect the most noble and precious part, the only substantial part of his being, which is the interior, the heart of the priest. Oh, the heart of a priest, what a marvellous word, and what riches, what an inestimable treasure it connotes! The Tabernacle of the Jews was a composite of marvels on account of the elegance of design and the preciousness of its materials, but especially on account of the dignity of its Designer, who was God Himself.

But what comparison could that material tabernacle, rich and beautiful and precious as it was, bear with the spiritual tabernacle, which is the heart of a priest adorned, not with gold and precious stones like the ancient tabernacle, but with every kind of merit and virtue, and destined, not merely to contain the symbols of the Divinity upon earth, but to become the royal palace and the throne of that God living on earth? It belongs to God to form this heart, to build this celestial tabernacle, to perfect this work more divine than human; nothing else remains for us but to give our material cooperation like Moses, and to use the means to execute this great design.

I   FIRST MEANS: FLIGHT FROM THE WORLD

The first means, without which all others will be useless, is to put far away everything that is not in conformity with that heart. There is question of forming an internal, spiritual, celestial abode: away then with whatever is external, superficial, mundane and earthly!

God and the world cannot exist in the heart together; the spirit of the one is incompatible with the spirit of the other. It is absolutely necessary for the priest to be convinced of this; he cannot be of the world and be the temple of God, nor can he be half of one and half of the other. God neither accepts a divided heart nor any conditions. The ecclesiastic who has decided to be, who really wishes to be the temple of God, must come of necessity to this severing, this divorce, this separation from the world; separation of heart by detachment from, and contempt for, its follies; separation of body and of person, as far as is possible, by flight, by seclusion and by solitude. This is the theme and argument of the present conference. We shall see firstly, the necessity for this double separation from the world in an ecclesiastic; secondly, the advantages that he will gain from it for himself and for others; finally, we shall add some means that will help us to defend ourselves and keep us far away from the world and its distractions.

Let us pray our Divine Redeemer that He may repeat to us from that tabernacle what He repeated so many times to His first priests, His Apostles: *"You are not of the world, but I have chosen you out of the world."* [1] I have separated you from it: remember therefore that you are not of it and that you do not belong to it. Let us ask Him to say to us: My son, you are no longer of this world, recognize it, believe it, and keep it well in mind; you are not of the world, the world is no longer for you: I have selected you, I have divided you, I have separated you.

(1)   *Separation of the Heart from the World*

Our separation from the world must be twofold: separation of the heart, and separation of the body. Let us first speak of separation of the heart and affections. Of what use to an ecclesiastic would mere material separation from the world be if there was wanting that of the mind and heart? Of what advantage would it be for a priest to be all the day shut up in a room and thus made invisible to the world, if his mind and head were in the meantime filled with worldly ideas and concerns? What good would it do him not to allow himself to see with the eyes of body, if in the interior of his heart and soul, he was longing, sighing and seeking for what the world loves, seeks and sighs for?

When we speak therefore of a detached priest, we mean primarily a man who not merely by bodily presence—which is the least—flees from and hides from the world, but in his ideas, thoughts, affections and desires separates and divides himself from it; who does not think as the world thinks, who does not esteem what the world esteems, who does not seek or desire what the world eagerly longs for and sighs for. What the spirit of world is, what are the things it strives for, what are its aims and desires we know already: "*For all that is in the world is the concupiscence of the flesh and the concupiscence of the eyes and the pride of life, which is not of the Father but is of the world.*"[2] Sound the hearts and desires of worldly men as much as you like, and you will find that everything is of the flesh: the desire for pleasure and riches, vanity and pride, and the will to dominate. If a man cannot obtain these things in fact he desires them with the heart, he uses all his energy to get them, he strives after them passionately and does not stop until he obtains them; and when he does not succeed, he torments himself, he despairs, he goes mad and sometimes he either shortens his life or commits suicide. Just say to worldly people that they are not made for this world, that all that is in the world is but smoke and vanity, that everything is passing and transitory, that there is another world, another country which is our real home awaiting us, that it is finer, immensely greater than this world and that it is eternal; and they will tell you that this is a language that they do not understand. They do not wish to understand, because for them, "*This saying is hard.*"[3] And by their deeds, and indeed often in word, they say as the Athenians said to St. Paul: "*We will hear thee again concerning this matter,*"[4] and in the meantime, they enjoy the world.

But if worldlings do not understand and do not want to understand because they are so blind, "*They are blind and leaders of the blind,*"[5] we priests should take it in and understand it for: "*We have received not the spirit of this world, but the Spirit that is of God.*"[6] Selected out of the world and, in a manner wrenched from it, we have been placed in our state as in a secluded place, sheltered and protected from all those snares and pitfalls. Therefore casting a glance of sorrow and compassion on the world, as our Divine Redeemer cast on the doomed city of Jerusalem, we also should exclaim: O blind and miserable worldlings! If you did but know the danger hidden beneath the ground on which you are walking, the folly of your desires, the madness of this world, the vanity of all, its pleasures, how much better it would be for you! Happy are we who, by a special light disillusioned about the outward appearance of earthly things and, by our vocation placed above them, have turned our backs upon them, and have taken God as our inheritance, and want to have nothing to do with this world and its folly. Let him who wishes have it. As for me, with all my heart and will, I select and take the Lord as my portion, as my inheritance: *Dominus pars haereditatis meae.* The choice is made, the choice could not be better, I have therefore divined the right course. But, my dear Fathers, let not this choice be one only in name. We have said that we want to have nothing to do with this world. Let then the step we took and the promise we made become a reality and not remain a mere high-sounding phrase. Before we begin the external act, let it be a reality in our internal sentiments.

The beatitudes and the happiness that Our Lord promised with them in the Sermon on the Mount are an object of derision and laughter for the world, but for the priest they should be the guide of all his conduct. He should be fully and totally convinced about the truth contained in them. Let each one then enter into himself, let him think well and say to himself honestly: I know that my senses and my passions want to make me believe what the world says and thinks about the beatitudes. But am I really convinced, do I really hold as certain in the bottom of my heart, that those are truly blessed and fortunate in the sight of the Lord—not with a mere apparent happiness in name but truly and really happy—who are not attached in any way to the riches and pleasures of this world? Am I convinced that those people who do not seek them, who know how to suffer, to be silent and to endure; who are contradicted, blamed and despised unjustly by the world, and who mourn and lament under the weight of crosses and tribulations are blessed? When there is in me this spirit, this persuasion, this belief, then I can be sure that I truly possess the Spirit of the Lord. Then I shall be able to say that I am divided and separated from this world in heart, since my manner of seeing and thinking is so different from that of the world that there is no hope of bridging the gulf between us, because we think in a manner totally opposed.

But in order not to be mistaken in a matter so important, let each one observe the signs and indications of his division and separation from the world, which are his judgments and sentiments. I mean, let each one note in practice the importance and weight he gives to things of the world, the way in which he occupies himself with them, and the effects he feels from them. Tell me, dear Fathers, can it be hoped for, or can it be said that a priest is detached from the world when, in his conversations and pastimes, there is no more frequent or welcome subject than secular and profane affairs, parties and amusements, and when he speaks of them from experience and with such heat as to show that he attaches great importance to them. Can we say that a priest is filled with that spirit of detachment who, on every occasion that presents itself—if indeed he does not go in search for occasions—mixes himself up and occupies himself with such worldly affairs, as contracts, purchases, sales and objects of gain, to the detriment of his ministry and of that piety and recollection which are so necessary for the interior life of a priest? Can a person say of a priest that he is not bound hands and feet to the world, if he cannot remain in his house or pass a single day without going here and there, to meetings of cliques, or parties of amusement? And this brings us to the second part of our conference, which is flight from the world.

(2) *Separation of Body from the World*

It is true that for us separation from the world in heart is the most necessary and substantial part, since it is indispensable, but it does not follow that we can neglect corporal separation, which is flight from the world itself. It is impossible for a priest to arrive at the first and be really separated from the world in heart and mind if he is given to gadding about, looking at everything, wanting to know everything, chatting and amusing himself in the midst of the world. It is impossible for him to be an interior man with the priestly spirit if he is not able to control himself so as to remain in the seclusion of his house or room when possible. I say, when possible, for I do not want you to forget that discretion must be used, nor do I want to put the secular priest in the same class as the religious. I will merely note that it will cost a secular priest more to maintain fitting seclusion than a religious, because the latter has doors, rules and superiors to keep him within. The secular priest has only his own virtue to serve him as cloister, door and rule. And if this virtue is lacking, he is threatened with ruin. Like a river that has broken the banks which keep it in its bed, he rushes here and there wherever the weathercock turns, or inclination or whim carries him, and then he has reason to lament and grieve over his disorders, as the prophet Jeremias lamented when he said: *"The stones of the sanctuary are scattered in the top of every street."*[7] "What are those stones" asks St. Gregory "specially chiseled, because they were destined to serve as ornament and decoration in the house of the Lord, which are seen scattered here and there, mixed and confused with every kind of rubbish?" And the Saint in grief replies; *"These stones of the Sanctuary lie scattered over the streets, when persons in holy orders abandon themselves to lives of pleasure and become immersed in world affairs."*[8] These scattered stones are the priests who rove about through the most public and frequented places and indulge in the business transactions and amusements of the most worldly-minded people of the world. If you want to find them you need not go to their houses to look for them, for they use them only to sleep in; nor need you seek for them in the church, which they do not use even to make a little preparation for, or thanksgiving after Mass. Will you find them perhaps at some meeting of studious companions intent on improving themselves with useful study and the cultivation of virtue? Far from it, for they have no inclination for such places. I will tell you where they are if you want to find them. They are there in that house, at that corner, at a meeting of that clique, on that bench, in that shop; sitting there idle, joking and laughing, listening to the news and discussing it and thus losing whole days: *"The stones of the Sanctuary are scattered in the top of every street."*[9] If you do not find them there, they will have gone off to the country to a hunt, or to a party, or to transact some business that belongs more to a merchant than to an ecclesiastic. Behold realized to the letter the disorders over which the Prophet lamented. These men, like the stones of the sanctuary, had been formed and chiseled during many years in college with great care and labor, in order to be placed in the Church of the Lord to edify the people; now all their beauty and lustre are gone, and they lie here and there like stones mixed and confused with earth and mud. What a pity, what a heartbreak, in these times when there is such a want for true priests, to see these men who, weary of themselves and of their state, give the impression that they cannot live if they are not speaking of the world, if they are not jesting with the world. "Flee then," I repeat with the Prophet Jeremias. "*flee ye from the midst of Babylon and let every one save his own life.*"[10] This is the only way that is left to the priest in the midst of the sea of this world: retirement, solitude, and flight from the world. In order not to be too diffuse, I shall dwell on two motives only which absolutely demand this retirement and separation from the world; which are our conscience and our reputation.

II   Motives for Separation from the World

(1) *In Order to Keep the Conscience Pure*

The roads of the world are dirty and muddy. It is impossible therefore for those who frequently travel on them to avoid being covered with dirt and mud. Observe the difference in personal cleanliness between a person who is always at home, and another who travels through the country at every time and season. The person who remains at home easily keeps his clothes clean, and if they get soiled, it will be but lightly and he will immediately brush the dust or dirt away without difficulty. But he that travels on the roads will get his clothes soiled with mud in a short time, and as he continues doing so, there will be mud upon mud; and what is worse, he himself will not even notice it, so much is he distracted by and occupied with what he sees and meets. And perhaps he will even think that he is cutting a very fine figure, whereas he is in a pitiable state. Apply this comparison to the spiritual lives of the priest who lives a retired life, and the worldly priest. The priest who loves his cell is, says St. Ambrose, like the river that remains tranquil in its bed and keeps its waters limpid and pure, while the one that goes out and rambles here and there is like the river that overflows its banks and rushes furiously through the country, and then the water which, in its natural channel, was clear and limpid, becomes dirty and muddy and carries with it every kind of filth and dirt, for a river that bursts its banks quickly collects mud.

Oh! I know how to look after myself, the worldly priest will reply immediately. I know what I am doing, and certainly that will not happen to me. What shall we say to these pillars who regard themselves so solid as to trust themselves to every kind of wind? Is it that they should test themselves against the world? I will leave reasoning apart and say: let us proceed to the proof. Let us take two priests, one different from the other; one given to solitude, to passing his life as far as possible in the quiet and silence of his room; the other, accustomed to spend the whole or almost the whole day away from home at games, parties, gossip, buffoonery and such like. Let us compare their conduct, their spirit, their method of fulfilling their duties of preaching, of hearing Confessions. Let us consider the conduct of these two in their relation with the world, in speaking, laughing, recreation. I am quite sure that there will be no need of any discussion or reasoning to convince ourselves which of the two has gathered most mud and dirt. *Even the Religious has need to cleanse his heart from the dust of the world.*[11] If the heart of a devout and pious religious living in solitude cannot escape being soiled with the dust of this world, just think with how much dust, or rather with how much mud, that priest will be covered who cannot bring himself to remain at home but goes out exposed to every wind that blows.

The dialogue between two old monks treating of this very subject that we find recorded is both interesting and instructive. There was a certain monk who could never stay at home, his cell had become a most irksome prison for him, and hence he was frequently abroad. And, not content with going round the countryside, he was wont to go into the villages and even into the city, and there, as is the custom of vagrants, he gazed at everybody, he looked at everything, he amused himself and chatted with everyone. Another monk who observed his wanderings and foresaw the consequences, thought it his duty to admonish him, and one day took him apart and said to him: "You know, my dear brother, that it is not good that a religious should allow himself to be seen so often in public, that he should stop to talk and amuse himself with everything and everybody. You know that the people observe it and are scandalized. Recollect that the world is full of pitfalls and dangers, and think what may happen to you if you do not take more precautions? Remember also that by talking with and mixing with the people of the world, a religious is always the loser. Therefore take my advice if you wish to be safe from danger, leave the world and live a little more retired." The other monk listened to him and what was his reply? Did he profit by the advice? Oh! it is very difficult for a religious, whether he be a priest or a brother, to profit by a correction, even though it is conveyed in the kindest and sweetest manner. "That is all melancholy," replied the idle monk, "mere pettiness and scruples; sanctity does not consist in those things. It is necessary to be simple in heart, to have a right intention and a clear conscience; that is what pleases the good God. What you say is the effect of a small heart and a narrow mind. Consider the sublime discourses, the wise lessons that those who frequent the world are able to give! And not only is it true that monks can give such discourses, but priests of our day often repeat them. What need is there then to remain shut up so much? Have not we also to live in the world and in society? And what harm is there in it? We know well that a priest ought to be virtuous and holy, but does virtue and holiness consist in what you say? Those are just melancholic ideas that pass through your head. A right intention, simplicity in everything, a clear conscience, that is what is necessary, the rest is foolish nonsense." "Ah, Lord," exclaimed the other monk raising his hands to Heaven, "may Thou be blessed and praised for the great virtue of my fellow monk here! I, in the desert, confined to my cell without seeing the world and without intercourse with anyone, have to fatigue myself much and, only with great efforts, can I keep my heart pure, have a right intention in everything and maintain my conscience clean and free from every stain. This man, unlike me, living in the midst of the world, seeing and talking with everyone, with his eyes and ears full of the scandals and allurements of the world, has, in spite of all, arrived at such perfection; he fears nothing at all, nothing gives him trouble, nothing worries him and he says that always and in everything his conscience is clear and pure!"

Well! I should say to those broad-minded ecclesiastics: allow me to make just a little examination of that conscience so frank and clear. A clear conscience! But in the midst of so much dissipation how can the duties of celebrating Mass, reading the Divine Office, and administering the Sacraments be carried out properly? How can you have the knowledge necessary for preaching, hearing Confessions or even for teaching catechism properly and with fruit, if you are always away from home and do not study? Where will you get the strength to resist so many temptations if you do not pray? Will you continue, nevertheless, to say that you have a clear and unblemished conscience? God grant that you may not be like the man who, knowing that his clothes were covered with mud, pretended not to notice it or see it, and went forward as if he was the best groomed and the best dressed man in the country: *"And they were mingled among the heathens, and learned their works: and served their idols."* [12]

Thus it happened to the Jews, because by mixing with the pagans and living among them they contracted their vices, and adopted their habits and even went so far as to adore their gods, with the result that they became a cause of scandal to those same pagans whose vices they had adopted: *"And they became a scandal to them."* [13] This is what the Jews gained by mixing with the pagans, and this is what the priest gains when he abandons recollection and solitude and frequents the haunts of the world. He learns the maxims of the world, he adopts its views, his mind becomes immersed in mundane affairs, his heart becomes entangled with friendships, attachments and pursuits that are all of the world. He begins to love, to adore what the world loves and adores; riches, games, amusements, vanities, rivalries and even worse. And when he has contracted the vices and adopted the customs of the world the priest becomes to worldly people an object of scandal: *Commixtus est inter gentes et didicit opera eorum . . . et factus est illis in scandalum.* [14] And this is another very strong motive for cultivating retirement in order that we may not lose our reputation in the eyes of the world and with it the means of being able to do good in it.

(2) *In Order to Protect Our Reputation*

By a special disposition of Providence, the world, even though wicked, has a very high, almost a divine idea of the priest until it knows him. Knowing that he is a person destined entirely for sacred things, it imagines him to be a man all sanctity, so that whether he works, or speaks, or looks, everything in him is pure and holy. In proof of this, there are found some among the very ignorant people who are under the impression that the priest has no need to eat and drink like other people in order to live; to such a degree are they convinced that the priest is different from, and superior to all other men. But leaving aside the extravagant idea that some simple country people form of us, it is certain that the world has a very high idea of us, far higher than our merits deserve. From this there results a greater authority and force in our words and deeds and consequently greater power to do good. But suppose people of the world are constantly coming in contact with us, particularly if some of us fail to use circumspection and reserve, they will gradually come to know that we are men like themselves and, since it suffices to be men to have defects, they will lose that high idea of us which they had, they will become accustomed to look upon us as one of themselves, and thus our ascendency will be lost.

Let us cultivate retirement therefore, my dear Fathers, and love for our houses where, says St. Bernard, the air is purer for the soul, the Heavens more open and the Lord nearer and more familiar: *Aer purior, coelum apertius, familior Deus.* In this way we will be more secure and tranquil, for believe me, the world is spoiled and corrupt, and it is impossible to keep ourselves healthy if we breathe foul and corrupt air. Living in retirement, we will have greater peace and tranquility, less dangers and pitfalls, and what is more important, we will be in a position to do great good. The sole presence, the sole appearance of a priest who cultivates retirement and flees from the noise and dissipation of the world is already a sermon which will produce a great effect. Whoever sees him, whoever meets him, and much more, whoever is able to hear a word from his mouth, regards himself fortunate and is content. He remembers it, he repeats it to others, and he desires to meet that man and hear him another time, and if he cannot do so, he will be satisfied with seeing him. On the contrary, if a priest is met with at every crossroads, if he is seen continually here and there, laughing and joking, people avoid him, they even wish not to meet him, and they experience discontent if they have him always among them; so much so that a Council of the Church had to make the pronouncement: *There is nothing that does more injury to the dignity of the clergy than too great familiarity with the laity.*[15]

✛ What Will Others Say

But some one may object: in my country, in my town, in the place where I am, I would be severely criticized if I acted in that way and if I did not do as others do; God knows what people would say about me, all the more so because there are other good priests who make no scruple about conducting themselves as I do. Well! What nonsense to have to reply to! However, I reply that when the method of life of others is not compatible with the retirement so necessary and indispensable for a priest, it cannot be followed, it must be abandoned. Let the world say what is likes, let other priests do as they think fit, the frequenting of that house, of those public places, of those persons is not proper. The world about which there is question here is but a group, a handful of people, idle and lazy, and to be despised. The world with all its flattery and all its raillery will not change us or make us either better or worse, says St. Gregory Nazianzen: *Nec laudatores nec vituperatores nos immutabunt; nec enim meliores, nec pejores efficiunt.* Other people will, on the contrary, be edified and those same people who, in the case given, were inclined to censure the retired conduct of the priest would, when necessity arises to speak of serious matters, be the first to praise him, and would give proof of their esteem for him when they find themselves in need of a priest to pray for them, to advise them, to provide for the needs of their souls. In those cases, they will not apply to their companions in dissipation, to priests they meet in public places, but they will go to find the priest who lives hidden and retired.

✣ Other People Do As I Do

But there is the further objection: other priests, and good priests too, have no scruple about those matters. I will not enter into a discussion about whether they are good or bad. I say that it is impossible for an ecclesiastic to be good unless he is a man of retirement in the sense that we have explained; besides, since this is so, whoever wishes to be a good priest must not take as his standard what other priests do. Look at little Samuel! He too had before his eyes the bad example of other priests, Ophni and Phinees, who were older than he, and of greater authority because they occupied a higher place; but what did the good youth do? He closed his eyes and acted as if he did not see them; he let them do as they wished, and led a devout, retired life; he attended to the temple, to the acts of worship, to the service of the Lord and, by that manner of life, the Scriptures tell us: *"the child Samuel advanced, and grew, and pleased both the Lord and men."*[16] It would have been otherwise if he had reasoned as so many people of our day do. Others older, more gifted and occupying higher places than I, act in such and such a manner, why cannot I do so? Instead of looking at these mundane and worldly priests, let us look at the great number of other priests whose lives we can read, and who have traced out for us the true life a priest ought to lead. Let us observe also the multitude of good priests who live in our own time, let us enquire how they spend their day and see whether they have much time to lose with mundane affairs: these living mirrors of our duties, these sermons by their deeds, will help us not a little to get a disgust for the world and to make us watchful over ourselves and fond of retirement and solitude.

Am I then never to go out, another will ask? I have already stated that there is a difference between the monk in the cloister and the secular priest, and that the latter can fittingly and indeed will be obliged to go out and appear in public, and that absolute, material retirement would be for him impossible and perhaps harmful. What then do we mean by a retired ecclesiastic? We mean a man who loves retirement, and who, as St. Bonaventure says: prefers to remain in the seclusion of his house as far as circumstances permit, than to go out in public; who therefore does not go out without a true and valid reason, and when for such a motive he has to leave his retirement, he prepares himself and takes the proper precautions both to keep his conscience clear and not to give any scandal, but to edify the people by his presence. Let us examine the retired priest with regard to this matter.

In the first place, he should love retirement, and this is essential, otherwise he will never be disposed to remain at home. Love is a weight that a person drags after him, and the person goes where love draws him. In the second place, he does not go out without a reasonable motive such as for business, for a social function, for health reasons, or, of course, for the duties of his ministry.

Finally, when he goes out he always uses the proper precautions of time, place, persons, according to the circumstances and the reason for which he goes out. He does not remain out longer than is necessary. He selects places where there is least dissipation and, if possible, he takes with him some companion with whom to converse on the way on some useful and edifying subject. Thus act those priests who are true lovers of retired life and solitude.

In order to incite ourselves the more to adopt this life of retirement, let us see briefly the means that will help us in the practice of it.

III Means

(1) *Association with Pious Priests*

In the first place, let us make sure to associate habitually with good companions, with priests of interior spirit and retired life. In such priests everything speaks to us, preaches to us, instructs us: the sight of them, their demeanor, their example, their conversation. Almost without noticing it we become like one of them and learn their spirit. It was the course of action recommended by St. Bernard, "that we should select, love and associate with those priests, whom we know by experience to be men who despised the world, and kept away from it, to be men who practiced virtue and loved retirement, good order and discipline."

(2) *Reflection*

Another means that will help is to habituate ourselves to think, reflect and meditate. All the disorders in priests as well as in lay folk arise because they do not think. A priest who from time to time meditates seriously on the burdens of his office, its great dignity, the account that he will have to give of it, the reward that he may expect; who meditates on what a priest is in the world, how he must conduct himself in a calling which is of all others the most fatal if he fails, and the most glorious if he conquers, on how he is destined to bring with him a host of others to a happy eternity; a priest, I say, who meditates on these things will certainly spare no effort to assure for himself such a glorious future by a truly priestly life.

(3) *Occupation*

Finally, the indispensable means to succeed in becoming a man of retired life is occupation. Let us suppose that a priest sets about the work with good will, does violence to himself, leaves his worldly companions and remains at home, he will before long give himself to serious occupation. But if someone says that he does not know how to occupy his time I will say just this: if that is so it is a true sign that he does not know his state in life, that he does not know how to pray or the necessity for it, that he does not know how to study, or the necessity of study. I do not intend here to dwell on the evils and consequences of idleness, I will merely explain a doubt concerning a question of morals. Is a person who suspects evil in the life of a priest who lives idly guilty of a rash judgment? I reply that ordinarily he is not, and I think you will agree with me, for there are many good reasons for the conclusion. The priest living in idleness in the world is like a ship without rudder or anchor in the midst of the sea; we can therefore foretell how he is going to end up. Let us conclude that the priest will never be a man of retirement unless he becomes a man of labor and occupation. This occupation will be like a chain binding him to his room, and from that room there will go forth one day a priest who will be the light of the world, the edification of the people, the ornament of the Church and the port of salvation for a multitude of souls whom he will one day lead to the Heavenly city, to the glory of Heaven. Amen.

---

1 John 15:9.
2 1. John 2:16.
3 John 6:61.
4 Acts 17:32.
5 Matt. 15:14.
6 1 Corinth. 2:12.
7 Lament. 4:1.
8 Past part. II, cap. 7.
9 Ibid.
10 Jerem. 51:6.
11 Leo Papa. Serm. IV de Quadrag.
12 Psalm. 105:35, 36.
13 Ibid.
14 Ibid.
15 Concil. Aquil. cap. XI, De Vita Cler.
16 1 Kgs. 2:26.

The Priest Must Be a Man of Prayer

E HAVE SEEN that the priest must be a special man distinct and different from all others: an interior, spiritual man, separated from the entanglements of the world and consecrated entirely to the interests of God; a being more divine than human, a true mirror of the divinity upon earth. Now among the means to be employed to bring about that result, besides retirement, which we have already considered, the most necessary is prayer. We read in the Gospels of our Divine Redeemer, the Head and Master of all priests, that whenever He had a moment of rest from His continuous labors, He retired and He prayed. Retirement and prayer: these are the two friends that will raise the priest so high as to make him like a god upon earth. Retirement and prayer are two inseparable qualities, one the result of the other; I speak of pious virtuous retirement, and not of retirement that is merely natural or capricious. The retired man naturally loves prayer. The man who prays keeps away necessarily from the din of the world, and seeks quiet and solitude. Retirement and prayer are two virtues which are sufficient, for they carry with them and support all that is required to form a worthy, holy priest. It is impossible that a man who lives retired and prays should not have his heart detached from this world and filled with the spirit of the Lord: it is impossible that he be not occupied, given to study and labor. It is therefore impossible for him not to be holy for himself and useful and profitable for others and, by these two things, he will fulfill his destiny as a priest. It is therefore of the highest importance, that having considered the necessity, advantage and form of retirement in the priest, we should consider this other companion virtue akin to it, namely prayer. It brings the priest so near God and binds him so closely to Him that it almost makes him one with Him; it shows him how to deal with God, to converse with Him. It obtains from God all those helps and lights and comforts that are necessary for him.

We shall not stop here to consider what prayer is; we know already that, considered in its object, it is a petition that we make to God for the things we need; *Oratio est petitio decentium Deo,*[1] and that, regarded in its form, it is a bound, a flight of the heart towards the throne of God: *Ascensus mentis in Deum.*[2] Nor shall we discuss the necessity of prayer in general or its qualities. We shall, instead, consider three things that concern ourselves more closely: (1) what is the need, the absolute necessity of prayer in a priest; (2) who among priests can be truly called men of prayer; (3) of what kind and how great is the influence of the priest who prays. You will hear nothing new, but what you will hear will not be less useful and important for that. From one end of the year to the other we are telling the faithful about the need to pray and explaining to them how to pray; reason therefore demands that we should look well into ourselves and see if we really know that art which we have to teach to others every day.

✣   NECESSITY OF PRAYER

(1) Should a priest pray? To convince ourselves of this necessity, of this duty, it will be sufficient to ask. Did the Apostles, who were the first priests, pray? Did the priests who succeeded them for so many centuries pray? Do all those good priests whom we ourselves know pray? It is beyond doubt that all those prayed, that they prayed much, and we are quite certain of this, therefore there is no need to bring forward proofs. There is nothing more true and necessary than that we also should pray, unless we want to say that we are exempt from that common necessity.

Besides the general reasons which oblige all the faithful to pray, and besides the fact that the priest is in greater need of special helps to fulfill the duties of the grave office that he holds, and therefore is under greater necessity to ask for those helps by prayer, there are two special reasons that bind a priest to this duty so closely as to take away every excuse or pretext that could be put forward: the first is that prayer has been made the duty of a priest; the second, that on the subject of prayer the priest should be a master.

(1) *Because Prayer is the Priest's Office*

Among the duties and offices of the priest that of praying may, without hesitation, be said to be the first: ". . . every high priest," says St. Paul, "taken from among men is ordained for men in the things that appertain to God."[3] Now the principal means, indeed the only one that he has to keep open this way, this relation, this communication with God, in order to fulfill his great mission, his sublime embassy, is prayer. Take away prayer, and you will at the same time take away all intercourse between Heaven and earth, between God and man. You will take away the priesthood itself, for the priesthood consists in this: to present to God the needs and interests of man, and to represent God among men, wherefore it is that we find a common, harmonious and unanimous language among the Fathers and Doctors of the Church with regard to prayer and the duty of praying for a priest.

"*Priests,*" says St. Ambrose, "*should pray day and night for the people entrusted to them.*"[4] "*The priest,*" adds St. Augustine, "*should be such a man, that what the people are not able to obtain from God for themselves, he will merit for them whatever he wishes to be obtained.*"[5] And the Lord said of the Levites of old that He had selected them expressly for this office. "*I have taken the Levites for all the firstborn of the children of Israel . . . to pray for them, lest there should be a plague among the people if they should presume to approach to My sanctuary.*"[6] Hence the Council of Cologne stated that the office of the priest consisted in praying to the Lord for the needs and prosperity of all the people: *Presbyterorum officium in orando Deum pro totius Ecclesiae et populi christiani prosperitate situm est.*[7] This is quite natural, since if the material churches are destined solely and totally for this purpose and are called houses of prayer, should those who belong to the family of these houses, their owners and chief dwellers, who are the priests, be destined for anything else? The spirit of prayer, the habit of praying should be ingrained and ardent in the priest. The Fathers of the Church are unanimous in saying that each and every priest should be a man of prayer, so that whoever is not, cannot properly be called a priest. The learned and gifted Archdeacon Peter Blesense gave the following reply to a priest who, being requested to assist in a certain work of the ministry, refused, saying that it did not belong to him; "Yes, it does not belong to you, and do you know why? It does not belong to you because you do not pray and, because you do not pray, you are not a priest."[8] *The priest,* says St. Gregory, *is a man who, by the use and experience of prayer, has learned that he can obtain from God whatever he asks.*[9] You all know the saying of the Venerable Father Avila: "Let him not be considered suitable for the priesthood who has not the spirit of prayer and meditation." And St. Bernard recommended Pope Eugenius not to accept or promote to holy orders anyone who had not cultivated and practiced prayer: *Illos assumito qui orandi studium gerant et usum habeant.*[10] "Take care," he adds, "to select candidates for the priesthood from among those who in every case trust more in prayer that in their own industry"; *Illos assumito qui de omni re orationie plus fidant, quam suae industria vel labori.*[11] And St. Charles before ordaining a priest was accustomed to examine him carefully on this point: whether he understood clearly the nature of prayer, the need for it, the times he should pray and the mode of praying: *Quis orationis modus, quot quibusive partibus illa constet; quae regulae et coetera ejusdem generis.*[12] Even if the candidate was most gifted and talented, the Saint expected nothing from him and did not ordain him unless he had proofs that he was to become a man of prayer. Prayer is therefore the office of the priest.

(2) *The Priest Should Be a Master of Prayer*

But there is the further consideration: The priest by his profession should be master of the great art of prayer, and should teach it constantly to others. How will he be able to do so, if he scarcely understands it and does not practice it himself? Have you ever observed what an accomplished teacher does when he wishes to instruct a pupil or disciple in a profession or teach him an art? He commences by explaining the principles and the theory. He tells him the why and the wherefore of everything in order that the pupil may know the utility and force of what he is teaching, but he does not stop there. He himself does the first part of the work in question under the eyes of the disciple, as if he were a beginner, and then he gives him the work that has been begun and makes him continue it in his presence in order that he may be able to correct him and help him, and thus bit by bit, and part by part, the two continue the work between them as if they were one person, and they finish it to the satisfaction of both; of the master who is pleased at the progress of his disciple, of the disciple who learns through the goodness and energy of his master. That is how the priest should act with his people to teach them the great art of prayer, whether in the pulpit, in the confessional, in the school-room at catechetical instruction or in familiar discourses. If we wish our people, like apt pupils to learn the art of prayer and profit by it, we should imitate the master of whom I have just spoken. We should first of all impress on their minds the theory of prayer, its need, its efficacy, the ease with which it can be made. But mere reasoning and explanation are not enough; we should come down to practice and suggest to them what they have to do in their own circumstances. We should imagine ourselves in their shoes and put into their mouths the words that they have to use, teach them how to make them their own and when to say them. If they should get discouraged or tired and wish to give it up, we should encourage them, urge them on, suggest other ways of prayer easier and less exacting. This will require time, labor and patience, but you may be sure that our people will gain by it and that we shall see the fruit. Happy will we be and happy will they be if they succeed in learning this great art. But to accomplish all this, to succeed in becoming a master who will produce such results, it is absolutely indispensable, as you know already, that the priest himself should know well how to pray, know it by practice, by the use and exercise of it, which is the only means of acquiring full knowledge and full mastery of it.

After all that, what reply are we to give to a priest who is not ashamed to say: let others pray as much as they wish, as for me, I cannot, I have not the head or the time for it, and I do not know how to go about it when I kneel down to pray; I am willing to do anything else, however burdensome and heavy, but for goodness sake do not ask me to pray; the very mention of it irritates me and almost makes me sick, such is the aversion and repugnance I have for it. What are we to reply to such language from a priest? And note well, of a person whose first and most indispensable duty is to pray, and to teach others how to pray and exhort them to pray? It may well be, and I am willing to suppose that all this is merely a mountain made of mist, an imaginary difficulty; that although this priest does experience antipathy to prayer, and aridity and nausea, in spite of all that he does do violence to himself and prays, and is therefore a man of prayer, as we shall see in a moment. To such a one

I would say frankly: have courage, my dear Father, do not be troubled; you pray more than you think, and you are a better priest than you imagine yourself to be; as you know, virtue and merit do not consist in taste and satisfaction, but in sincerity of heart and will. Now this is not wanting, when one overcomes weariness, conquers repugnance, and does the work in spite of them. But what are we to say where the case is different, when the priest does not pray as much as he ought, and in the way he ought, when he is a man of work, if you will, of study and learning, but not a man of prayer? Well, perhaps my reply may seem a little harsh, and that he will not like it; however, we are here to tell the truth. This priest says that he cannot pray, that he has not the head or the time for prayer; but when there is question of something necessary, something that must be done, there is no room for further discussion about it. When there is no way to avoid it, we must go forward whether through motive of love, or by doing violence to ourselves. Whether we have the inclination or not, if it is a thing that must be done, all excuses or pretexts are useless. Look at how people behave with regard to temporal affairs, when they are burdensome, complicated and difficult. These people's first reaction is to shirk the difficulty if possible, but seeing that this is not possible, they come quickly to the conclusion; it is useless to be thinking about it, it must be done, and what is the use of saying that it can't? We must do what we can. That is what I would say to a priest in this case: the practice of prayer is indispensable in a priest, and it is loss of time to be thinking of excuses to avoid it; you must either pray or cease to be a priest. Well, he replies, since that is so, I might try and make an effort, but what good will it do when at present I do not know how to pray? What a reason to give! What an excuse to bring forward! A master who when he is asked to teach replying that he does not know how! But then you should not call yourself a master; and why did you become a priest, when you knew that it would be your duty to teach others how to pray?

But if you do not know how to pray, plenty of the school children will be able to teach you what you do not know, and very many of the faithful will give you a method of prayer and tell you with what fervor you ought to pray. Do you really not know how to pray? Well, St. Augustine gives helpful and consoling directions. "Place yourself at the foot of the cross, prostrate yourself before that God who became man and died for you and then think on anything you wish, since all will be prayer. Whether you adore that God, or admire Him; whether you praise Him, love Him, thank Him, rejoice with Him; all will be prayer, and worship of Him": *Adoremus, admiremur, laudemus, amemus, gratias illi agamus, gratulemur.* What scope, what material for conversing with the Lord!

(3) *How Are We to Pray?*

But in what manner, with what frequency, up to what limit must we make our prayer, since it is the prayer of the priest? It would appear useless to insist so much on prayer for a priest, to repeat that he should pray, that it is necessary, that it is his office, his duty to pray, since a person might say that he does nothing else: he celebrates Mass every morning; many times in the day he reads his Breviary; he often assists at functions in choir, at processions, funeral services and other various offices. And it cannot be denied that all that is prayer. And is all that not sufficient? What more is required of us? On this point, we can distinguish three classes of priests. The first recite prayers, but they do not pray; they are those who recite prayers with voluntary distractions, with minds wandering and paying no attention to what they say. We need not speak of these because they are very far from fulfilling their proper duty of praying. There are others who can be said to pray, because they have sufficient attention, but they do so without fervor, and only just as often as they are obliged; when they can say that they have fulfilled their strict obligation materially, they do not think of doing any more. That I say is not sufficient; in order to be true priests, it is necessary to be men of prayer. These form the third class that we are going to consider now.

I   What Do We Mean By a Man of Prayer?

To express briefly and in clear terms what we mean by a man of prayer, it is sufficient to say that he is a man of his trade. Just as a man of arms, a man of commerce, a literary man, an agriculturalist, signifies literally, and in the estimation of all, a person dedicated, consecrated to the military profession, to commerce, to the study of literature, to the cultivation of the fields; in the same way, a man of prayer signifies a man who is dedicated and consecrated to prayer, not only in name, but a man who makes it his continual and daily occupation, his dominant thought, the subject of his discourses; a man whose operations are all directed towards prayer. And what wonder is there in that? The artist is naturally inclined to love his art. He experiences a relish, a pleasure in occupying himself with it, and far from being reluctant to tell people about it, he wishes and desires that everyone should know about it, and is happy only when people find him engaged in it; he is not fatigued or bored by the labor, he would be far more fatigued, and would suffer more, if he had to desist from it. Apply the comparison to our case, and you will see immediately who is the man of prayer. He is the man who, instead of consecrating himself to any other art, consecrates himself to prayer; he loves prayer, he relishes it, at least with a relish of the will, he cannot tear himself away from prayer or abandon it. Observe him in his house, in the church, and even in his walks in the country, and you will see him praying continually. If he studies, he prays, if he works, he prays, if he amuses himself he prays, if he eats or sleeps, he prays. But how can that be? Is he always on his knees? That is not necessary. He prays because whatever he does, he does it for the honor and glory of God; he prays because from time to time he remembers the presence of God, thinks of Him, makes an aspiration towards Him, speaks with Him. And do not imagine that it fatigues him; for him to pray is a delight and a joy more than a burden. You need not try to distract him from it or make him desist, because wherever he is, whatever he is doing, without you knowing or noticing it, he is praying, he is conversing with his Lord. That is the priest who is a man of prayer. Whether such priests are many or few, I am not going to decide; I will say merely: happy for the world, fortunate for the country if in every priest we could find such a man, a man of prayer!

II THE POWER OF A MAN OF PRAYER

And who can estimate or understand the force, the influence, the value of such a man of prayer? He is the object of admiration, a man above other men, an extraordinary man, and do not be surprised if I say also an omnipotent man. "*Let me alone, that my wrath may be kindled against them.*"[13] Whose voice is this? And who is He against whom force is used, and who suffers violence? Who is He who asks, who prays not to be stopped, not to be held back, who seems to want to do something and cannot? Who is He? He is God; bear that well in mind, but God whom nothing can resist in Heaven or on earth, at whose command, at Whose mere look, everything bows. Yes, that same God seems to have found an arm stronger, more irresistible, which holds Him, stops Him, and constrains Him to cry out; *Let me alone.* Yes, there is one who resists Him and succeeds in stopping Him. You know who is that great man who appears to be above God Himself; it is Moses praying; it is a man of prayer, who encounters God and stops Him. "He to whom it is said: *Let me alone,*" observes St. Jerome, "is shown by that to have the power of holding Him back."[14] It is certain that Moses could not hold back the hands of God except by prayer, and it was relying on the power of prayer that he entered into that contest with God like Jacob of old with the angel. Let me alone, said God to Moses, I wish to exterminate this ungrateful generation, their case is finished, let me go. No, my God, said Moses, Thou wilt not do so. And how did the contest end? Who won it? Moses, or if you wish prayer.

Prayer is more than a request, it is a command, as we see in the case of Josue: "*Move not, O sun . . . . nor thou, O moon,*" said Josue, "*And the sun and the moon stood still . . . . the Lord obeying the voice of a man.*"[15]

From this idea spring all those wonderful titles and names which the Fathers, with one accord, give to prayer. St. Augustine calls it the key of Heaven, and says that he who knows how to use it is master of all the treasures within; and he brings forward as proof the command and prayer of the Prophet Elias: *Elias orders and the Heavens are closed; he prays afterwards, and they are opened.* "And do not think," adds St. John Chrysostom, "that this is but one case, a rare and particular case; no, it is a general doctrine; *In order that it may be shown that the Saints can not only accomplish by their merits whatever they wish on earth, but that they can obtain whatever they ask for in Heaven.*"[16] The obtaining of everything one asks for is equivalent to a command on the part of the person who prays, and equivalent to a sort of obedience on the part of God who hears the prayers. Salvianus expresses himself in a similar manner, commenting on the words of the Psalm: *The eyes of the Lord are upon the just: and his ears unto their prayers.*[17] "What does it mean," he asks, "That God stands with his ears listening to the prayers of the just? By this it is indicated that He is not only listening to the prayers, but that He is obeying the person who asks." In such a sense, some piously call prayer ambitious; others, audacious; others, impudent and others, omnipotent, in order to show the marvellous efficacy it has with God. St. Peter Chrysologus, commenting on the words of Scripture where God said to Moses: "*Behold, I have appointed thee the God of Pharao,*"[18] asks: "What was the gift or quality that made Moses a sort of God on earth, putting him on a par with the omnipotence of God?" "I cannot find any other" he replies, "but prayer." *By prayer, Moses becomes a God, and he commands all the elements to aid him in his triumph.*

✣ The Efficacy of Official Prayer

Now, if that is true of prayer in general, what will not be the efficacy of prayer offered officially by the person expressly deputed to present petitions to God? Have you ever noticed the difference it makes whether it is an ordinary private subject who presents a petition to a king, or head of the State, or a person of high rank in an official position? The private individual may not even get an audience, while the person of rank and position will be announced and received with all the respect due to his position. He does not beseech, but represents his case. He does not beg, but makes his recommendations, and it is almost impossible that his recommendations be rejected or ignored.

Such, my dear Fathers, is our condition on earth; when one of the ordinary faithful prays, it is a private individual who supplicates and begs mercy, but when we pray, especially at the altar and whenever we offer the official prayers of the Church, we present ourselves, not as mere suppliants, but as persons who have the right to represent, to demand, to make recommendations. Imagine the case of a person who is charged with the duty of mediating between two parties, as we are. He does not limit himself to requesting the parties, but rather makes proposals, gives advice, persuades, and is accustomed to say: This is to be done, not that other thing; this is the right way to do it, not that other way, and so this is the way we shall do it. Observe how a minister of a sovereign speaks when he goes to have an audience. He does not begin to beg or beseech, rather he goes on to explain the case, to make clear the reasons for his proposals, but at the end he concludes: Your Majesty, this is what must be done. In these two personages we see the type or figure of a priest at prayer and the difference between us and the simple faithful. Could an ordinary person, even though good and holy, use such language with the Lord? But if a priest was fully conscious of his high position and animated with a lively faith, when he kneels down to pray, he would say to God: O Lord, Thou knowest me, I am Thy minister, I am he to whom Thou hast deigned to entrust the office of representing Thee on earth, of preventing sin, of saving souls, of converting sinners; now I am here to treat with Thee about these affairs. Thou knowest that there is that scandal, there is that soul that does not wish to know Thee, that chain which must be broken, that work for Thy glory which I am powerless to promote, that there are many difficulties in the way; I have done all in my power to persuade, to prevent, to overcome; it is useless, my puny strength is not sufficient. I have therefore come to Thee because I know that Thou canst by a single word finish the case. Tell me now, would God send away with empty hands His minister who would speak to Him in such a manner about such a case, when He Himself has entrusted the priest with the office, when His every desire is that he should succeed, and when He rejoices at his success? It is impossible that the Lord should refuse; it is a thing that we cannot even conceive.

✢ Efficacy of Prayer for Others

A person might here observe that when making petitions for others, a priest is not sure of obtaining conversions of sinners because they may put obstacles to God's grace. It is true that such can happen, and this is, according to theologians, the reason why prayer said for others is not infallible in effect. This fact can serve to reassure the priest who, after having done his duty, has not the consolation of obtaining the conversion for which he had prayed. But while such a failure can happen in theory, it is very rare that it will happen in practice, when the priest is truly a man of prayer and does not stop but perseveres in prayer even when it might be said that he has done his duty. Look at the example of Moses! Having prayed to the Lord to pardon his people, and having perceived that He was not willing to pardon them, Moses might have desisted, satisfied that he had done his duty, and thus the chastisement would certainly have fallen on his people. But no, he did not desist, he did what the priest should do in such a case, which was to continue to insist, to press his claim and not to yield, to say to the Lord as Jacob said to the angel: "*I will not let thee go except thou bless me*"[19]: it is useless for Thee to send me away, saying that these people do not deserve mercy, that Thy anger is just; I insist on what I ask for. Either grant me this favor or otherwise I will not leave this place. In like manner the priest should say: Either grant me this soul, the conversion of this sinner, the amendment of this penitent, the cessation of this scandal, the reconciliation of these enemies, peace and concord in these families, or I will remain here and will not depart.

The letter which St. Bernard wrote to Pope Eugenius about this subject is at the same time amazing and sublime. After numerating a long list of requests which, he said, were proper for a priest to make in prayer, he expressed himself thus: You, Holy Father, by virtue of Your office, have to deal with certain men who are not only wicked men, but monsters of iniquity; men who are not lacking in power and force to sustain their case against men. In dealing with such men, it will be necessary for Your Holiness to show yourself more than man: *Ubi malitiae juncta est potentia, aliquid tibi supra hominem praesumendum: vultus tuus super facientes mala.*[20] Far from retiring or covering your face in shame, or showing fear, you should rather hold your head high, with a fearless look such as becomes the Vicar of Christ, which you truly are. But what are we to do, you will ask, to obtain such courage and strength? Who will give them to us? They are to be obtained only through the spirit of prayer: *Let him who despises admonition fear prayer.*[21]

The spirit of prayer is the sign in which the priest will conquer, the fulcrum on which he must lean when he has to deal with perverse and obstinate sinners, when he meets with hearts hard as stone and unyielding as a rock. Instead of crying out, inveighing against them, fulminating and threatening chastisements, let us have recourse to prayer with such fervor and lively faith that it will be like a challenge to them. You do not wish to listen to reason, you are unwilling to yield, well, make your choice; either yield and cease committing that sin, change your life, break that chain, or I will have recourse to prayer. But remember that you are forcing me to have recourse to a powerful weapon, which is nothing less than handing your case over to God and dealing with Him about you. You will see what He will be able to do. He will expedite your case for me and finish it without delay. You are not willing to stop; I will therefore speak to the Lord and He will make you stop. *Timeat orationem qui admonitionem contempsit.*

A certain person could not make up his mind to break off a sinful relation. The confessor after trying all means finally decided to have recourse to prayer. He said to the penitent: "If you do not consent to promise me to amend, at least permit me to pray for you; do you agree?" "Oh! yes, I will be even grateful to you." "But remember that I will pray with all earnestness, and when a confessor sets himself to pray, it is a serious matter because God will not say no to him." "All the better," replied the penitent, "for if so I am sure you will be heard." "Very well, replied the Confessor, "be prepared therefore for anything that God may dispose." "And what do you mean by that?" asked the penitent immediately, a little alarmed. "Up to this I might as well be speaking to the wind as to you, you would not listen to me or give up your life of sin, now I am going to have recourse to God and He will finish you." "Finish me in what way?" asked the penitent. "It is easy to know," said the confessor, "what God will do. Since you are determined not to give up that sin but continue committing it if you live, the Lord will take you, and then it will be finished." "Oh!" replied the penitent, "if that is so, for Heaven's sake do not pray." "There is no middle course," concluded the Confessor; "either amend your life or I pray; I do not need to have your permission."

✣ Efficacy of Prayer for Ourselves

Such is the efficacy of prayer offered for others. When it is offered for ourselves, we are even more certain that it will be heard. I do not speak of praying to God for temporal favors, for in the eyes of the priest these things are worthless trifles; certainly God will not be wanting in providing us with all that we need, and defending us if the necessity arises. I go on to things of greater importance, which are spiritual blessings that conduce to the good of our souls and to the advantage of our ministry. In this matter, it is not necessary to seek for proofs, to cite witnesses or to advance reasons. It is a proposition rigorously logical that prayer made with the necessary qualities and with perseverance is of *infallible efficacy* when there is question of the interests of our own souls; when for example, we present ourselves before God and say to Him: O Lord, I am a priest and, as such, I have need of humility, mortification, detachment from the world, purity, faith, courage and confidence. When we make such a prayer not merely as an experiment or test to see whether God will hear us or not, but with absolute confidence, we can be certain that if we ask and continue to ask we will infallibly be heard; we can be even more certain when there is question of ceasing from committing sin. And what is more necessary for our salvation than to have done with this monster once for all? Let each of us, therefore, say during these days of retreat with the prayer and faith of a priest: "O Lord, it is time that I arise from sin once for all; I wish that the question be finished during these days; that for me there will never again be sin. Give me Thy hand, O Lord, let me lean on Thy arm, and from this day forward let there be between me and Thee an eternal alliance." St. Alphonsus was accustomed to repeat: Whoever prays shall be saved, whoever does not pray shall be lost. I repeat it: the priest who prays is certain to become good and virtuous, and will be saved; as for the priest who does not pray, although he may be an energetic man, a man who studies and becomes learned, I fear for his virtue and goodness, and I fear still more for his salvation.

Let us conclude therefore that the priest should not only pray, but that he should be a man of prayer. To become so, many words will not help him, nor will art or industry serve him. What is needed is detachment from the world, retirement, the practice of piety and mortification, but principally, the habit of reflection and meditation. And when our hearts are cleared of the mud and dirt of this world and full and warm with the things of the Lord, it will be no longer possible for us to live on this earth without frequently going up in spirit to Heaven to salute God, to speak to Him and to engage in familiar conversation with Him. Then we shall be men of prayer, marvellous men, extraordinary men, omnipotent men, and then we shall be able to say to those souls entrusted to our care: Beware of making us pray for you, do not force us to have recourse to the terrible weapon of prayer: *Timeat orationem qui admonitionem contemsit.*

1 S. Joan. Damasc. Orth. fid. 1. III, c. 24.
2 Ibid.
3 Hebr. 5:1.
4 Sup. II. Tim. 3.
5 Serm. II in Psalm. 36.
6 Num. 8:18, 19.
7 Tit. De Sacr. Ord.
8 Epist. 139.
9 De Cura Past. p. I, cap. 10.
10 De Cons. lib. IV, cap. 4.
11 Ibid.
12 Conc. Mediol. part. III. De Exam. Ordin.
13 Exod. 32:10.
14 Epist. 105.
15 Jos. 10:13, 14.
16 Lib. II. De orand. Deum.
17 Psalm. 33:16.
18 Exhod. 7:I.
19 Genes. 32:26.
20 De Consid. lib. IV. cap. 7.
21 Ibid.

Delicacy of Conscience

*R*ETIREMENT AND PRAYER are two great means, equally necessary and efficacious, to form in the priest that singular man that
we have been depicting for the last few days. Another virtue, however,
ought to accompany and adorn that illustrious personage, a virtue which
will keep him free from sin, and give him a clean heart and a pure, spotless and delicate conscience. Of what advantage to him would be his
high dignity, a well-ordered exterior, a life of retirement and prayer, if
he were to lack that cleanness of heart, that purity, in a word, that delicacy of conscience which make our hearts and souls like jewels in the
eyes of the Lord, and a shining example of virtue in the eyes of men.
Every priest should be worthy of having applied to him that wonderful
panegyric, that grand eulogy which God Himself spoke of His servant
Job: *"Hast thou considered My servant Job, that there is none like him in
the earth, a simple and upright man, and fearing God, and avoiding evil."*[1]
Have you not sometimes observed a good priest closely? Have you not
seen that he is an upright, just man, who keeps far from evil and fears
to offend God? *Homo rectus ac timens Deum et recedens a malo.* You will
find others more gifted than he, with more of this world's goods, more
esteemed and honored, but in the matter of purity of conscience, *non est
ei similis.* This, my dear Fathers, is the eulogy, this is the testimony that
each of us should merit from God and from men. It certainly will not
be an easy matter to keep ourselves pure and clean of heart in the midst
of the vanity and allurements of this life, clothed as we are with sinful
flesh and disturbed by so many passions; however, it is an indispensable
virtue, and there are so many good reasons why we should have it that
we ought to set ourselves to acquire it at any cost. Let us therefore make
it the subject of our conference. We shall see: (1) What is this purity
and delicacy of conscience, and in what it consists; (2) how important

and necessary it is that every ecclesiastic should possess it; and finally, the means to obtain it and preserve it.

It is possible that to some this argument might appear too subtle, to make excessive demands, to be much like hair-splitting; but against that there is the reflection that we priests are confronted with two courts of judgment, one more severe than the other; the court of the world that judges us without charity or mercy, and the judgment-seat of God, which will be strictly just. To anticipate these two dreaded tribunals and to protect ourselves from being condemned by them I see no means better than to put ourselves in the dock, and make that judgment beforehand, and make it more severely than either of the other two. If we enter into ourselves, and refuse to pass over any fault (which the Lord will one day discover, even if the world does not succeed in doing so), that alone will go far to make us those men of pure and delicate conscience that we are going to consider.

✧ WHAT IS MEANT BY DELICACY OF CONSCIENCE

When we speak of a man of delicate conscience, it appears to some the same as speaking of a scrupulous man, a man excessively timid, a man who fears when there is no need for fear and sees evil where there is none. But that is very far from the reality, for between the one and the other there is a vast difference. There is the difference between a calm sea and a sea in tempest, between night and day, between a person who sees clearly and another who sees in a blurred manner, between a mind that is accurate in its judgments and another oppressed and upset by turbid apprehensions and excessive fears; thus we distinguish between the man of delicate conscience and the scrupulous man.

Let us pay close attention to this difference for, in practice, among the imperfectly instructed, and indeed it may be said, even among priests, these two things are almost always confounded. A person, for example, is invited to a party, to some amusement, to some assembly; through delicacy of conscience he declines; the cry is raised immediately, what a scrupulous man! An ecclesiastic happens to be among a certain company where there is violation of charity in speech, or licentious conversation; because he is a man of principle and of delicate conscience he shows himself displeased; "Hush, be careful!" they say, "there are scrupulous people present." Don't be so quick to bandy these names about, and to call such conduct scrupulous! It is very true that a scruple is not a sin or even a defect that constitutes a real wrong, but that is not a full explanation. In the conscience it is necessary to distinguish between the judgment of the mind and what is done in consequence; the conscience consists properly in the judgment of moral good or evil that a man makes within himself; when a person errs in this judgment, and for insufficient motives sees evil where it is not, we call it a scruple, and it is so in fact.

But the effects and consequences of this judgment are a different matter, such as hatred of evil, aversion and repugnance to evil which are usually experienced from a true motive; that part of the conscience is right and just, and is properly called delicacy of conscience; and the conscience will be more or less delicate according to the degree of its aversion to evil and its care to avoid it.

But in order to make this argument more useful in practice, we shall develop it more fully; we shall see that delicacy of conscience in a priest supposes three things: (1) that he guards well against committing any fault; (2) that he is careful not to expose himself to what might be a beginning, a cause, or a disposition leading to a fault; (3) when he adverts to the fact that he has fallen into some fault, that he corrects it immediately and does not suffer it to remain. If you take away one of these precautions from a priest he may still be a good priest, if you wish, if indeed he can in practice persevere in that goodness—a question that we will discuss later on—but he can no longer be called a man of delicate conscience. Let us take an example from ordinary life. A man who is careful about the cleanliness and neatness of his clothes naturally not only avoids getting them stained, but he avoids also whatever might expose him to the danger of getting them stained, and if, by misfortune or accident, he happens to get them stained, he will not allow the stain to remain on them, but will have it removed as soon as possible; if, on the other hand, his clothes get stained a few times, and he does not trouble to have the stains removed, he will no longer be regarded as a man who is careful about his personal appearance, but rather as careless and negligent. Let us apply the comparison to the case of a priest. I do not here speak of a man who lives habitually in mortal sin or who falls into it easily and often, for such a person, far from having any right to be called a man of delicate conscience, should rather be called a man who has lost his conscience. I speak of a priest who, when there is not question directly of mortal sin, does not take much trouble to avoid committing a fault, and is accustomed to say: Oh! it is only a venial sin, a gratification of curiosity, a white lie, a joke, a display of exuberant spirits, a little human weakness. What great harm is in it? And without reflecting further whether it is only a venial sin or on the border line of mortal sin, he goes ahead saying, anyway, it does not amount to a mortal sin. I speak of the man who, knowing that he has fallen, even several times, into some sin, and fearing that it may have been a mortal sin, forces himself to believe that it is not, and passes days and weeks in that state, without caring to purify his heart and correct the fault; I speak of the man who, in spite of the fact that he suspects and has been warned, that such frequent visits, such carelessness about what he says, such want of proper behavior, and of guard on his eyes, may attract attention, and may lead to serious consequences and cause harm, despises these fears, calls them the effect of melancholy, rejects these warnings and continues to do as before. Now I state clearly that none of these can be put in the class of priests of delicate conscience. And how could you call them men who love and desire cleanness and purity of heart when they care so little about these faults and about the danger to the soul and the deformity that results from them? What then are we to say of these men? What judgment are we to pass on a priest who lacks delicacy of conscience? It can be put in a few words: such a want is very shameful for a priest, very dangerous for him and a source of scandal for others: three serious considerations which show the great necessity there is for a priest to acquire delicacy of conscience.

II The Importance of a Priest to Have a Delicate Conscience

Observe how in the world this delicacy is held in high esteem even in temporal matters. Professional men all boast, or at least make the claim, that they have a strict or delicate conscience in all matters that concern their profession; for example, the artist, the business man, the lawyer. If anyone expresses a suspicion to the contrary, they resent it, they show that they are offended, and reply immediately: "You do not know how scrupulous I am in these matters." In fact, the credit and reputation of these men and the confidence placed in them rest on this gift of delicacy. If we want to sell something or to make a purchase, to conclude a business deal or to treat of any matter whatever, the first thing we want to know is, of what sort is the person with whom we have to deal. If we are quite sure that he is a man of delicate conscience we may shut our eyes and go ahead, there is nothing to fear, and why? Because, if he is such a man, he will take care not to be guilty of the smallest wrong, the least injustice. He would rather expose himself to the risk of being at a loss than injure the other party; and if it should happen that he makes a mistake, you may be sure that he will be ready to correct it without any hesitation, even to his own disadvantage. Now I say: if in the world this virtue is so esteemed and prized, and if all boast and make it both their glory and their duty to be considered persons of delicate conscience, is the priest the only one to be indifferent to it?

Of what kind is our profession, my dear Fathers? It is one that demands of us that we should be holy, virtuous, perfect; that is our duty, the scope of our profession, our end. Take an example of a priest of delicate conscience. As long as you talk to him about property, health, duties, as long as there is question of pastimes, travels, or other temporal affairs, assuming of course that they are licit and becoming, he will not get excited or offended, and you will find even ready to see your viewpoint and to agree with you. But woe to you if you touch his conscience! For he will not allow even the slightest suggestion of evil or even the shadow of sin to be insinuated. That is what should be said of each of us if we do not wish to show ourselves inferior to laymen. And what could be more opprobrious for a man who makes profession of virtue, of holiness, of hatred of sin than to see him frequently contaminated with sin? And in addition, to see him live as lightheartedly as if he had the clearest conscience in the world? Would we not lose our respect for the sun if it appeared often partially covered with dirt and stains, which, though they did not blot out its light entirely, nevertheless diminished it and rendered it less clear and bright? Would it not be shameful, and indeed very shameful for a gentleman at court if he dared to present himself before the king with clothes, although not altogether ragged and dirty, yet soiled and stained. If it was one of the common people who was unexpectedly presented to the Sovereign, it would not be considered much harm if he allowed himself to be seen in such a state; but for a courtier, for a man devoted to the service of the king, and expected to be a credit to the royal palace, it would be unpardonable.

Now that is just our case. We are the light of the world, who should by our light illuminate the earth and shed light on those opaque and darkened bodies, which are the worldly people; will it not therefore be a great shame for us to show ourselves soiled even by small stains, and not caring to keep our light clear and resplendent? We are the gentlemen in the house of the Lord, destined to maintain its decorum by the beauty of our garments, that is by the purity of our hearts and the cleanness of our consciences. Our purity and cleanness should be of such a kind and in such a degree, according to St. Chrysostom, that we should not appear inferior in lustre even if we were to come to be placed among hierarchies of the angels: *Sacerdotium obeuntem ita purum esse decet, ac si in coelis inter potestates illas collocatus esset.*[2] How opprobrious, therefore, would it not be for us to be in that house, and stand before that Lord soiled and stained like the common herd! What confusion for us to be obliged to tell others to adjust their garments and remove the stains, if the stains on our own garments were clear and evident! Therefore, the profession of virtue and holiness which we embraced, the holiness of the house of the Lord in which we dwell, the dignity of the functions and ministrations which we must perform, the greatness and majesty of that God whom we are called to serve in His very house, all require great delicacy of conscience and cleanness of heart, which if we do not possess, we shall become worthy of blame and objects of shame and opprobrium.

❖ Dangers to Which Lack of this Quality Exposes the Priest

(1) *It Exposes Him to the Danger of Falling into Sin*

The lack of this quality would therefore expose the ecclesiastic to dangerous consequences. And note that we have not been speaking of a priest habitually bad, of a man who lives in mortal sin; but do you think that a priest who has not a delicate conscience is very far from it? Holy

Scripture, reason and experience make us fear that he is very near it; *"He that contemneth small things shall fall by little and little."*³ And observe that he does not say: He who *falls* in small things, but he who *contemneth*, he who attaches no importance to small things, which, as we have seen is precisely what the man does who has not a delicate conscience. And reason itself tells us that it cannot be otherwise; if the priest takes no care to avoid committing small faults; if he sleeps, as it were, on them, and makes no effort to avoid committing new ones, it is natural that horror of and aversion for sin, which is the great protection against committing it, should diminish in him, in much the same way as a person who is accustomed to deal with tame animals loses the sense of fear of dangerous animals, with the result that he sometimes goes too near them and, because he is not on his guard, gets mauled. At the same time the passions will become bolder, vanity and the allurements of the world will go on acquiring mastery and dominion over him. On the other hand, the Lord, although He will not withdraw His grace entirely, will begin to restrict it, and certain special helps and graces which would have kept him firm and constant in violent temptations will hardly be granted to a priest who is not reserved and who has not a delicate conscience.

Let us ask daily experience how that priest will end who, neglecting the warnings of others, and ashamed to follow their example, considers it a weakness to be guarded in his words and dealings and to avoid dangerous visits. And how will that other priest end who mocks at those who show themselves circumspect about attendance at parties, banquets and amusements and who frequent them as seldom as possible? It is not necessary to answer; the falls over which, alas! we are too often obliged to weep and deplore give us too certain a proof and too clear an explanation. It is almost impossible that a man, much more an ecclesiastic, should all at once precipitate himself into mortal sin. If we seek the origin of all falls, even the most grievous, we shall find that almost always the beginning was not a decisive fault, but rather the want of delicacy in avoiding a danger or a distant occasion of sin. A small fault, like a tiny sapling that, as St. Jerome says, would have been rooted out at the beginning by a man of delicate conscience, a slight attachment against which a good priest should be on his guard, or even a want of caution in fulfilling a duty towards relations or towards society, is capable of causing a great evil. And what is all that but a want of delicacy of conscience? How dangerous and even fatal then is this want!

(2) *To the Danger of Giving Scandal to the People*

Finally, want of delicacy of conscience cannot fail to be a source of scandal. I have said at the beginning of this conference that the lives of us priests are subjected to a terrible scrutiny by the world; a continuous, daily, hourly scrutiny, so that we may regard ourselves as always judged and always being judged, because we are always under that examination; a most severe judgment, because it is carried out either by the most prejudiced and malignant, or by good people of such delicate conscience that they notice even the smallest defect in us; and the former are always watching us and peeping at us with a hundred eyes. If an unguarded word or gesture or look escapes from us, the world makes capital out of it; we are immediately under suspicion and made the object of conjecture and gossip, and that goes on indefinitely. Now, if there is a priest who has not a delicate conscience in the sense that I have explained, who does not guard against every fault with the greatest care, against the very appearance and danger of sin, and who, if he stumbles or falls, does not take care to rise immediately, who takes no care to avoid levity in act and speech and jest, how will he fare from the judgments of the world? How will he avoid giving scandal frequently? And let us not go on saying that these are small things and insufficient to cause scandal, for we know what St. Bernard said: *Inter saeculares nugae, nugae sunt; in ore sacerdotis, blasphemiae.*[4] And the Council of Trent confirmed this at the time when, recommending to all priests that they should lead holy lives free from all blame, they based their recommendations on this very reason: *Levia etiam delicta, quae in ipsis maxima essent, effugiant.*[5] Just as our office as priests can make grave for us what would be only light for a layman, so it can render illicit for us what would not be a sin for another: *Quae in aliis non reputantur ad culpam in iis haberentur illicita.* Hence it can happen more than once that a priest who is invited to take part in some pastime, some game, a banquet, a conference or such like, which in themselves are not sinful, may have to decline saying frankly: "As for you, you can attend these functions, but it would be regarded as wrong for me to go"; and in the meantime, on account of certain circumstances of time, or place or persons, he should say to himself, I cannot go there: *Quia haec in me haberentur illicta.* A priest who has not a delicate conscience certainly will not make these distinctions nor will he give such questions so much consideration, and therefore God only knows what harm he will do and what scandal he will give.

Therefore, my dear Fathers, to conclude this point of our conference, there is every reason why we should become men jealous of our reputation, cautious about what we do, and of delicate conscience, not indeed in gallantry, etiquette and worldly prominence, but in our interior life, in our hearts. If we look around us we shall see that people form their consciences according to their state in life, their occupation, and that they regulate their conduct accordingly; the soldier has the conscience of a soldier, the sailor of a sailor, the artisan of an artisan, the merchant of a merchant. Let us also follow that usage; we are priests, let us therefore form for ourselves the conscience of a priest, and regulate ourselves according to it. By our position we should be those men spoken of in the Book of Ecclesiasticus, rich in virtue and eager to shine in its splendor and beauty: *Homines divites in virtute, pulchritudinis studium habentes*[6]; and, as we are no longer men of this world, our love and zeal for the beautiful must not be for the perishable and transient beauty of this world, but of another kind of beauty, immensely grander and more fitting for us, namely, spiritual beauty of the heart and soul, which will never fade or diminish but will make us glorious and resplendent, not indeed in the eyes of a treacherous and deceitful world, but before God, the Searcher of hearts and the just Judge of virtue.

Look at the people of the world; what eagerness, what exertion, what patience to preserve or augment mere earthly beauty! What adornment, what powders, perfumes, and such things, do they not employ for that purpose! And what time they spend in dressing, powdering and adorning themselves! It might well be called a martyrdom, an ordeal calculated to drive the most patient person in the world out of his wits, if it were not for that insane eagerness to appear beautiful. However, all that is done willingly and gladly by these people madly eager to surpass, not only others, but themselves in splendor and beauty, and to show forth in all details an exquisite touch, a delicate, refined taste. Let us, my dear Fathers, learn from these blind, worldly people to use at least equal care, equal eagerness, equal delicacy to procure for our souls that internal candor and beauty which so far surpass all the beauty of this earth.

III MEANS TO ACQUIRE DELICACY OF CONSCIENCE:

(1) *To Meditate Often on the Gravity of Sin*

The first means to keep ourselves delicate in conscience, with an ever-increasing aversion for and horror of all sin, is to meditate frequently on how great the evil of sin is, and how unbecoming it is for a priest who serves God in His own house, and who treats and converses continually with Him to be always adding insult to insult, even though small, to his Lord and Master. Until we fully comprehend this great truth, it will be difficult, in fact, impossible, for us to succeed in conceiving that hatred and aversion for all sin which is so necessary for a priest who wishes to keep himself pure, because, as long as sin, even though venial, enters freely into our hearts, and we sleep tranquilly on it, it will be useless even to enquire whether we are men of delicate conscience or not; it would be like the case of the man covered with dust and stains, trying to persuade people that he was clean.

(2) *To Mortify Ourselves in Things Lawful*

Another means that will help us to avoid falling into disfiguring faults and to keep us clean and pure in conscience is to make an act of mortification from time to time, and deprive ourselves of something that is licit, so that we will not transgress in what is illicit. You may regard a person as already fallen, who wishes to satisfy himself excessively in everything, and to abstain only from what is certainly sinful. In theory, we can make subtle distinctions and fix the boundary between what is sinful and what is not, but in practice these very often deceive us, and they become traps into which we fall.

In the first place, circumstances of fact vary *ad infinitum*, and it is very difficult to see clearly enough, especially in our own case, so as to be able to form a certain conscience sufficiently secure to act upon; in most cases of this kind, a person remains uncertain and wavering and, in the end, acts with a doubtful conscience, and that is a sin. In the second place, once we have commenced an action, it is not so easy to stop at the point that we have fixed; our passions, the world, the flesh, companions, rashness, will drag us along and bring us where perhaps we would never have thought we would go; and how many there are who every day are deceived in this manner. Then there is the final consideration that the extreme point where safety ends is dangerous. Imagine a person who is travelling along a safe road but near the edge of a precipice (like the road by which we are travelling in this world), and that nothing will serve him but to walk on the side of the road next to the precipice and keep as near the precipice as possible. At any moment there may be disaster, and one day or another he will fall over the edge. The same thing happens in all similar cases. The owner of a farm who ploughs up to the boundary mark of his property easily comes to usurp a portion of his neighbor's property; the person who always insists on all his rights will in the end, without wishing it perhaps, be guilty of arrogance and injustice. That is what will happen to the priest who goes through life with a measuring rod in his hand to mark the boundary between right and wrong, going to the extreme limit of what is right without taking care not to cross the boundary. These looks, these words, these books and periodicals, these visits, taken separately, appear to contain nothing dangerous; in these affections, these dealings, there does not yet appear to be sin; therefore the priest in question will say: What harm is there? It is not a sin; I can go ahead. The poor man will soon discover whether there was danger or not, and sooner or later disaster will come. On this point experience teaches only too clearly, and gives us very painful proofs.

Besides, that mean stingy way of dealing with our Divine Lord cannot be excused from ingratitude and rudeness towards Him who has poured out on us the treasures of His divine grace. And since this is so, is it not to be feared that in punishment for our niggardliness and refusal to give God anything except what we cannot help, He will allow us to pass from what is licit to what is illicit, to our great humiliation and confusion? Therefore, I repeat, whoever wishes to be a man of delicate conscience and not to fall easily into what is illicit, let him strengthen his will by depriving himself from time to time of what is licit; whoever wishes not to be guilty of excess in speaking or in eating or drinking, let him, from time to time leave a word unspoken or a morsel or two on his plate at meals; whoever wishes to be able to restrain his eyes when there is real need, let him mortify his curiosity to see what is licit; whoever wishes to be able to restrict his appearances in the world to strict necessity, and to avoid snares and pitfalls when duty calls him to go out, let him exercise himself in restraint by remaining at home of his own free will. In this manner, he will go on acquiring that mastery and control over himself, his senses and his passions, so that he will be able to withstand any trial or assault.

(3) *Frequent Examination of Conscience*

The third means to acquire the delicacy of which we have been speaking is the frequent examination of conscience. How many times does not the merchant who wants to be accurate in all details in the conduct of his affairs, such as in receiving and dispatching goods, examine what he is doing to secure that there may be no mistake; how often does he not check bills and invoices to see that everything corresponds; to see that his obligations have been met, and his bills paid. The priest should do the same thing if he wishes to keep his conscience in a healthy condition. And could a priest's conscience be delicate and clear if he passes whole days and weeks without ever thinking on what he is doing or what he has done? After all, we are human, and it is almost impossible for us to avoid making mistakes in some things, and if when occasion arises we do not apply a remedy immediately, one fault will bring on another; after a light one, another more serious will follow, and in the end we will find ourselves covered with stains.

I do not mean that we should interrupt our work frequently and go on our knees to make our examination, but that we should accustom ourselves during the day, and even in the midst of our occupations, to cast a glance over our principal actions and think for a moment on how we have conducted ourselves; whether there is anything to be corrected, anything to be sorry for. We have, for example, celebrated Mass, heard Confessions, administered other Sacraments; we will have to go to a certain house, to deal with certain business, to be with certain persons. Well, without anyone noticing us and without giving up what we are doing, it is very easy to reflect for a moment on how far we have succeeded or failed in these occupations. If we have nothing with which to reproach ourselves, if our heart is at ease, both about what we have been doing and how we have done it, let us thank the Lord; if not, let us correct whatever is wrong immediately. Let us then say: "O Lord, I see now that this word, this impatient act, this haste was wrong; pardon me, I will be more careful in future. O Lord, I now advert to the fact that I was not sufficiently reserved, that I spoke too much, that I was too distracted; I ask pardon." Now what great time or effort does this demand? Every evening let us not deprive ourselves of the consolation of passing a few moments at the foot of the crucifix to lay our day's work before Our Lord, spoiled, alas! by so many stains. "O Lord," let us frankly say to Him, "Thou canst cleanse these stains with one drop of Thy precious Blood; I place this day's work in Thy sacred wounds, judge it, correct what is wrong, so that my accounts with Thee may be in perfect order."

(4) *Frequent Confession*

Finally, the most efficacious and indispensable means to keep our conscience clean and pure is the proper use of the Sacrament of Penance. I regret that I have not time to speak of this subject at length, but I shall touch on the principal points. There are three dominant defects common to us priests with regard to our use of this Sacrament, which are: that we do not use it frequently enough, that our Confessions are superficial, and that we have not sufficient confidence in our confessors.

I am presuming that all priests make use of this Sacrament. If, by chance, there is any priest who says he can do without Confession because, not having any mortal sin, he is not obliged to go to Confession, we can easily reply to him by saying that although there is no direct obligation, there is an indirect one because of the scandal he would give. And indeed if there be such a priest who never confesses we may be sure that there will be more than venial sins. But leaving that supposition aside let us come to our first point: how often should priests go to Confession? There will not be the same rule for all; some confess every week, some every fortnight, some every month, and others at longer intervals; however all these go to Confession. You all already know which of these methods should be followed. It is most fitting and most useful that the priest should go to Confession every week; this is the practice of good priests, the Church recommends it, and as we know, gives this weekly Confession the privilege that it suffices for gaining all the indulgences which, taken singly, would require Confession every day, so she regards it as equivalent to daily Confession.* And this does not appear to be too frequent, for we ourselves would be unwilling to allow people, even good people, to continue receiving Holy Communion for more than eight days without going to Confession again; and besides other dangers that might arise, reverence and respect for the Blessed Sacrament would seem to demand it.** "Why go so often," some priest will perhaps exclaim, "it seems to me that I can have an easy conscience as long as I have no mortal sin." Ah, my dear man, are we to wait to go to Confession until we have fallen? Will he who wishes to keep his body and his clothes clean wait to wash himself and brush his clothes until he is all covered with mud? No indeed; whenever either his body or his clothes get soiled, he will wash or clean them and, even when there is no necessity, he will wash himself and brush his clothes to ensure that he will be always clean. Thus also will the priest act who wishes to be a man of delicate conscience, always spotlessly clean; for, you remember, I have not made delicacy of conscience consist in being exempt from defects, from imperfections or even from venial sin, but rather in watching over ourselves with great care. If, in spite of our vigilance, we fall, we have the remedy at hand, which is to go to Confession immediately.

That is all very well, someone says, but I cannot go so often, I live too far away from another priest. I willingly admit that there are difficulties, but whatever the difficulties or obstacles may be, Confession should not be deferred for longer than a month; and so, cost whatever it may, a priest should confess once or twice a month. In the second place, if a priest cannot confess every week, let him at least have the desire and will to do so; in order to keep this desire alive and sincere I suggest the following means: let the priest arrange to perform some pious exercise during that week in which he cannot make his weekly Confession, a useful exercise, and one that will cost him something; such an exercise might be, for example, a day's fast or an abstinence, a Holy Hour, the

---

*Can. 931 deals with the Confession required for gaining Indulgences.

**Can. 863 urges the faithful to frequent and even daily Communion and Can. 856 deals with the dispositions required. This passage was written before the Decrees of Pope Saint Pius X on frequent Communion.

giving up of some excursion or amusement, especially for one who is accustomed to attend parties.

The second defect in our Confessions, which is superficiality, results perhaps from having no grave sin to confess, or from confessing often, or from the fact that we are confessors ourselves, we know these things from practice, or as is sometimes said, by trade. Sometimes we kneel down to make our Confession as if we were going to table; it is time for Confession, I have an opportunity, therefore I will go to Confession. I do not mean to say that such Confessions would be bad ones, no, but there is great danger that they might be null and of no advantage; for, even for venial sins and in what is free matter, sorrow for some of them is required, and that may be sometimes wanting, if a priest accustoms himself to confess in this manner.

Finally, there is the defect of want of confidence, which I fear is rather common in our Confessions. Of the person who would conceal what is grave and necessary matter, I will not speak here; I rather intend to speak of the person who, having something a little humiliating to confess, does not conceal it, but prepares and plans the terms in which he confesses it in such a way that the confessor has difficulty in understanding him. Such Confessions do not leave the person satisfied and cannot bear the fruit that they would if they were more sincere. The same might be said of the person who, having confessed what is strictly matter for the Sacrament, allows the confessor to know nothing else to guide him in giving direction, such as tendencies, inclinations, temptations, projects, etc. It is true that such things are not matter for Confession and that it is not a sin to omit them, but by omitting to tell them, we deprive ourselves of a great help towards our sanctification, and towards making us advance in that cleanness and delicacy of conscience which is the subject of our conference.

Those, my dear Fathers, are the means that will help us to acquire this great gift of a good clear and delicate conscience, which St. Paul calls the glory of the priest: "*Our glory is this; the testimony of our conscience, that in simplicity of heart and sincerity of God . . . . we have conversed in this world.*"[7] And such is the relief, the consolation, the nourishment that the voice of such a conscience gives us that it has come to be called "a continuous and abundant feast."[8] To this, you are to add the recompense promised to the man, to the priest of pure and delicate heart:

"*Blessed are the clean of heart; for they shall see God.*"[9] May God grant that our hearts may be such as to merit on earth that glory and that peace, and to arrive one day in Heaven to see Him, to love Him and to praise Him for all eternity.

1 Job. 1:8.
2 De Sacerd. L. III, Cap. 4.
3 Ecclus 19:1.
4 De Consid. lib. II. cap. XIII.
5 Conc. Trid. Sess. XXII de Ref. cap. 1°.
6 Ecclus. 44:6.
7 2 Corinth. 1:12.
8 Prov. 15:15.
9 Matt. 5:8.

SEVENTH CONFERENCE

The Spirit of Religion

*F*LIGHT FROM THE WORLD, love of solitude, prayer and delicacy of conscience in a priest cannot fail to generate in him another virtue, another spirit akin to these and of not less importance; this virtue is the spirit of religion. If we ask a layman whether he possesses this spirit, perhaps he will reply to us that he does not even know what it is; and up to a certain point he will be excusable; he is a layman who knows more about the things of this world than the things of the spirit. The priest, however, who is a master in the things of religion cannot and must not be ignorant of it; and if he is unable to tell what it is, the reproach can be made to him: "*Art thou a master in Israel, and knowest not these things?*"[1] Religion, as you know, is the exercise of all that belongs to the worship and honor of God, and of everything pertaining to Him; but that which renders such an exercise virtuous and makes religion a virtue is the spirit, the affection that a person cultivates towards what forms the material object of this worship, the esteem that he has for it, the way that he shows it and the end for which he offers it. The priest, therefore, will be filled with that spirit when he loves and esteems in his heart all that can honor his God externally, practices it, and exercises it with all due respect and veneration, and with the special end of rendering to the Lord the homage and honor due to Him.

Certainly, this will not be a new or strange subject for a priest; but the object of our conference, if not to instruct, will be to admonish, to urge, to revive that spirit; to increase it, nourish it, perfect it according to the advice given by St. Paul to Timothy: "*Neglect not the grace that is in thee, which was given thee by prophecy, with imposition of the hands.*"[2] *This is,* as Cornelius à Lapide says, *the office and order of bishop which is an office of prayer.*[3] We shall then, in this conference consider three things: the importance of this spirit in the priesthood; in what things principally he should make it shine out; and the losses and evils that will come on the priest who neglects it. We shall enter into minute details of everyday affairs, because we shall have to examine all that the priest does in the course of the day; in the church, in his house and in the performance of his duties, in order to see how, without much labor, he can, by each one of his acts, do great good, if he is animated with this spirit of religion; and on the contrary, how he can be the cause or the occasion of great evil, when he has not that spirit of which we are speaking.

I THE IMPORTANCE FOR A PRIEST TO POSSESS THIS SPIRIT OF RELIGION

The possession of this spirit of religion for a priest is of equal importance with his vocation; the one is inseparable from the other. If you find a priest who has no taste or love for the performance of the functions of his office and goes through them as if under compulsion; who, when actually engaged in them, does not show that zeal, and gravity, and decorum which these functions require; who, when there is no strict obligation to perform them declines them and avoids them; in a word, who shows a total lack of the spirit of religion; and I will tell you frankly that I very much fear that such a man was not made for the priesthood. Such priests are like those columns that are sometimes put in front of great buildings for the purpose of ornament. At some distance away they are a most imposing sight and appear to be supporting the whole building, but no, they are empty inside, they are there purely for appearance; and if you go up beside them and tap them, their sound will discover the secret to you immediately. Of such kind are certain ecclesiastics; at first sight they appear to be solid columns capable of holding up by themselves alone the great edifice of the Church, or at least of affording genuine support by their preaching, by the administration of the Sacraments, by the exercise of the sacred functions, by their example; but no, it is all appearance and nothing more. Whether they labor, or do not labor, if they lack the spirit, the unction proper to their state, their labors will be purely material; they will produce no fruit, but very often will be more of scandal than edification to the faithful. And what is the reason for all this? It is because these men are empty inside;

they are void of that spirit that gives life and worth to our external actions; they are void of love and esteem for their state, for their ministry, for that which in general concerns the worship which they are called upon to offer to God. Just observe their deportment while they are engaged in carrying out Church functions, and see whether it is proper for ecclesiastics. What dissipation! What levity! What haste! What disorder! Their deportment is more calculated to bring contempt on our religion and give people a disgust for our ministry than to inspire love and respect. And it cannot be otherwise, because they are priests who are wanting in the spirit of religion.

Take the case of a servant. I take that example because it is most expressive and is most applicable to us priests, who are really servants in the house of the Lord and in the great family of the Church. Let us suppose that the servant in question has not the spirit of his state, that he has no will or inclination to serve his master, that he has no esteem or affection for him and therefore cares little whether he pleases him or not. It is easy to see what kind of service such a man will give his master. Not unfrequently, under various pretexts, he will refuse to do the work given to him; whenever possible, he will evade his work or leave it to someone else, and when there is no possibility of evading it, there is every reason to fear that he will do it in such a surly fashion, that it will be an insult, rather than a service to his master. You can say the same of a priest who has not the spirit of his state, the spirit of religion. You can prove this for yourself by saying to one of them that he should not say Mass with such haste; that he should say it with more external decorum, and with proper preparation and thanksgiving: he will reply at once that God looks at the heart, not the exterior, and that a priest must not abuse the patience of the faithful by spending too long a time in celebrating. You need not wonder if you get such replies, my dear Fathers, those priests are empty columns: *intrinsicus sunt cavi.* Continue to tap them, tell them that they should perform the functions of the Church in a more modest, becoming way, and they will reply that such advice is motivated by scrupulosity, that they do like everybody else. They give out the same sound every time because they are empty within. Ask them to lend a hand in some laborious work, and they will tell you at once that they cannot, that they have not time, that it is not their business, that there is no obligation, unless perhaps they ask how much is the honorarium. Alas! they are always the same, so long as they have not got that spirit of religion, every attempt will be useless; reason with them, persuade them as much as you wish, even get them to make the Exercises several times, they will not change, they are always the same, because they are hollow inside.

✣ THE MEANS TO OBTAIN THE SPIRIT OF RELIGION

But what are we to do, you will ask, what means are we to employ in order to become filled with this spirit, since it is so important and necessary. A few words will suffice to reply to this necessary question, for these means have already been mentioned in previous conferences, as well as the reasons for adopting them, and the assurance that they are efficacious, so that anyone who is disposed to make use of them can be sure of success. They are briefly: first of all, the priest should have a proper idea of himself and his state; next, he should be convinced that he ought to be a man different from others, that the state of the priesthood is one of labor, of sacrifice and of subjection; and finally, he should flee from the world, love solitude and give himself to prayer. If the priest adopts these means he will, without any doubt, soon become filled with the spirit of his state, with the spirit of religion, the spirit of true virtue which will make him prompt and eager to serve the Lord and to perform the ecclesiastical functions in a becoming manner.

II IN WHAT PLACES IS THE SPIRIT OF RELIGION TO BE SHOWN?

But in what place and at what times should that spirit of religion shine forth most in the priest, and what should be the promptness, facility, and decorum with which he should display it?

(1) *In the Church*

The principal place where it is to be exercised is the church, for the church is the place where fitting worship is offered to the Lord; the principal ways for offering that worship and homage are the functions established by the Church and the pious practices approved by her. Such is the material object of the spirit of religion: love and respect for sacred places, which are our churches; love and respect for the functions that are celebrated in them; love and esteem for the practices of piety and worship promoted and recommended by the Church.

It might appear to be useless and even insulting to tell a priest that he should love and respect the church, since the church may be said to be his own house. Whoever loves a place goes there often and remains there willingly. Take for instance that place, that house, that company in which a priest has his whole heart, because he plays, laughs, jests there, because there are companions of pleasure there, persons of genius, objects that please him. How often he goes there! Scarcely a day passes that he does not go and perhaps he goes several times a day; and with what impatience he waits for the time to go there! And how short the time that he spends there appears to him! And how reluctantly he leaves it! And why is all this? The reason is clear: because he loves the place. To the church, however, to that place which should be for him the object of his desires and affections, he goes with an effort, and that only to celebrate Mass; outside that time, no one will see him there and when he goes there, what reluctance, what ennui he shows both in going there and remaining there! One would imagine that it was a purgatory; the minutes seem hours to him. And what is all that the sign of? There is no need to tell you, you know already.

✧ REVERENCE AND RESPECT DUE TO THE CHURCH

Priests should therefore have love for the church and at the same time reverence. In a house that we know is destined for important functions, in which persons of high dignity dwell, who would not willingly present himself with all due regard for the place and persons, and show the greatest respect and reverence while he remained there, especially at the times when most important affairs are transacted by persons of the highest rank and authority? It does not require much learning or culture for anyone to be able to conduct himself properly on such occasions. All people know the respect that is due, and they show it in their own way. Now what place was ever destined for higher functions than the church in which the Lord Himself dwells; in which are transacted affairs, not earthly and passing, but divine and eternal? What place was ever inhabited by personages of greater authority or higher dignity? In the church you have persons of the highest rank on earth; in it you have men of rare goodness and exemplary virtue; in it you have pure, innocent souls; in it you have hearts all on fire with charity; and what is much more, in it you have Angels, Archangels, Seraphim and members of the whole nine choirs of angels who descend from Heaven, remain there, and take up their abode there, because the King of kings, the Lord of lords, the great God Himself descends, remains and dwells there: "*Behold the tabernacle of God with men.*"[4] Behold that wonder, that prodigy! Heaven and earth, God and man, angels and saints dwell together, converse together and live on familiar terms in one great family. Behold the tabernacle of God with men! What is it but a land of delights and pleasures! Heaven itself may be said to come there, to be transplanted to earth. Ah! if God made His voice heard when Moses, ignorant of the mystery, was about to approach the burning bush, and called out to him saying: "*Come not nigh hither. Put off the shoes from thy feet: for the place whereon thou standest is holy ground*"[5] what does He not expect of the person who advances, not like Moses of old to a symbol, to a figure, but to that which was signified by the figure, to God Himself? *Reverence my sanctuary: I am the Lord,*[6] God had already said to the priests of the Old Law and had threatened dire penalties to any of them wanting in due respect!

We are accustomed to denounce from the pulpit the irreverences committed by the faithful in the holy place; distractions, conversations, etc; but let us just look at the conduct of some of our brethren. It is heartbreaking to see some of them coming into the church: besides removing their hat—which even a Protestant will do—one might say that they show no other sign of respect, except perhaps, a half genuflection and a hurried Sign of the Cross made with less devotion than the most ordinary layman. Then they go up the church turning their head now to one side now to the other, as if they were in a museum. You can guess from their manner of entering that they will remain only a short time, and that their behavior when going out will be similar. Those are only a few, you will say to me, but I wish that there was not even one such, because these few are sufficient to make people lose their respect and reverence for the holy places. And how can you expect rude, ignorant, superficial people to conceive a great idea of our churches, if they see the priest showing such little reverence for them? It would be better if they did not go there at all rather than behave in that manner; if they did not honor the church by going, at least they would not profane it by staying away.

But I don't notice anything wrong, says a priest, I do that without thinking of it. Worse still! for in that case it is to be feared that he behaves habitually in this way, for it is the habit not the individual act that dominates one's conduct in practice. And what great harm is done by such conduct! What scandal is given! A priest irreverent in church! A certain priest who was accustomed to enter the church, walk through it and go out in the manner described, was seen by a layman and not a very pious man either; he turned round and said to those standing near: that man should have been a soldier, not a priest.

We should therefore have respect for the church; our manner of entering it should be always grave, devout and dignified: *Ingressus ad ecclesiam sit humilis et devotus.*[7] On entering, let each one remember that in the church he is dealing, not with men but with God, and therefore he should endeavor to comport himself in such a manner as not to render himself unworthy of an audience with God: *Omnes in templo ita se componant, ut sibi non cum homine, sed cum Deo rem esse intelligant.*[8] And the Council of Milan sums up by saying: "Let priests bear in mind that while in church they are to show respect to the church and at the same time to teach the laity who frequent it to do in like manner."

❖ REVERENCE AND RESPECT DUE TO CHURCH FUNCTIONS

The priest should show love and respect for the functions in the church. Among these some are considered honorable and dignified, others are of lesser importance in the eyes of the world; there is an honorarium for attending some, for others there is none; some require little effort and impose no inconvenience, others are heavy and wearying. If we want to know the priest who has the spirit of religion in what regards the attachment to and love for the exercise of his functions, let us observe whether he attends all functions without making any distinction, and how he conducts himself. If we see him making distinctions between function and function, and behaving differently in different cases; if we see him ready and eager to attend only when there is some material advantage or honor to be gained, and no inconvenience; but if there is no such motive, if we see him avoiding them, seeking exemption, and only attending when compelled, then you can say that he loves gain, honor and his own convenience more than the worship and honor of the Lord. This is a manner of testing that never fails. If, on the contrary, you see a priest who in the course of his day makes no distinction between function and function and, as far as his state and occupation allow him, shows as much eagerness to attend at one as at the other and, when possible, is never absent whether he is obliged to attend or not, you can say that such a priest cannot fail to possess this affection, this spirit of which we are speaking. And what edification will not the faithful get from that alone!

Wherefore, we may say that as long as we say Mass and attend these functions for which there is something to be gained, the people will not be impressed, even though we are devout; at best, they will say that we do things nicely, but as they are aware that money considerations or self-interest enters in, they will conclude that these are the principal motives of our devotion. If, on the contrary, they see that we are always equally assiduous and prompt; if they see us like one of themselves, listening to the sermons, assisting at Mass, Vespers and Benediction, taking part in functions and processions; however ill-disposed towards us they may be, they cannot fail to come to the conclusion that we have the Faith, that we know the excellence and the value of these functions, and that we are acting through the spirit of religion; and much more so, if they see us attend at these functions with promptness, gravity and reverence; about which I will now say a few words.

In the exercise of the functions of the Church the most important element, insofar as the merit of the priest before God and the edification of the faithful are concerned, is the manner in which they are exercised. But in order to be able to show the external respect and reverence that will edify the people, the priest must first acquire an esteem for these functions. When we wish to ascertain the amount of importance that a person attaches to what he is doing, we observe the care and attention with which he does it, and we deduce the degree of importance that he attaches to it from the greater or less degree in which his attention is absorbed in it to the exclusion of other things. When people want to know the importance and value of the functions we perform, they watch our face, our eyes, they study the composure and gravity of our whole person, and if they see us grave and composed, with our whole attention concentrated on what we are doing, they will say among themselves: that priest is really in earnest; they will understand from his demeanor that the church is no place for joking or laughing and that they too must be serious. "What a grand Mass," said one of these laymen of the good old times to his companions as they were leaving the church! "It was just a little long, but what does that matter, a person goes away satisfied." This man was, of course, alluding to the gravity and modesty with which it was celebrated. We read of a pagan priest who, when he was engaged in performing his pagan rites, had a person standing by who was to raise his voice from time to time and say: "Pay attention to what you are doing." *Age quod agis.* How useful and opportune it would be in our times also if we had some one standing near the priest when he is performing the sacred functions who would repeat from time to time: "Pay attention to what you are doing": *Age quod agis.*

Time does not permit me today to go over in detail the faults that are committed during the various functions. However, I will touch on a few of the most common. Is that rough manner of putting on and taking off the sacred vestment proper? Can that laughing or jesting at such a time be said to be fitting a priest who wishes to show love and esteem for the sacred functions? Can a priest who goes to the altar and returns from it with hurried steps, looking round to right and left, casting glances that speak for themselves, be said to be showing proper respect and reverence to the sacred place, and to the sacred functions that he has performed, or that he is going to perform? Can that manner of giving Holy Communion be called reverent, when the priest distributes the sacred particles with such haste that a person would think they were made of fire and that they burned his fingers; with an attempt at a Sign of the Cross that no one could recognize and with the words mumbled in such a way that they would give the impression that he was distribut-ing some object for fun? It would be well if there was someone present who would raise his voice and say: "Pay attention to what you are doing, your Reverence, and to how you are treating your Divine Lord." And in the administration of Baptism and the other Sacraments, is not want of controlling the eyes, and allowing them to wander in all directions a thing that will be noticed by the faithful? Not only is it noticed, but it is made a subject for joking and laughter at our expense, or rather at the expense of the Lord and of holy things.

✣ The Celebration of the Mass

In the short time that remains, I shall say a few words more about the celebration of the Mass. In the first place let us remember that the rubrics regarding the celebration of the Holy Sacrifice are not merely for directing us, but that they are all obligatory; that, therefore, whoever omits them, mutilates them, mixes them up or confuses them cannot be excused from sin, and that, by both natural and divine law, all these Heavenly ceremonies should be performed in a grave and reverent manner. To secure that this be so, a certain length of time is required. You are all aware that a priest cannot be excused from mortal sin who celebrates Mass in less than a quarter of an hour, and with difficulty from venial sin, if he celebrates in less than twenty minutes; this is the opinion of Pope Benedict XIV. Each priest should make sure that he keeps within these limits. On the other hand, he is to try not to take longer than a half-hour as St. Philip advised. By the same law which requires due reverence for the Mass, a priest is bound to make proper preparation before Mass and suitable thanksgiving after Mass, so that I cannot see how a priest who habitually omits preparation and thanksgiving can be excused from grave sin* on account of the irreverence shown to the Blessed Sacrament, and the scandal given to the faithful. The minimum time usually laid down for thanksgiving is a quarter of an hour. It is not necessary for me to mention here that there is a most grave obligation on any priest who has fallen into mortal sin to go to Confession before celebrating Mass; that want of confidence in the confessor available will not excuse from the obligation; that whenever a priest is unhappily in that state he must confess if possible; that when it is not possible, there must be a grave reason for celebrating before he is justified in doing so, and then he must make an act of perfect contrition before celebrating and must go to Confession as soon as possible after celebrating even though there be not necessity to celebrate again.**

* See Code of Canon Law, No. 810.
**See Code of Canon Law, No. 807.

✠   Love and Esteem for Pious Practices

Finally, the spirit of religion requires that the priest should have love and esteem for all the acts of worship and pious practices which the Church recognizes, promotes and recommends. Among these are to be placed the use of the Sacramentals, especially of holy water, the exercise of the Stations of the Cross, the recitation of the Angelus, enrollment in pious associations, grace before and after meals. Oh! some priests may say, these practices are all right for lay people who have need of some external helps to make them concentrate their attention, but a priest has something else to do; he has other more important and substantial matters with which to occupy his time, all the more so, because he can become a holy priest without so many external practices. In reply it should be sufficient to say that a priest who has the spirit of religion will not speak in such a manner; when time or circumstances do not permit him to carry out all his devotional practices, he will omit what has to be omitted, but he will not reject them all indiscriminately. The Church has made no distinction between priests and laity in regard to these pious practices; on the contrary, she has approved them for all, granted privileges and favors for all, conceded indulgences for all, why then contend that these practices are intended for the laity only?

If the priest has not time, if there are more important things to be done, if, on account of some particular circumstances, any of these practices be inconvenient, then some of them may be omitted, But if there be no such excusing causes a priest should practice them. That a priest might become holy without these pious practices may be conceded in theory, but in practice we see quite the contrary: good, virtuous, holy priests attach great importance to them and are assiduous in practicing them. Let us give just a passing glance at the pious practices of the simple faithful. Practically all, even those not very devout, take holy water and bless themselves on entering a church; all the faithful with any pretense to devotion keep holy water in their houses and make use of it. Is the priest to be the only one who thinks that it is of no efficacy, and that he can do without it? In pious families the Rosary is recited each evening, would it not be fitting that the house of the priest should be among the number of those who offer Our Blessed Lady this daily act of homage? We mean, of course, that the priest himself should join in the recitation of it, and that it should never be said of his house what alas! is sometimes said: that the Rosary is indeed said, but by the servants, and when the priest is not there. The same may be said about the recitation of the Angelus; we see that this practice is still alive among the common people, especially in the country, where at the sound of the Angelus bell the people cease work and say it; they even lay down the mouthful of food about to be put into their mouth in order to salute Our Lady at the first sound of the bell; can we say that among priests there is the same esteem for the Angelus and the same eagerness to say it?

❖ The Priest Should Avail of His Opportunities to Gain Indulgences

In order to avoid being tedious I shall not here give a long list of pious practices but I cannot omit a reference to works of piety and religion to which indulgences are attached, for respect for the indulgences granted by the Church and eagerness to gain them are comprehended under the name of spirit of religion. And in this connection, I may remark that we priests have to include ourselves among those who, generally speaking, do not avail themselves sufficiently of the opportunities to gain indulgences. It should be quite the contrary, for we priests know their value, having learned when in college that indulgences have all the value mentioned in connection with them: *Indulgentiae tantum valent quantum pronuntiantur,*[9] and that, when it is said that there is a full and total remission, it is so in fact. We priests can gain indulgences more conveniently than any of the laity, and we have more opportunities, because we live at the church and are by profession men of prayer, and in most cases, all we have to do is to form the intention of gaining the indulgences attached to the works we do, or to the prayers we say. Finally, it is our duty to instruct the faithful about the doctrine of indulgences and tell them how to gain them, and how easy it is to gain them. And priests should not excuse themselves by saying that some of the conditions necessary to gain indulgences are very difficult; for instance, the condition for gaining a plenary indulgence presents the difficulty that to gain it in full a person must be free from all affection to venial sin. I am willing to concede that this condition might present a difficulty for people of the world, but not for a priest; even though he may fall into some venial sin, he can in a moment make an act of sorrow and repent, and then the affection for sin will cease immediately.

✛ MOTIVES FOR ACQUIRING THE SPIRIT OF RELIGION

(1) *Want of it Exposes the Priest to Danger*

It remains to say a few words about what a priest has to fear when he has not this spirit of religion or when he neglects it. What has a servant to expect who takes no care of his master's house, who omits or does badly the work allotted to him? The least he has to expect is to be corrected, threatened, and if that does not suffice, to be punished. God deals with us in like manner: He warns us, He threatens us, and if His warnings and threats are ignored, then He chastises.

We cannot have the slightest doubt about the fact that God regards irreverence in church committed by us as a serious offense; the castigation that Our Saviour gave those who profaned the Temple of Jerusalem suffices to prove this; and in that case we are not told that the profaners were priests. If they had been priests, we may presume that He would have treated them even more severely; for it is certain that irreverences committed by us priests are more sinful than those committed by the laity, and that they will be more severely punished, just as irreverence on the part of courtiers or ministers of a king are more offensive to him than those committed by people outside. The chastisements fulminated against the priests of the Old Law are terrible. The language of Sacred Scripture about the two priests, Ohpni and Phinees, who were guilty of scandal and irreverence in the house of the Lord fill us with dread. After calling them sons of the devil, the Sacred Scripture said that their sin was too great: *Grande nimis,* because they turned the people away from the worship of the Lord. And that is exactly the effect produced by irreverences committed by us in the church; if the people see us distracted, disorderly, wanting in respect, some go away and come no more, some continue to come but become irreverent and undevout like us, that person who had promised some work or gift for the glory of God, seeing us so negligent about His glory, will break his promise and keep back his gift, so that the words of Holy Scripture could be applied to us also: "*The sons of Heli were children of Belial . . . the sin of the young men was exceeding great before the Lord; because they withdrew men from the sacrifice of the Lord.*"[10] The Lord speaks no less clearly about functions of the Sanctuary done badly and carelessly: "*I am full, I desire not holocausts . . . . incense is an abomination to Me . . . . I am weary of bearing them.*"[11] The manner in which you serve Me fills me with nausea, I can stand it no longer. "*I . . . . will curse your blessings . . . . I will scatter upon your face the dung of your solemnities.*"[12] In general, therefore, God has already pronounced his judgment, and it is nothing less than a malediction against whoever does badly or disrespectfully a work of the Lord. "*Cursed be he that doth the work of the Lord deceitfully.*"[13] And a person who is dilatory or negligent in carrying out his obligations, although he does not omit them entirely, is reckoned by the Lord among transgressors and workers of iniquity: *Declinantes in obligationes, adducet Dominus cum operantibus iniquitatem.*"[14]

(2) *The Priest Is the Representative of Jesus Christ*

But let us leave aside these motives of fear, and end with a thought that should have greater effect on us: the thought that in our ministry we represent the person of Our Lord Jesus Christ; that we work for Him and in His place; and that we should therefore, on our part, perform our acts of service in the same way as Jesus Christ Himself would perform them. This reflection may perhaps appear to contain an exaggeration, or to be the pious imagination of a small mind: that is not so; it should be our daily endeavor to remember whom we represent, and to do our actions as He would do them. We know that we are truly and really the representatives, the vicegerents of Jesus Christ, so that in a certain sense it can be said of every priest: behold another Redeemer of the world, behold another Jesus Christ, who therefore is destined and commanded to do what Jesus Christ does! And is it too much to expect, is it too extraordinary a demand, that one invested with such dignity and power should exert all his energy to carry out the ministry of Jesus as He carried it out when on earth, and as the same Divine Redeemer, who has deigned to make us His representatives, would carry it out again today?

A great lord, if left to act as representative of his king for a certain period of time in a certain place, would not only count it a pleasure, but a duty to put on, as it were, the king's person, to uphold its decorum and gravity; to imitate his sovereign's manners and customs in such a way that it could be said that sovereign and representative formed, as it were, but one person, and if there was difference in name and identity, there was no difference in actions and sentiments. It should be possible to say the same of us. If there is a difference between us and Jesus Christ, a difference in name and person, which is infinite, we should endeavor that there be no difference in the works and in the manner of performing them. Ah, if that thought came often to our mind, and if it was applied to our actions, what benefit would result from it! Suppose a priest were to reason and meditate in the following manner: I am in the confessional, but if Jesus Christ were here in my place how would He welcome those souls, how would He deal with them? I am going to celebrate Mass, to recite the Breviary, to study, to preach, to teach cathechism; I am called to a sick person, I am at the bedside of a dying man, I have to deal with some poor person in great trouble, but if Jesus Christ were in my place, if He were called for those cases, if He dealt with them instead of me, would He deal with them in the way that I am dealing with them, or would He put more zeal, more fervor, greater gravity and exactness into these things than I am putting? What pressure such reflections would exercise upon us, and how they would discover to us any imperfections in our actions! What material they would provide us with for daily examination, and how they would make us reform our lives! And at the same time, what a stimulus they would provide, and what hope of spiritual fruit and advancement they would give!

In all our works, therefore, let us act under the influence of this spirit of religion, a spirit that will make us respect holy places, a spirit that will make us perform our functions in a worthy manner and hold in high esteem all that can conduce to the honor and glory of God, so that the people in admiration and astonishment at our devotion, gravity and composure will cry out: Oh, how great our God must be who has such worthy, such splendid ministers on earth! *Ut qui ministrum videt, Dominum praedicet et veneretur, qui tales servulos habet.*

1 John. 3:10.
2 1 Tim. 4:14.
3 Comm. in Epist. I ad Tim. IV, 14.
4 Apoc. 21:3.
5 Ex. 3:5.
6 Levit. 26:2.
7 Conc. Rom.
8 Conc. Burd.
9 S. Thom. Suppl. p. 3. q. XXX, a. 2.
10 1 Kgs. 2:12, 17.
11 Is. 1:11, 13, 14.
12 Malach 2:2, 3.
13 Jerem. 48:10.
14 Psalm. 124:5.

The Priest's Recreations

W E HAVE CONSIDERED a good part of the life and duties of a priest during these last few days and have gone through a great part of his day exhaustively. We have him now resolved and determined to become a true and holy priest; we have him persuaded that his life is one of labor and sacrifice, and that, being placed on a pinacle by his dignity and character, he is obliged to surpass others in virtue and perfection; that in order to do so he must flee from the noise and din of the world as much as possible, live a mortified life and attend to prayer and works of virtue and religion.

Now you will ask me, cannot the priest every day, or at least some times, rest a little, have some entertainment, relax sometimes from his labors and occupations in order to acquire new strength and vigor? It is true that the priest is a special and distinct man separated from the rest of men, and in a manner transformed into a new creature between God and man; but with all that, he is still a man and, as such, has need of rest and recreation; cannot he therefore relax at times and take recreation? There is no reason why he should not: search as you will, you will find neither canonist, nor theologian, nor ascetical writer who prohibits it; and, in addition, repose, recreation, amusement, besides being lawful in itself, may sometimes be beneficial and even necessary. The difficulty is to decide what kind the recreation should be and how it should be taken. For some priests, it consisted, and does still, in prayer, in familiar conversation with God: that was the recreation of the Saints, for example, of St. Francis Xavier, St. Francis de Sales, St. Francis Regis, and of many holy priests, but for us perhaps it would not suffice. For others, it consisted in suspending the more grave and serious occupations and turning to something lighter and more superficial, such as reading, or the exercise of some mechanical or liberal art; but for us, perhaps not even that would suffice. Others might take their recreation by going on an excursion to some quiet place, by visiting the sick or by attending to some temporal affairs. That is a common form of relaxation for many and does not require any special virtue, so that anyone could easily adapt himself to it. However, I fear that for certain people, any or all of the above methods of recreation would still not be sufficient. For those, then what kind of recreation is required?

Since we have come here to study how the true priest should spend the day and all its parts, let us say everything and say it at once. There are certain people who cannot get recreation from anything, unless they can give their tongue a little exercise; unless they are among congenial company, or in some gathering, chatting, laughing and joking. Now may a priest lawfully take his recreation in that way? No direct answer can be given to this question, for various circumstances have to be taken into account that may affect the morality of these actions; it will be necessary to consider these circumstances, and that will form the subject matter of this conference. We shall consider the nature of the conversations that takes place at various meeting-places with the defects and dangers that may accompany them; and from that we shall see the way in which a priest must conduct himself, so as not to burden his conscience or lose his esteem and reputation.

✢ Different Kinds of Recreations

When we speak of going out to have a talk, we do not mean a casual visit to some layman's house or a visit for some purpose, because if there is anything wrong in such visits, it will be from some aspect other than that which we are considering. The talks or conversations I mean are those that take place at assemblies or gatherings where several people meet frequently in some place, whether private or public, for familiar conversation and where the priest goes for recreation. What are we to say about attending such assemblies? We may distinguish three kinds of assemblies: the first, evil and dangerous, and therefore to be avoided by priests; the second, licit and honest, at which the priest may attend if he takes the proper precautions; the third useful and good, and to be approved of without reserve.

✣   GATHERINGS THAT ARE EVIL OR DANGEROUS

With regard then to assemblies or meetings, some are evil and dangerous, and to be avoided, either because their object is bad or the conversations that take place at them are bad. Under this first heading, a great
number of meetings or gatherings must be regarded as places unfit for a
priest to attend. Let us come down to particulars.

I   ON ACCOUNT OF THE BUSINESS THAT
TAKES PLACE

The first reason why a gathering or society is bad is on account of the
business that takes place at it. For instance, there are houses where certain people meet to examine, not indeed their own consciences or private affairs, but the private affairs, faults and failings etc. of the people
of the neighborhood, and where, having, so to speak, erected a platform
they make the various people appear on it, in order that each member
of the conventicle may pronounce his sentence on them. Such houses or
such meeting places are not suitable for a priest. Nor can such attacks
on people's character be excused by saying that the things said are true
and often public, besides those who meet are prudent people and will
not divulge secrets. These are mere pretexts, and do not excuse such
conversations, and when they take place habitually, it is inevitable that
what is untrue will be mixed with what is true and, if the substance of
what is said is not false, the consequence drawn from it will be false.
Then one thing leads to another, what is private will be told as well as
what is public. Various excuses for divulging people's secret affairs will
be given; it will be said that those present are prudent people and will
keep the information secret and that if people can't talk about what is
true, they may talk about something worse. In reply to this we can say
that there is no reasonable hope that such secrets will be kept, and that
it is not lawful to do evil in order to avoid another evil. We can conclude
that meetings of such kind where people's secret faults will be discussed
and their characters injured are not suitable for a priest, and that consequently he is not free to attend them.

Then there is a house of some relatives or friends or acquaintances of the priest to which he is invited. He says that it would be rudeness on his part to refuse, and that there is really no other house in which he can relax and enjoy himself. But in the house in question the conversation generally begins by laughing and joking about some pious people and ridiculing their piety; from that they go on to casting ridicule on pious practices, without however openly denying defined doctrine; then they discuss love affairs, curious, but unseemly and suggestive stories are told, there are even improper glances; enough has been said, we will not pursue the unsavory subject. But what does the priest do? Is it possible that he has fallen so low, that he has so far lost his dignity and reputation that people will dare to talk and jest in that manner in his presence? However, there he is! Look at him in the midst of that coterie, enjoying such company. I am presuming that he does not speak and joke in the same manner as the others; the very thought of such a thing horrifies us. "How," says St. Bernard, "can you make such use of the tongue which has been consecrated to the Lord to proclaim His doctrine, to announce His precepts!" How can you profane it and sully it with such language! Do you not know that this is a detestable sacrilege? *Consecrasti os tuum evangelio, talibus jam aperiri illicitum assuescere sacrilegium est.*[1] And note that the Saint was not speaking of such serious and delicate matters, but of profane things.

But I don't speak, I don't take part in the conversation, the priest says. But then what do you do, I ask? Even though you don't speak, it would be impossible to avoid smiling or giving some sign of enjoying what is going on, and, in a priest, that would suffice to make you guilty. I do not even do that, he replies, I keep completely silent. That is hard to believe, I reply; you might do so once or twice at most, and after that you will fall, for if a priest tries to act that way habitually, his attendance at such a gathering will no longer be a recreation for him but a penance, and therefore either he will cease going there, or the others will not allow him. They will make him see clearly that he is not in his own house. But even suppose that he can keep silent and show no sign of approval, I would not say that he can be easy in his conscience.

Silence can suffice to clear oneself from blame and to correct offenders when a person has a valid reason for being present; for in that case everyone will understand that if the priest is present it is because he is forced by necessity or because there is some interest at stake and, not being able to prevent what is being said or done in any other way, he keeps silent, and that may be enough. But this does not hold when a priest goes spontaneously, urged on by his own desire and curiosity, because in such a case people will believe that the reason why he does not give some external sign of approval is that he is afraid or does not dare, but that what is being said or done is not displeasing to him. At any rate, they will say, if he was really displeased he would not come any more. And this is true, for suppose he was insulted in such a house and was deeply offended, you will see that he will keep away immediately and will not try to go there any more. Instead of the priest, it is really his Divine Master who is being repeatedly offended and insulted in the person of the priest, and the insult is aggravated by the laughter and jeers; and can a priest remain present and be witness of such a thing, even though he does not take part?

But in my case, it would be useless to speak, I would only do harm. Well then, adopt another weapon, for our armory has many; if these people will not listen to you, get out of there, leave them, and pray for them, for a priest must never remain present while his Lord is being insulted, when it is possible to depart. Such pastime, far from being a recreation, should be a martyrdom, an agony, just as it would be for a dutiful son to see his father beaten and torn without being able to prevent it. It is not merely an advice that I give to a priest to keep away from such places, it is a precept; it is a duty imposed on him by charity and much more by his position as priest, and by justice also, if he is under an obligation to correct. "*I beheld the transgressors, and I pined away,*" said the Royal Psalmist, and what was the reason for such grief? "*Because they kept not thy word.*"[2] You need not expect to find such a spirit in the priest who frequents the company that I have described, and who seeks to tranquilize his conscience by saying: "I don't take part in the conversation." Anyone can see how far that is from doing his duty.

(2) *Gatherings Dangerous on Account of the People Present*

Another reason why a priest should abstain from going to certain gatherings is the kind of people who attend them. I reduce these to two classes: gatherings composed of men who are known to be bad, and the company of women.

I Gatherings of Bad Men

As regards gatherings composed of openly bad men, we may repeat what we have said already: it is one thing to find oneself casually with such people for some just cause, such as a prudent attempt to convert them; it is quite another thing to associate with them, and make oneself their familiar companion by attending their meetings. I lay aside for the moment the danger that can gradually arise for the priest from associating with such people and I merely ask, what effect, what impression will be produced on the public by seeing and knowing that the priest seems not to be able to find more suitable associates or places of amusement. The least evil construction that can be put on such conduct is that it is a matter of complete indifference whether people live good or bad lives, seeing that the priest shows such esteem for and attachment to people of that sort.

But in my parish, says a priest, if I don't go and have a talk with these people, I don't know where to go, for I can find no others able to put two words together; I must make the best of what I have. You must! It is not a duty that you have to fulfill; no law obliges you to go to such gatherings. You can indeed show these people signs of friendship, even special signs, but not to the extent of joining their social gatherings to take your recreation with them. And I ask, do these people whose houses you frequent and who pass for your friends make their Easter duty? Of what kind is their conversation? What kind of reputation have they in the country in matters of purity and religion? It is well known that they have very little of either. Well then, neither the company nor the conversation of such people is suitable for a priest. If he can find no others with whom to converse, let him resign himself to do without any. After all, the priest should be a mortified man; he should therefore make a sacrifice and seek some other kind of relaxation. What company or what conversation had our Divine Redeemer, the Head and Model of all priests, He who was wisdom incarnate associated with a few rude, ignorant fishermen. What enjoyment could be found in the speech and conversation of such men? And we do not read that Our Divine Lord went to seek others. He went sometimes to the houses of public sinners, but for what end did He go, what object had He in view? We know that it was in order to convert them; and in fact every time He went to such people we read that He converted them. When we have such an end in view and such a hope, let us go too; but of that we shall speak before finishing.

II THE COMPANY OF WOMEN

The second class of people with whom too great familiarity or too frequent association is harmful for the priest are women. I would gladly pass over this subject, for I think it must be painful for us priests to speak of it or hear it discussed, but it would leave too great a gap to omit the subject altogether; I shall therefore deal with it as briefly as I can and with the greatest possible reserve. I shall not stop to quote the many passages from Sacred Scripture and from the Fathers and Doctors of the Church telling priests to be on their guard against visiting women, and remaining in their company. They all cry out, threaten, and grieve over the inevitable ruin of the priest who is not on his guard. It is useless for him to put forward pretexts of relationship, suitability, urbanity, good motives, honest intentions, blameless life, irreprehensible conduct, not even the shadow of danger. No one will listen to such excuses, and people will just repeat: woe to the priest who trusts himself to them, who does not seek safety in flight; he is lost! The strongest columns and the stoutest oaks have fallen, and how can you expect that the frail reed is going to survive? Ah! how many priests have had to lament, and how many lament daily because they would not listen to reason! The days which they pass sad, melancholy and sorrowful, objects of jests and mockery, the deaths brought on prematurely through this bread of pain, are all so many additional proofs of the truth of the words spoken for so many centuries on this subject in warning and sermons, but all to no purpose because these men would not listen. In this matter the devil has always plausible reason to deceive the poor priest; and he is able to represent the affair in such a way and clothe it in such deceitful colors as to make the unfortunate man believe that his case is not the one that has been condemned by the voice and pen of men of long experience. Women and priests have to be as distant from each other as two opposite poles, if not in actual distance apart at least in heart and will. Let women come to the church, to the confessional, if they have need of a priest; let them meet him outside these places, if it is necessary; but let it be as rarely as possible and with proper precautions; for the rest, let them keep their own places, and look after their own business; and when a necessity to speak occurs let the priest remember: *Sermo brevis cum mulieribus et rigidus est habendus,*[3] and as St. Bonaventure says; *"let the conversation be dignified and serious."* "Woman what is that to me and to thee?"[4] These words were used by our Divine Redeemer in a different sense from that above; but in the above sense I recommend them to every priest who has to deal with women. I don't mean that he should actually say these words but that he should think them. A lady for example comes to me and begins a rambling conversation. I ask myself what have I to do with her? In what way can I be useful to her? Let us therefore come to the point at once.

A lady was going often to the priest's residence; she was well behaved but the priest could see no reason for the visits. He therefore thought that it would be better if they ceased. What was he to do? He tried to make her understand indirectly, but it was no use, she either did not understand him, or pretended that she did not. Then he spoke plainly to her and told her to stay in her own house. She took it badly and, one day that she met him, she complained in presence of other people and asked him if that was his ordinary way of dealing with ladies. He replied that it was. And why? she asked. Because, as you ought to know, the priest's house is not made for women. She remained mute, and those who were listening said: Fine! What more does she want to know? That reason is worth a hundred. Vice versa, we can say: the houses of women are not made for priests. "Let him go and say his Breviary, this is not the place for him," was said by a lady about a priest who wanted to prolong his visit.

Those laymen who know no restraint, those men dissipated and worldly who know nothing of God or spiritual things, but only of the flesh and the world, who lose their time and their reason after women, excite our compassion, but do not surprise or astonish us much; but that a priest trained in the school of the Divine Master, modelled after Him, a man separated from the rest and distinct, who should have nothing to do with this world, a man destined to represent the Divinity upon earth, that this man, I say, should lower himself, debase himself, so cover himself with the mire of the world as to look after a woman, think on a woman, visit her frequently, become familiar with her, is such an ignominy, such an opprobrium, that I say frankly that I can find no words to express myself, and if I could, I would not have the heart to use them. Let these people therefore, be kept as far away from our persons as possible. *Quid mihi et tibi, mulier?* What has the woman to do with the priest, her affairs with our affairs? Let us therefore keep far asunder; the farther the better.

Nor will it serve us to put forward the common reason, or rather the common pretext, that we are tranquil in conscience and that we have nothing with which to reproach ourselves before God. We shall see on another occasion whether that holds good in theology; for the present, I will confine myself to saying, even granted that this is true with regard to the danger to chastity, is there not the consideration of suspicion, of gossip, of accusation? We read in ancient pagan history of a young girl who had been sold into slavery, and whose virtue was placed in danger by the man who purchased her. She was so firm in will and strong of arm that she succeeded in killing her insolent aggressor. She was brought to trial and accused of homicide; she defended herself so well that she was not only acquitted but highly praised. Emboldened by such praise, she asked to be allowed to become a priestess. Oh! no, not that, was the reply, although your virtue is so strong, the fact that you were with suspicious characters, in fact, with people known to be bad, is alone sufficient in the eyes of the people to leave such a stain on your character as to exclude you, and render you unworthy of such an office. O my dear Fathers, would to God that we should get that warning into our heads once for all: it is not enough to be innocent, especially in this matter of chastity, but it is necessary, it is indispensable to avoid giving ground for the slightest suspicion. The people confound what is done with what can be done; they do not see what is done or whether it has been done, but that it can be done or can have been done: *Nescimus quid faciat, sed quid facere possit, bene scimus.*

I shall not add any more, perhaps I have even said too much, but I hope that we are all convinced about this truth. Wherefore, I recommend that we should go on ever increasing our precautions to guard inviolate this beautiful virtue and keep it free from all suspicion. No care, no sacrifice will be too great when there is question of preserving a priest's purity and his good name unblemished. In order to guard and protect himself, St. Jerome thought it necessary to retire into a cave, St. Benedict rolled among thorns, St. Thomas Aquinas had recourse to a firebrand, St. Philip Neri ran precipitately down a staircase; there were others who, having no other means of defending themselves, bit out their tongue with their teeth and spat it contemptuously into the face of their assailants; there were others, in fine, who disfigured their faces and tore their flesh as if they were executioners; would it then be too much for us to observe modesty, to practice a little mortification, to avoid the company of, and familiar conversation with women?

II Lawful Recreations

There are other groups or assemblies of people which, as we have said, are licit and honest and which the priest can attend, if he uses the proper precautions. They are those which are free from the dangers and vices referred to; that is to say, they present no evil or danger of evil either from their nature and object or from the people who frequent them. That is easily said, but in practice it would be difficult to find a place, a group, an assembly of lay people in which each one controls his tongue so effectively as not to transgress, but always keeps it within the bounds of honesty, charity and religion. Usually those who frequent such places, if they are not irreligious, are gossipers; and how will it be possible among so many tongues of that kind to keep always within the limits of what is licit and becoming? If it is regarded as a miracle for one person to do so, what about a number? But let us for the moment lay aside the question whether those faults are few or many, let us suppose that the priest is at some gathering where he can legitimately be present, what precautions is he to observe? They may be reduced to three:

✛ Precautions to Be Observed
the Time Spent Must Not Be Excessive

In the first place, let him take care that the time spent at these gatherings or with groups of friends is not excessive, for this in itself is reprehensible, and cannot fail to have baneful consequences; and even if it is not excessive, let him see that it be not time required for other occupations.

In the second place, let him take care that there be nothing in his speech or conduct unworthy of a priest; and let him put into practice the advice of St. Hillary, that he should always have in his mouth and on his lips words of peace, purity, piety and charity: *Nunquam in ore tuo, nisi pax, nisi castitas, nisi pietas, nisi charitas.*[5] The third warning is: with all these precautions, let him know and remember that from such places and from such conversations with seculars he will return always the loser: in his interior life he will lose quiet and recollection, and with the people, even with those familiar friends, he will lose some of the ascendancy and dignity of his state. This appears to be an exaggeration, however, such is the truth; the *Imitation* says: "As often as I was among men I returned less a man." *Quoties inter homines fui, minor homo redii.*[6] St. Bonaventure says that conversation with the world always lessens and sometimes even extinguishes that interior devotion in our mind, which consists in internal peace and union with the Lord; it weakens our eagerness to advance in virtue, it gives an appetite and relish for the pleasures of the world and a distaste and ennui during prayer,[7] and he adds, that he had often experienced this in himself and had seen it in others; and perhaps more than one of ourselves here can bear witness to the truth of this. During those days in which we frequented the diversions of the world more and had more dealings with seculars, our spiritual life was certainly more tepid, colder and more dissipated. The reason that induced St. Basil to retire from the world and cut off relations with it was because he found them to be sources of many evils, as he himself confesses: *Urbis conversationes reliqui velut infinitorum malorum occasiones.*[8]

We have already spoken on the subject of the retired life that the priest ought to lead, but it will not be amiss to repeat here that not only will the priest lose by the very fact that he frequents the world, but he will lower his reputation in the eyes of the faithful and thus he will have a means less for, and an obstacle more to doing all the good that he would otherwise have done. The very sight and presence of the priest repeated several times, the familiarity and liberty with him that it occasions, the slight defects, harmless in themselves, which will inevitably be discovered in him, defects if not in manners, at least in culture, prudence, caution, judgment—all this will serve to make the people lose the high idea they had of him. And how, asks Tertullian, could the Hebrew people ever dare to rise up against Moses, a man so great as he was, a man who conversed familiarly and visibly with God? How did they dare to rebel against such a personage whom even the elements respected, who changed the water of the rivers into blood, divided the sea, made water gush forth from the very rocks, made the ground open and swallow evil doers? How could the Jews go so far as even to attempt to stone him? Moses allowed himself to be seen, he treated with the people, talked to them, was familiar with them and, although he conducted himself in a blameless manner, the fact that the people saw him frequently and conversed with him was sufficient to lose for him that respect and reverence that he deserved.

We find confirmation of this in another passage of Sacred Scripture. An angel appeared to the wife of Manue (and mother of Samson). Filled with joy she ran to tell her husband the great news saying: *"A man of God came to me, having the countenance of an angel."* [9] Manue prayed to the Lord asking Him to send back that man of God in order that he might tell them what they should do. The angel returned and appeared to the woman again. She again ran in haste and said to her husband: "Behold the man hath appeared to me, whom I saw before." [10] Remark the difference of the words used by that woman; the first time she called the messenger *"a man of God having the countenance of an angel."* When telling her husband of his second appearance she referred to him simply as: *"the man whom I saw before,"* without adding either that he was *a man of God* or that he had *the countenance of an angel.* The angel at the second apparition to the woman no longer conveyed the same high idea of his dignity, and the woman's esteem of him diminished.

The same happens every day in the world; the first time a priest visits that house, the first time he is introduced to those people, what a sensation! What a joy! He is a man of God, he is a priest, his visit is regarded as a great event, all look on him as an angel; his words are gathered like Manna and preserved as a treasure. They are quoted: "So said the priest." But suppose that priest goes other times, that he continues to go frequently, you will see how that *man of God having the countenance of an angel* will end, you will find that the great idea first formed will go on diminishing in proportion to the frequency of his visits until he becomes a man like the rest of men. And then when he is announced, the people of the house take no more notice of him than they would of any ordinary person; soon his visits may even become irksome and the people will begin to say: he is haunting our house, he must have nowhere else to go; and they make plans how get rid of him, so that he may not come again.

That certainly does not happen in my case, some priest will say, because the people complain that I visit them too seldom. Ah! my dear man, you ought to know the ways of the world; these people invite you to come often with words, but they mean something quite different, and when you are gone they will say: by this time, he should understand what we mean and go and attend to his duties! We priests are like water; as long as water remains in its channel and does not disturb anyone, all esteem it a great benefit to have some near them, as it is in fact, and each one profits by the proximity and derives advantages from it. But suppose the water breaks its banks and goes rushing through the country and enters the houses of people, the case is suddenly reversed: all flee from it, they try to protect themselves from the harm that it causes, and they regard the occurrence as a great calamity. Let us apply this comparison to the priest who loses his time in useless visits; we can apply it literally without changing any detail; and then let us pass on to consider useful, praiseworthy, holy visits.

⁜ Visits That are a Form of Apostolate

In this class of good visits or conversations, I wish to include every means by which the zealous priest seeks dexterously to put himself in contact with the people, with seculars, in order to exercise an apostolate among them and, by services to them whether material or spiritual, to gain them for the Lord, or to confirm them in His service if they are good already. Whether he does this by talking to them when he meets them on the road, or whether he goes to their houses and talks familiarly to them there, and even laughs and jokes with them, it is a visit of a holy man, of a priest, of an apostle, and consequently it is a good, holy visit; it is also a visit that belongs to his duty, and is at the same time most useful and sometimes very difficult. In what we have just said, we have the three qualities of that familiar, domestic apostolate; firstly, it is an essential part of every secular priest's duty; secondly it is difficult; and thirdly, it is of the greatest utility.

✢ These Visits are Part of a Priest's Duty

When Our Lord ordered His Apostles to go into the world and preach: *Euntes praedicate,*[11] He certainly did not intend that they should preach in the churches and pulpits only, for these did not exist, or that they should preach only a few times and in a few places. They preached in the synagogues of the Jews, in the meeting places of the pagans; but the principal means they adopted to carry out their mission was to join in the conversations of the people, to mingle with them, to speak to them of the doctrine of Christ wherever opportunity offered, thus when we read: *Going forth they preached,* it was the same as to say, *going forth they conversed with the people.* St. Paul recommended this manner of evangelizing to Timothy: "*Be thou an example of the faithful, in word, in conversation.*"[12] The priest is, as you know, the light of the world, the salt of the earth; and these qualities should be part of his being, he should carry them with him everywhere; in the church, in his house, on the street, throughout the country, his light should shine, he should season the masses by good example, by word, by advice and by correction, if occasion should arise, and this is a continuous exercise of apostolate. That beautiful eulogy which the Church makes of St. Catherine of Siena should be capable of application to each one of us: no one ever approached her, without going away the better for it: *Nemo ad eam accessit, qui non melior abierit.*[13] And if those who deal with us, who see us, who speak to us, do not always profit by it, let them at least have a motive, an incitement to do so and to become better.

✢ A Most Useful Form of Apostolate

In the second place, this form of apostolate is most useful, because we can exercise it continually and in every place; everyone, in one way or another, can benefit from it when the priest wishes to exercise it. The other ways of evangelizing can be exercised only on certain days and at certain hours, and all cannot share in them. With this form, it is quite the contrary; at every moment, in every place, there will be opportunities for exercising it. The preaching that is done by it is usually much more useful that that which is heard from the pulpit, for people regard the latter as a priest's trade, and very often they listen to it either badly disposed or prejudiced; but the preaching done on the spur of the moment when people do not expect it and cannot escape from it cannot fail to touch men's hearts.

✢ A Difficult Form of An Apostolate

It is therefore a most useful form of apostolate, but it is at the same time a difficult apostolate, for it requires many solid virtues. In the first place, it requires prudence, discretion and dexterity, in order to know how to present ourselves, to show ourselves amiable and to attain our objective. Our plan of campaign must be carefully prepared, but without letting anyone know, for if our plans leak out and people get to know them it will spoil all; our plan will have failed and our efforts may even have done harm. In these conversations a word used at the right time is often worth a hundred in a sermon; but a word too many or too few, or a wrong word used may lose the battle. Next, we need the virtue of fortitude in order not to yield to human respect, but to show ourselves firm against the dangers that we may meet with in the world; the virtue of patience and long-suffering in order not to consider our own conveniences, but to bear patiently repeated repulses and humiliations; the virtues, however, that we need above all are great zeal and charity, which will make us study our methods, discover the means of attaining success, keep us alert and prepared for this way of preaching to the people, and give impulse and soul and fire to what we say; for it will not be the reasons we give, the time spent, the great knowledge we display that will ensure victory in this kind of assault, but great charity.

✢ To Exercise this Apostolate the Priest Must Be a Man of Prayer

And what are we to do, you will ask me in order to have all these virtues? How are we to make ourselves skilled in the exercise of this continuous apostolate, so suitable for a priest and so useful for souls? I shall only add one means common to all, easy and secure; it is to converse with the Lord before conversing with men: *"For his conversation hath no bitterness, nor his company any tediousness;"*[14] pray, continue to pray and become a man of prayer. In the house, in church, at the feet of the crucifix and principally before the Blessed Sacrament, let us study and meditate on our state, our obligations and our duties; let us study and meditate on the value of souls, the various ways of saving them, the great reward in store for those who save them; let us study and meditate on the counsels and example which our Head and Master has given us. When our heart is filled with these maxims and with His spirit, you may be sure that it will pour them forth in all directions, at all times, and to all people. Every word, every remark, every act, every look, will be a word of piety, purity and charity, a remark, an act which will touch the heart, conquer opposition, and save souls, so that the people in admiration and amazement cannot help saying: that priest is certainly a man of God because he acts, speaks, converses in that manner: *Ut qui vident, stupeant, admirentur et dicant: Hi sunt homines Dei, quorum talis est conversatio. Amen.*

---

1 De Consid. lib. II cap. 13.
2 Ps. 118:158.
3 De purit. consc. cap. 14.
4 John 2:4.
5 Hom. de S. Honor.
6 Lib. I cap. 20.
7 De Inst. novit. part. I. cap. 34.
8 De laud. eremi.
9 Judges 13:6.
10 Ibid. 10.
11 Mark 16:15.
12 1 Tim. 4:12.
13 Lect. 2 noct. in fest. S. Cathar.
14 Wisd. 8:16.

Concerning Games and Public Spectacles

*A*NOTHER KIND of recreation akin to visits, which is common among priests is card-playing in some form. We may add another more uncommon, but one at which we sometimes see priests present—especially on occasions of excursions, to the country or the neighboring city, or of voyages, or at certain seasons of the year—I refer to the presence of priests at public spectacles, which, as an extraordinary form of recreation, may be permitted sometimes; at least it is not to be gravely condemned. By the experience and knowledge gained through our ministry, we know better than anyone else the grave evils, the many inconveniences produced by both these forms of amusement: the quarrels, the discord, the blasphemy, the squandering, the ruin of families which result from gambling; the dissipation, immorality, irreligion which take place at public amusements, as the world calls them. Matters do not go to such extremes among priests, but although such abuses can happen even among us, they are not very common. I will therefore leave them aside and treat the subject under a different aspect, which is: up to what point can the one and the other of these amusements be approved of for a priest?

A great saint speaking about the recreation a person might take gave the following rule about amusement in general: the person should first examine whether it is licit, next, whether it is becoming, and lastly whether it is wise: *An liceat, an deceat, an expediat . . . .* I seem to hear someone saying on hearing the above: If we must look so closely into the matter, I for one would be afraid to play cards at all or to go near any place where card-playing is carried on. Well, my dear man, if every priest, including ourselves here, were to take that resolution, I would thank God, for I am sure that we would never have reason to be sorry, but I do not mean to propose such a thing or to make any pronouncement before examining the question. We should be slow about making laws for others based on our own likes or dislikes. It has always been the maxim of good men and of the saints that we should be liberal when dealing with others, but strict with ourselves. We shall then consider the morality of the various cases that can arise and see in theory how far certain actions are licit; we shall next apply the principles to us priests in order to see what must be forbidden and what may be permitted, so that our conference will take the form of a discussion on certain points of Moral Theology, and a solution of some cases to serve as a guide for ourselves.

Perhaps someone will say: this conference does not concern me at all, for I never play cards and I never go to see any kind of public spectacles at all. That is all the better, and is most consoling for us; may the Lord keep you so! What we are going to say will provide you with motives for thanking God who has kept you far from those habits which, at best, are dangerous, and will help to strengthen you in your good resolution; and the benefit that you gain from it can serve you as a guide in judging and providing for the good of those souls, especially of the priests whom the Lord will entrust to your charity. Let us then proceed to the examination of the question.

Any game may be considered under two aspects: as a contract and as a form of amusement. We shall take it in the latter sense and consider it a form of relaxation. What are the conditions required by moral theologians that games be licit and that they may be indulged in with safe conscience? Six conditions are laid down: (1) *that the primary intention of the person playing must not be gain;* (2) *that the stake be moderate;* (3) *that too much time be not spent at the game;* (4) *that the player does not expose himself to the danger of sin;* (5) *that the game played is becoming both for the person and the place;* (6) *that the form of the game be not prohibited.* And here let us remark that these are not conditions laid down by some isolated author with rigorous views, they are required by all theologians without exception. If therefore the game in which we indulge lacks any one of these conditions, it is certain that there is sin, and the sin will be grave or light in proportion to the matter and the consequences. Let us run over these conditions one by one.

The first condition is that the primary intention of the person playing must not be gain. Gaming cannot be lawful except in so far as it is
directed towards the relaxation and recreation of the mind, and only in
a reasonable degree; when it is directed to making gain, that is to say, to
satisfying the passion aroused by gambling, according to all theologians
it is sinful. We would like to know from certain priests who indulge in
games often or habitually, what is their intention in playing and whether
their health and their occupations really require so much repose and relaxation? I fear they would be embarrassed to give an answer. But it is
not necessary to have their answer in order to judge the case: the facts
speak for themselves; the eagerness with which they play, the anxiety
they experience, the amount of time that they spend, the depression of
spirits when they lose, all show clearly what is their intention: that it is
neither their health nor their mind that needs such relaxation, that on
the contrary there are evil effects for both, that it becomes a burden, a
labor and that it occupies their attention more than the duties of their
ministry. We may conclude therefore that whoever plays in this manner
cannot escape fault under the heading of intention, although otherwise
the game be licit.

The second condition is that a moderate sum of money be staked.
Under this heading, a person is guilty of sin who exposes to risk money
destined for some other end, either in justice, charity, or religion; this
concerns chiefly priests who have benefices or ecclesiastical pensions.
A priest who has a benefice can of course take reasonable recreation,
but I ask whether he can be easy in conscience when, having the option
of having a game at little or no expense, he prefers to play another in
which he risks the loss of a considerable sum of money? I respect the
opinions of others, but for myself in such a case I would not feel easy in
conscience. In the second place, a person sins who risks the loss of a notable or excessive amount. This is quite certain, but it remains to determine what is in practice an excessive sum, since it may vary according to
the nature of the players. The common rule is that it is lawful to expose
such a sum of money as will make the game interesting and enjoyable
for the players so that they will get that relaxation which the game is intended to give, but when the sum exposed exceeds that which ordinary
good people not addicted to gambling spend on parties of pleasure, it
may be regarded as excessive and is to be condemned, all the more so

that excessively high stakes are usually the cause of other evils and other sins, which we shall now consider.

But some priest says, I don't know what to do with myself on certain days in summer, and on long winter nights; I feel weary and tired, and have no mind for anything. But my friend, your reasons appear to be so frivolous as to set a person thinking. A priest who does not know what to do gives grounds for certain suspicions: we might ask him whether during those days that he feels the urge for gaming he has ever tried just a little study; whether he is sure that he has prepared his Sunday sermon; whether it is long since he revised his Moral Theology; whether he has made his meditation; whether he has visited the Blessed Sacrament and recited his Rosary. It is difficult to find a priest who does not know what to do with himself among those who live in the spirit of their calling, who realize the importance of being faithful to their spiritual exercises and of doing a little study, and who are devoted to the works of their ministry. But even though zealous priests may sometimes suffer from ennui and feel the weight of so many privations, what compensations will they not have, and what consolations and advantages! They will have peace of heart, because they are giving good example to their people, they will enjoy the reputation of being good, devout priests, and when they come to die they will be spared a certain panegyric that does not do much honor to those who receive it: Father so-and-so who played cards so wonderfully has died; it will be long before we have his equal again, and now that he is no longer with us, I fear our little card party will break up! It would be better for us to live in such a way as to keep far from us such a eulogy after our death; it would be much better for us if it could be said: That Father who has died was not one often seen playing, in fact he was the only one of us who did not play, but it was not because he did not know how, or that he could not enjoy a game; however, he deprived himself of the pleasure except when he was required to make up a party to give others recreation. We would all, I am sure, prefer that people would speak of us after our death in the latter rather than in the former manner. But how will people speak of us here after our death with regard to this matter? Just as they speak now: if the whole country knows that we are fond of playing, that there can hardly be a card party without us, knows how much we win, and whether we win or lose, they will say after our death what they say now:

That they have a priest very fond of card parties; a good man, zealous too, but very fond of the cards, in fact he couldn't live without them. Well! everyone has his weak point; except for that he was not bad. Thus the people will talk over our grave, and this will be the last fruit that we will reap from any card parties, when we are dead.

The fourth condition is that the person who plays does not expose himself to any danger of sin. Some of these dangers have already been referred to. They are: the danger of scandal to the people; the danger to ourselves of becoming dissipated or too much attached to playing; the danger of squandering money; and the danger of neglecting our duties or carrying them out badly. A priest who was accustomed to play after meals was one day, while engaged in a game, called out to anoint a dying man. He replied that he would go, but he waited to finish the game and then he went in all haste. When he entered the room he heard the words: "The man is dead, the priest can go and continue his game, and we hope that he will at least profit by the lesson." As for me, some priest may say, those dangers simply don't exist; I can have a game, and keep my position and my duties in mind; I would not for anything in the world let my ministry suffer by it. If there are priests who can combine all these things, although I personally don't like card-playing, I have nothing to say against them. However, a priest who has such virtue and strength of character as to be able to overcome all these dangers should be able, at least now and again, to make the sacrifice of abstaining from playing.

Let us pass on to the two last conditions which are the principal ones. The game played should be in keeping with the person, time and place, and must not be prohibited by any law; it should be for the sake of honest and necessary recreation, and should take place at a suitable time and in a fitting place. Under these conditions it will be lawful to play; this is the opinion of St. Thomas who says, *Congruat personae et tempori et loco, et secundum alias circumstancias debite ordinetur.* It must therefore be for the sake of recreation that a priest plays, and the conditions already mentioned must be fulfilled: it remains to see of what kind of game there is question, and what are the circumstances of person, time and place; that is to say: with whom he plays, at what time, and in what place. We know that games of hazard, with the exception of some for small stakes in favor of which there is a custom that makes them lawful, are severely prohibited to all priests. Many passages might be quoted from Canon Law in proof of this, in which Popes, and General and Particular Council have prohibited this manner of playing. Such games have been strictly forbidden by our diocesan synod of Turin, and all offenders are threatened with severe penalties: penalties will be incurred by those actually taking part in such games; those who assist at, participate in or cooperate in these games are also liable to severe penalties, because all these concur in the violation of a law.

It is not sufficient for a priest to avoid prohibited games, he must also avoid playing in prohibited places, at unseasonable times and with persons of bad reputation. Prohibited places are public places such as casinos, cafes, etc. for such places are evidently not suitable for a priest: *ne chartis lusoriis ludant ubi publici hi ludi habentur,* says again the Synod of Turin. Certain other places in the country which are not strictly public, but which are frequented by people who make gambling a trade, are also unbecoming for a priest to attend, because the games are played, not for recreation or amusement, but for the sake of gain. With regard to the time for playing, we do not refer here to the length of time spent, as we have already dealt with that, we refer rather to the quality of the time. The times when Mass or Benediction are going on are evidently times not suitable for a priest, so also are the late hours of the night and the early hours of the morning. With regard to persons, priests should not take part in games with women, nor with men of evil reputation, such as men addicted to immorality, nor with people with no religion, who neither go to Mass nor to the Sacraments. It would certainly give grave scandal to the faithful to see a minister of the Lord sitting at one side of a gaming table and His sworn enemy at the other, as familiar, confidential friends and equals contending with one another about money. If it were done in order to gain a sinner for the Lord, as St. Francis Xavier was accustomed to do, I'too would say: by all means play with him. But you all know as well as I do what God will gain from priests playing with such people; for these evil men, knowing the weakness of the priest, often invite him to take part in their game in order to make himself and his ministry a butt for their jokes and sneers later on.

So far we have been speaking of games considered as recreation, and we have noted the abuses that may easily arise from them. We have not gone further than that, for a priest who allows the passion for gambling to get mastery over him is on the road to ruin. A priest given to gambling and possessed by the passion for it! How ugly that sounds, and what fatal consequences result from it! We know the evils that occur in families: the wailing and lamentation, and ruin caused by this accursed passion. You can say the same of a priest who allows himself to be overcome by it: learning, piety, devotion, recollection, obedience are all lost; and in a short time, you have nothing left but a useless, ignorant, undisciplined, sacrilegious man, and God grant that it may not be even worse. A reference to this extreme case is sufficient, for, thank God, gamblers of that kind are very rare among priests. I have touched on it because the thought that such can happen will serve as a restraint, as a brake for us, and will help to keep us as far away as possible from this form of recreation.

What then are the conclusions that we should draw from what has been said. They are: let those who have not been accustomed to such games and have kept far away from them continue to do so and take their recreation in some other manner; let whoever wishes to be more content in mind and more secure have nothing to do with gaming; let those who are more or less accustomed to playing not forget to practice a little mortification and abstain from time to time if they do not wish to give up playing altogether; and when they do play, let them take care that there be nothing unbecoming of a priest, whether in the end, the mode, the time, the place or the persons. I shall repeat what St. Thomas has said: *Gratia honestae et necessariae recreationis congruat personae, tempori et loco et secundum alias circumstantias debite ordinetur.*

✣ Public Spectacles

It remains for us to say a few words about public games and spectacles, and discuss whether a priest may be present or not. And why not? If the priest lives in the world and is a member of the human family like anyone else; if he feels the weight of, and bears his share of the burdens of civil society, why can he not take part in the recreations which society provides? That sounds fine, but he is a priest, and therefore a man different from other men—as you should remember from what we have said in the beginning—who has renounced everything that savors of the profane in order to live consecrated entirely to the interests of God.

However, I do not intend to pronounce these forms of amusement to be all unbecoming for a priest without examining them. You will find reference to these forms of amusement in Canon Law, and in all local statutes for priests and therefore I cannot avoid saying something about them, and I ask you to excuse me if what I am about to say appears rigorous or offensive. These public games and spectacles may be divided into two classes; theatrical performances, and dances which are public. Under these two headings I wish to include all spectacles of either kind, and I say that religion, reason, and the standard of life prescribed for a priest should keep him far away from them. You all know better than I do the evils that arise from these amusements, the sins that are committed in these places, and how they are generally condemned by the Fathers and by theologians. It is true that these things are indifferent in themselves and non-sinful; but in practice we are very far from this indifference, especially in modern times. It would be almost impossible to keep these public amusements from being tainted with both immorality and irreligion, when we consider the number and the kind of people who attend them, their manner of dress and speech, and general conduct; everything about these amusements appears to be an incentive to sin. Ecclesiastics may say that they do not consent, but there is the question whether it is lawful for them to expose themselves to temptation even though they hope they will not consent. Consult any theologian you wish, and you will find that it is not lawful to do so. Besides, whoever, without any reason, rashly exposes himself to temptation has every reason to fear that God will humiliate him by a shameful fall. And then what are we to say about the disedification, the scandal that is given to the laity by the attendance of priests in such places? But someone will say: many priests go to them, and why cannot I also go? But I ask: are those priests doing right or wrong? Are they excused? I answer that they are doing wrong; and I ask you whether you would call one of these priests, if you were on your deathbed and were to make your last Confession? But some priest might add: I attended these performances many times, and as far as I could see, no one noticed my presence or wondered at it. You cannot be sure of that, my dear man, for it sometimes even happens that a layman, out of charity, will say to a priest: if you take my advice you will get out of here, it is no place for a priest. Most people will say nothing, but you must not conclude from that that the priest has escaped notice, for when the people go home they will most likely tell about the priest whom they saw at the public spectacle to the detriment of his character and of our ministry.

Then there are some priests who go dressed as laymen, in order to escape notice, as they say, but rather in order to escape correction and punishment. I would like to ask some of these who think themselves at liberty to attend public amusements without distinction; dances, plays, comedies, etc.: Tell me if an accident were to occur while you were in one of these places and you were about to die as the result of it, would you be as well satisfied to die there, as to die in your house, in your church, while at prayer, while engaged in the discharge of your duties? I hardly think that any priest would be a slave to his passions and to human respect to such a degree as to say that is was a matter of indifference to him whether he died in such a place or not. If then he says that he certainly would not like to die in such a place, I would be bound to agree with him; however, I should ask him why he is so imprudent to go to a place, to put himself in a situation in which he would not like that death should come upon him by surprise. Who has assured you that the hour you spend at that club may not be your last? You are right in saying that you would not like that death should overtake you in that place, because if it did, you would die in flagrant violation of the law. And even if nothing wrong was done, even if both reason and the moral law did not forbid your presence in such places, and there were no danger, we have more rigorous laws which forbid it, and which admit of no exception, laws both ancient and modern, local and universal, that have been enforced on all priests. There is no need for me to make lengthy quotations for you all know these laws: I will merely remind you of the prohibition which our Synod has made and which has been renewed in more recent laws: *Neque ... pectatores intersint clerici theatris, choreis, profanisque ludis omnibus quae voluptatem, otium, vanitatem fovent ac sapiunt.* The law has been made, the law continues, the law does not distinguish, the law necessarily should bind: excuses and pretexts are therefore useless; whoever violates it, whoever does not observe it sins, that is certain.

The only question that can be raised is the kind of sin committed by the priest who goes often to such places, goes seldom, or goes only once. I will not make any statement on that point to you, Fathers, for you are capable of judging for yourselves; I will confine myself to reminding you of what we have studied in Moral Theology. Two conditions are required that a law bind *sub grave,* and that it make the person who violates it guilty of mortal sin: the legislator must intend to impose a grave obligation and the amount of violation must be notable and grave. How are we to know the intention of the legislator and measure the gravity of the matter? The intention is known from the terms more or less severe in which the law is framed; from the penalties threatened for violation; from the gravity of the material and from the abuses which the fault in question produces, and which the law wishes to prevent: such is the teaching of all theologians on the subject of laws. Applying this rule to our case, we see that laws on this question, both common and special, use most rigid and pressing terms, and the penalties threatened are not light; it is impossible, therefore, to doubt about the intention of the legislators. The abuses against which the law is directed and which it intends to repair are the scandal of the people, the contempt brought on the priestly character, and the danger to the priest himself. If it is to be feared that one of these three abuses or inconveniences is present and is grave, even though in a particular case it does not happen, that is sufficient to render the matter grave. It is useless therefore to go on saying that it is not a sin, that it is done everywhere by many without scruple, that it is tolerated, that great importance is not attached to such things in modern times, and that it would be strange if it were a mortal sin, for persons of piety and good judgment do not condemn it, at least gravely.

Perhaps it may appear to some of you that the views expressed in this conference on amusements and especially on games and spectacles are a little too rigid. It is necessary to distinguish first of all between what is obligatory and what is of counsel. I have endeavored to measure what is of obligation and precept strictly according to the rules laid down by theologians; you can put the most benign interpretation on it, and if I have made a mistake in anything or in any application of principles, I pray you to correct it. I would be happy to be able to lessen obligations in order that occasions of committing sin might be diminished proportionately. There is a reproof which I should justly address to myself, and it is to have discussed a question that was unnecessary for you. Such a reproof to myself is a eulogy for you, and it is a consolation for myself to have an opportunity of speaking to priests who know themselves and the high dignity of their state; and who know so well how to live up to the great end of their vocation. Let the conference rather serve as a guide to help you to direct those priests whom the Lord will send to you; let it serve as an incitement to urge you to increase ever in that spirit of piety and devotion which are the greatest glory of an ecclesiastic; let it serve in fine to make you ever more faithful imitators of our Divine Model and ministers worthy to represent the Divinity on earth. The spiritual theatres and places of amusement for Christians should be the sanctuaries and basilicas, and the tombs of the martyrs, as Tertullian said to the Christians of his day: "The festivals that we ought to attend should be the functions of the Church and the prayers in common." *Haec voluptates et spectacula christianorum: sancta, perpetua et gratuita.* I repeat the same this evening for you and myself: the theatres, the spectacles, the festive halls for us priests to relax and take our recreation in, ought to be our churches, our oratories, our studies; our relaxations should be the administration of the Sacraments, visits to the sick, the works of our ministry. "Leave to seculars," said St. Jerome to a priest, "all that madness: those songs and dances and spectacles and every form of folly, and recognize that they are not suitable for a priest. Let us leave levity and vanity, dancing and noisy festivities to worldlings; let us take for ourselves retirement, piety and devotion so that the people, edified by our example, may learn to keep away from and despise the follies and the transitory things of this world, and to seek to gain for themselves those festivities and joys of Heaven that will never end."

NOTE: Canon 140 of the Code of Canon Law says: *Spectaculis, choreis, et pom pis quae eos dedecent vel quibus clericos interesse scandalo sit, praesertim in public theatris, ne intersint.*

The Zeal of a Priest

*I*N THE PRIEST, as we have said at the beginning, we can distinguish two personages: one private, interested primarily in sanctifying himself and reaching that standard of holiness which his sublime dignity as a priest demands; the other public, consecrated to the spiritual well-being and advantage of others. It is this second personage who will occupy our attention during the few days of our retreat that remain. As it is most certain that God wishes all men to be saved: *Deus omnes homines vult salvos fieri,*[1] it is also a most indisputable truth that He has placed a man on earth, in order that others may be saved, and this man is the priest. Our Divine Redeemer came and lived in that world in order to procure honor and glory for His Father and extend His reign over the whole earth: "*I honour my Father.... I seek not my own glory,*"[2] and when He was leaving the world, He entrusted the same mission to the priest: "*Go ye into the whole world and preach the gospel to every creature.*"[3] The same Redeemer came to destroy the reign of sin, as the Archangel predicted to the Prophet Daniel: "*That.... sin may have an end and iniquity may be abolished,*"[4] and to drive from the face of the earth our capital enemy: *Now shall the prince of this world be cast out.*"[5] When hanging on the Cross, before dying, He left this mission and His thirst for the glory of His Father and for the salvation of souls in the heart and in the hands of His priests. In these few words we have indicated the end, the scope, the mission of the priest on earth: to fight, to fight continually, to fight energetically, against sin; in these words are comprehended all the duties and obligations of this man destined for the good of others. The priest should put his zeal and energy into this great struggle; in this battle he should use up all his strength and should continue fighting up to the last breath of his mortal life.

Oh! how many things are to be said when we consider the priest in this field of action: the fitness, the importance, the obligation, the necessity of zeal in a priest; its efficacy and value; the merit that accompanies it and the means to exercise it properly! On this ample and important subject, I intend to propose some thoughts for your consideration, thoughts which, I hope, will make it more interesting and more consoling for you. These thoughts are: (1) in the world, the great evil of sin is not known or recognized because so many are committed and souls are lost in such enormous numbers; (2) no one more than the priest is more strictly obliged or has greater opportunities to prevent these sins; (3) if the priest has only the will, he can be certain that he will be able to prevent sins being committed to a greater or less degree; (4) by preventing the commission of even one sin he will perform the greatest and most meritorious action that a person on earth can do. Happy shall I be, if some of us prevent the commission of one single sin in the world; the time spent in this consideration will be well repaid both for that priest and for me.

I   Sin Is the Greatest Evil in the World

Among all the evils, disasters and miseries that abound in the world, one thing alone merits the name of evil, because it attempts and seeks to destroy the true and only good: *there is one good, which is God, and one evil which is sin.* Sin! This is the monster that has emptied Heaven, for which Hell was created, on account of which there has been wailing and lamentation for so many centuries that will go on for all eternity and never have an end; this is the great evil to be avoided at all costs, as the Holy Spirit says in the Book of Ecclesiasticus: *"Flee from sins as from the face of a serpent. . . . The teeth thereof are the teeth of a lion, killing the souls of men. All iniquity is a two-edged sword: there is no remedy for the wound thereof."*[6]

❖   The World Ignores the Evil of Sin

However, there is another great evil in the world, and in a certain sense still greater, and it is this; that the great evil of sin is not known or recognized. People have lost the sense of sin, and from this arises an immense, incalculable evil. Sin is committed with the greatest facility and, as it were, for fun; people sleep tranquilly in sin and, in a manner, armor themselves with it; they even go so far as to make sin their glory, to boast of having committed it and of intending to continue in their evil life. Cast a look round the world, just observe the manner of living, of speaking, and you will see immediately whether the evil of sin is known in the world or whether any attention is paid to it. Not to speak of those who live decidedly irreligious and wicked lives, how few of those who pass for good and who approach the Sacraments are aware of the great evil that sin is, and the great ruin it brings with it. It must necessarily happen that, on account of this certainly culpable ignorance in which most men live, an enormous number will come to be damned, because no sin is pardoned which is not detested, and it is impossible to detest sin properly if it is not known as such.

II It is the Duty of the Priest to Wage War Against Sin

"*A necessity lieth upon me. For woe is unto me if I preach not the gospel,*" exclaimed a great Apostle, St. Paul."[7] Woe to the priest who does not aim at this end, who does not strive towards it and labor for it! He is guilty, and must answer for every sin that he could have prevented and did not try to do so: "*I will require his blood at thy hand.*"[8] It was such a priest's duty to preach, but if he had used more diligence and put more labor into his sermons, how much greater fruit he would have reaped! Many more souls would have been touched by them and would have repented and would have ceased to sin, or at least would have sinned less often. But if through his fault there be one soul that has not profited, even for that one he will have to answer to the Lord. If that priest had been a little more diligent in the confessional, and had shown more patience and charity, how much reduced would have been the number of sins committed! If instead of being diligent and patient, he is careless or rough with the penitents, they will come more rarely and will show no improvement. Who will answer for this consequence? Naturally, it is the priest. If he had been more wide-awake, if he had put more heart and spirit into his work and had given more edification to the people, how many sins would have certainly been prevented! But he did not: let him prepare therefore to give an account!

And let not this appear an exaggeration to us; it is the strict truth. A son is not only answerable to his father for the injuries and insults done by himself but also for those which he permits to be done by others, and for those which he could have prevented and did not. A servant or employee is not only accountable for the loss which he himself causes to the property of his master, but also for the work that he omitted and for the losses that others cause to whatever is entrusted to his care. It is not sufficient for a person entrusted with the care of another's property to abstain from squandering it, he must see that profit is made out of it, and he will be bound to repair the losses caused by his carelessness and negligence. So it is with us priests: independently of what office we hold, by the very fact that we have the state and character of priests, we are bound not only in charity, but by the office we hold and duty that accompanies it, to look after the interests of our God zealously, and, among these duties, the greatest is to see that no one outrages Him or offends Him.

I am not able to say whether the priests of our time have this zeal or to what degree; but I know the laments uttered by St. Bernard when he considered the priests of his own time and found that they had indeed zeal for insisting on the respect due to their own dignity, and for amassing money, but not for preventing the commission of sin and for saving souls. *Fervet ecclesiasticus zelus pro dignitate tuenda, pro divitiis congregandis.* My dear Fathers, if we too look around for priests fired with zeal to preserve their own rights, to get a good position, to succeed in some affair, to gain money, I believe that we shall find many zealous for their own esteem, their own honor, for the interests of their relatives. But shall we find as easily and in as great numbers, priests who, fully conscious of the great evil which sin is and filled with horror of that monster; priests who, spurred on by the great sorrow which they feel, will, I do not say die of heartbreak, as so many apostolic men like St. Gaetanus have done, but will most earnestly seek through their status as priests, through their ministry, and if they have no other way, by good example and prayer, to prevent the commission of sin, and make reparation for the offenses against the Lord? I pray that it may be so, for otherwise we will be merely statues, or priests in appearance, in appearance and nothing more.

Yes, my dear Fathers, that fire, that eagerness, that zeal is so necessary for us priests that it constitutes our *raison d'etre*, the very marrow and substance of our state. In us priests, the dignity, honor and character of the priest is one thing; quite another thing is the true, practical priesthood which consists in our apostolate, and in the exercise of our ministry to attain the ends for which it was instituted. This is so true that without the spirit of zeal and charity urging us on to the exercise of our ministry we shall be priests and apostles in name only, but not in deed. God and man are like two extreme points; between them a certain intercourse and communication must be maintained, and God has selected among men a certain class of persons and has appointed them mediators between Himself and men. He has made them priests and charged them with the duty of looking after His interests with men, and the interests of men with Him; and in this consists the essence of our state. But if the spirit of zeal be wanting in us; if we neglect those interests and allow them to suffer, as far as in us lies we despoil ourselves of the quality of priests, which is to say, of the office of mediators between God and the people, and we try to reduce ourselves to the common state of other men. And what a shame and humiliation that is for a priest who has any respect for his sublime calling!

✢ The Priest Is the Guardian of the Honor of God

We priests by our character, are, in relation to God, like the guard of honor round a prince. Now what would you say of the soldiers of that guard who, seeing their prince insulted, despised and treated contumeliously by rebellious subjects would stand idly by and allow them to carry on, and worse still, who would laugh at the indignity to which he was subjected? Ah! vile, ungrateful, worthless fellows, someone would cry out, why do you wear that uniform, why do you occupy that position and accept that pay if you will not defend your lord? Such, and with much stronger reason, would be the reproof that a priest would merit who has zeal and who does nothing to prevent, as far as in him lies, offenses to his Divine Master. Consider those brave soldiers who remained to defend King David, and who accompanied him in his flight: when they heard the insults which the rash Semei dared to hurl against the good king, they burned with indignation, and immediately the valiant Abisai cried out: "Why should this dead dog curse my lord and king?"[9] They wanted to stop him immediately and thus prevent the insult to their king, and when they were not allowed to do so by order of the king himself, their blood boiled with indignation at every insult which Semei uttered against him, such was the love they bore to their king, and such the zeal that burned in their hearts for his honor. So every priest should do, and so should every priest conduct himself, whenever he sees, or hears or comes to know of any offense offered to his God: he should in the first place experience a lively sorrow, and then he should burn with holy indignation, with just resentment, and seek to prevent it, not indeed by violent methods, as Abisai wished to do for David, for this is altogether alien to our mission, but by peaceful means, by charity, by prayer and, when occasion arises, by the use of legitimate authority so that no means will be left untried. And when it is not in our power to prevent the insult, we should shudder, we should grieve and sigh and lament for the offense that we see being done to our God, and for the hard necessity in which we find ourselves of having to look on without being able to prevent it.

Give me a priest of this mettle, full of religious spirit and zeal, put him in any office of the ministry, and you will see the prodigies of valor that he will perform in the defense of His God. Let him be a pastor, an assistant, a chaplain, or a professor; let him be in the city, in a small village or countryside; let him be engaged in the confessional, in the pulpit, in his house, in attending a sick person, and you will find everywhere evident signs of the effects of his work. He may not be a very learned man or very gifted or very eloquent; he may not be robust in health or have a pleasing appearance, but none of these things matter; it is sufficient if he has zeal. With zealous priests at their disposal, we can truly say that God and His Church have their own men, true soldiers, true apostles, loyal guards of honor on whom they can rely in a crisis or encounter. On the other hand, if you take away zeal from priests, you have nothing more than priests in appearance, soldiers who may look fine on parade, but nothing else; you need not calculate their number, or take notice of their boasting, or attach any importance to their decorations or mere external signs of bravery; if zeal is wanting, the marrow and substance is wanting. If a contrary wind arises, you will see their bravery vanish like smoke, and the combined lot of them will not be capable of preventing a single sin, or remedying a single disorder.

Even the enemies of the Church know this, for when in any country they wish to attempt some criminal design, to promote some abuse or disorder, in evaluating the obstacles that may stop them, their first care is to study us priests, whose office is to be the vigilant guards of the Lord. Their first question will be: are there many priests in that place? If they oppose us what are we to do? They often give a reply themselves something like this: There is a small number who will give us trouble; they will not give in; they will not compromise; but we need not worry much about the rest; even if their number was twice as great it would not take long to dispose of their opposition; if there were question of gain, of high offices, of banquets or amusements, they might be interested, but they will not put their heart into opposing what we are planning to do. That is how seculars are able to distinguish between priests and priests; between true priests of zeal and virtue always ready to prevent insult being offered to their Divine Master, and priests who are only so in name and external appearance. It is therefore an absolute obligation, it is an indispensable necessity for a priest to be zealous for the honor and glory of God and to show that zeal by preventing offenses to Him; and when he possesses that zeal, you may be certain that he will succeed to a greater or less degree, a thought which is very consoling for us.

III In His Efforts to Prevent Sin the Priest Is Certain of Success

People in the world work, labor and sweat with the object, and in the hope of gaining success, but their best efforts very often meet with failure, hence they are in constant fear and uncertainty. The businessman is uncertain about his business, the country-man about his crops, the soldier about the result of his battles and the traveller about the success of his voyage. This one goes to great trouble to get a position but he does not know whether he will get it; that other one is ill and does his best to get well, but who knows but he may get worse; that other one is engaged in a lawsuit and leaves nothing undone to gain it, but it is quite possible that he may lose; thus it is with almost everyone and in nearly everything; they live on and struggle buoyed up by hope only. The priest, on the contrary, if he really wishes, is sure to succeed in the great work for which he is destined; and how grand a thing it is to labor, when one labors and fatigues himself with the certainty of success! How happy the farmer would be if he was equally sure of a good harvest!

That, then, is the happiness of the priest: he is in this world to prevent, to lessen the number of offenses to his Divine Master and he can be certain of attaining his object when he sets himself to the work in earnest. It is not necessary for me to say that even though in a particular case some obstacle may prevent visible success, the failure to achieve it will not turn to his loss in any way, for before the Lord he will have equal merit: but I repeat that he may be certain that he will succeed. It is impossible that the labor of a zealous priest continued for a little time, and much more so if continued for months and years, will not produce fruit of some kind, will not prevent some sin. In a priest of true zeal everything is directed to this end, and the least effort possesses marvellous efficacy in the attainment of it. I do not speak of preaching and the administration of the Sacraments by means of which sins can be diminished by hundreds and by thousands, but even a simple word, a look, the very presence of a zealous priest can at times help to prevent sin though he is unaware of it. Observe a priest of virtue and character who goes through the country and visits the houses: although he does not preach or declaim, there will be force and power in his very presence; if a person is using bad language, he will immediately become silent; if there is any unseemly conduct the culprit will go away; if anyone is quarrelling, he will stop. And what causes this? It is the appearance of the priest, and that is sufficient to prevent sin. A priest was accustomed to go often to the prisons and, as anyone may well imagine, he very often obtained very little visible results from the inmates. An old man who saw him go frequently one day stopped him and said to him: "Look here, you are going to great trouble in coming here so often, but are you not afraid of losing your time doing nothing?" "No," he replied, "the very presence of a priest in these places, his very virtue, is certain to produce some fruit."

❖ The Effect of the Presence of a Good Priest

The sight of a priest in the world, all the more if he is known to be a good priest, has what we might call a magic force, and speaks in a thousand ways to the hearts of those who see him, especially of those who are in the state of sin. Hello! there is the priest, says one of these, I wish I were a little more like him; I wish I had done what he told me to do, what he recommended in his sermon last Sunday; I don't know how it was that I paid no attention to it, but I must begin in earnest to do it now. A meeting with such a priest will give rise to agitation of conscience, to the most poignant remorse, to good resolutions, to repentence, which will mean so many sins less. Some will be truly converted through the work of that priest and will remain firm and constant on the right path, others will sincerely repent although they may fall again, others will not go as far as to truly repent and to amend their lives. Nevertheless, even for these latter the visit of the priest and his exhortation will not have been useless, especially if they afterwards avail of his ministry, which will then bear great fruit. The result will be that they will fall more rarely, they will find it more difficult to remain in sin, and thus there will be so many sins less.

✢ The Consolation to Be Obtained From Waging War On Sin

And what consolation must it not be for a priest to he able to say to himself every evening: I hope the Lord will be satisfied with my work this day; even though I may not have accomplished anything, I have made it the object of my actions and my visits, and the intention of my prayers, to prevent offenses to God, and I feel confident that I have spared Him some offenses! Let anyone else in the world, however gifted or great he may be come forward and say whether he has done as much as this priest. Some have labored in the fields, others have worked in offices or factories, others have made money in business, this one has won a great lawsuit, that other has made a great fortune, this man has obtained a high position, that other has gained a kingdom or an empire; well, I say that there is one person who has done more than all these; one who has spent a better day; and who is he? He is the priest who has prevented one sin, who has spared the Lord one offense. What are all the gains, all the fortunes, all the offices and careers, even all the kingdoms of the world, compared to preventing an offense against God, to preventing a sin which is the greatest evil in the world? There is no work greater or more noble either in Heaven or on earth that this: to prevent offenses against God. This is the last thought on which we will meditate in order to excite ourselves to greater zeal and to comfort ourselves.

IV It Is a Most Noble Work

To go to the ends of the earth, to save one soul, and then to die is a lot worthy to be envied: this was an exclamation often uttered by St. Francis Xavier. For a priest to save one soul, to prevent one sin and then die is the most beautiful life, the sweetest death in the world. I say sincerely that I have no words, that I find no sentiments sufficient to express the grandeur, the nobility of this work of the priest; it is a thing of which we are all convinced, but which we will be able to understand only in Heaven. I invite you therefore to ponder well on these words: *I have prevented a sin, and by that alone I have saved the honor and glory, and I can even say in a sense, the life of my God!* It is an eminently great work to save the fame, the life of another, especially of a person of great service to others, for example, of a king. That is nothing at all compared to the case I have made. I have prevented a disaster in a family, the ruin of a countryside, of a city, an entire kingdom; that is certainly a great achievement; but it bears no comparison to the colossal work of a priest. Let us leave this world and go to the other; if, by an impossible hypothesis, someone had such power and virtue as to be able to deliver a soul from Hell, what a prodigy, what a miracle, what a great blessing for that lost soul! However, not even that could equal the work of a priest who spares God one offense, for in the latter case, sin has not been committed and the honor and glory of God has not been violated, and His justice has been glorified, while by sin it would have been outraged. It is sufficient to say that neither the angels nor the saints nor Our Blessed Lady herself could do a work greater than that which the priest does when he opposes the commission of sin and prevents it.

Happy is the priest who is called for so noble and so grand an enterprise! but happier still, if he devotes all his days to it and attends to it with all his strength. By that alone, he becomes the terror of Hell and sets it into a rage, he becomes the joy and delight of Heaven and the envy of its inhabitants. Yes, my dear Fathers, if a soul in Heaven could have a longing or desire, it would certainly be to be in our place, to have a day, an hour, or even a moment to prevent an offense against God, and to enjoy in Heaven the comfort of having once saved the honor and glory of his God. And, my dear Fathers, what are we doing? Shall we lose our time with the trifles and follies of this world? Let it therefore be the firm resolution from the considerations of this retreat, to live from now onwards, with this one end, with this one aim, to prevent sin in the world. Oh, if all priests had this spirit, this zeal, how many sins less there would be in the world, and how greatly the Lord would be glorified! If only every priest succeeded in preventing one sin every day, think of how many offenses would be spared our God every day. What consolation in life for a priest who would do that, what comfort on his bed of death, and what glory and happiness in Heaven! The glory which the good priest will have labored to procure for his God on earth, that same, God will render to him a thousandfold in Heaven for all eternity, for the Holy Spirit says: *They that instruct many to justice, (shine) as stars for all eternity!*[10]

---

1 1 Tim. 2:4.
2 John 8:49-50.
3 Mark 16:15.
4 Dan. 9:24.
5 John 12:31.
6 Ecclus. 21:2-4.
7 1 Cor. 9:16.
8 Ezech. 3:18.
9 2 Kgs. 16:9.
10 Dan. 12:3.

Good Example

*T*HE DESTINY of the priest is to struggle against sin; if he lives, he lives to combat sin; whether he studies, prays, labors, all should tend to this end; everything should be directed to exterminate, if possible, this monster from the earth. Among the many means which the priest has to fight this battle with good success, the first and indispensable means, without which all the others will avail little, or even nothing, is his own blameless conduct and exemplary life. There is no subject on which it is more fitting to speak to priests than good example; it constitutes a gift, an endowment, which is in a special way suitable for us priests, because in itself alone it includes a comprehensive way to all the other virtues. To be a priest should mean the same thing as to be an exemplary man, and a person may in a certain sense say of whoever is not so, that he is not a priest at all; in the sense that anything that does not shine cannot be called a light, anything that does not preserve cannot be called salt, any person who does not teach cannot be called a master. Good example is everything in a priest, and a priest is everything if he has it. With it, he shines, he preserves, he teaches; with it, he is retired, devoted, patient; with it he prays, studies, labors; in short, with it he is everything, because it suffices for everything. He is exemplary, that is, he is blameless; therefore there is no need to look for more.

Holy Scripture, the Fathers and Doctors of the Church and those who have spoken or speak of the priesthood have all without exception recommended, inculcated, insisted absolutely that the priest should be a man of exemplary life: "*So let your light shine before men,*"[1] said Our Lord to His Apostles: "*Be thou an example of the faithful.*"[2] "*In all things show thyself an example of good works,*"[3] the great Apostle, St. Paul repeated to his two disciples, Titus and Timothy: "*It behoveth therefore a bishop to be blameless,*"[4] he said to Timothy, and all commentators are agreed that all grades of ecclesiastics are included here under the name, "bishop." Every other profession or career may enjoy fame and esteem without this quality; thus a literateur, an officer, a painter, a sculptor, an artist of any kind may be renowned, may have reputation and fame in his art or profession without being exemplary in his conduct. But not so with a priest: he will never enjoy credit, he will never have the reputation of being a good priest, if he is not exemplary and blameless in conduct. I therefore choose this very necessary subject as the matter for our present conference. We shall consider: (1) in what this quality consists, what does the exemplariness require of the priest, and of what kind should it be; (2) how great its necessity and importance is. God, the Church, and the faithful will all bless us if we become priests of such a kind that no one can point the finger of blame at us.

I   In What Does Good Example Consist?

This quality of exemplariness in a priest embraces two things; the priest's conduct should be such that it cannot give an occasion of sin to anyone, and it should serve as an incitement and stimulus to spur on others to the exercise of virtue, so that whoever does what the priest does, whoever speaks as the priest speaks, whoever thinks as the priest thinks, is certain to walk free from blame and to live a life pleasing to God.

(1) *In Not Giving Any Occasion For Sin*

The first duty then in this connection is not to give any occasion for sin. An occasion for sin may be given in various ways: either by doing an act that is bad, from which others take or may take an excuse for doing the same; in that case the person who does the bad act is truly a scandal-giver; or by doing an act which is indifferent or even good, but which, on account of some circumstance, may appear bad in the eyes of the simple and delicate of conscience, who are offended by it and interpret it in a bad sense, although the act really contains nothing bad and the evil interpretation put on it arises solely from the ignorance of others: this kind of scandal is called the scandal of the little ones. An occasion for sin may be taken by evil men from an act which neither in itself or in its circumstances contains anything evil, but may be even good, by men who solely on account of their wickedness make it an occasion for committing sin: this is called pharisaical scandal.

I shall not delay to speak here of real scandal, or of a scandalous priest. Ah, my dear Fathers, may the Lord protect us from being sinful priests! But if by misfortune we should ever become so, may the Lord preserve us from being scandal-givers, and from being lost for the sin of scandal. I do not think that it is possible to imagine any sin or disorder more fatal than scandal in a priest, whether it be considered in relation to God or with respect to our neighbor or to the unfortunate priest who commits it. It would have been better if he had never been born, if he had never heard of the ecclesiastical state; it would have been a thousand times better if he had laid aside the clerical garb when there was yet time rather than stain his hands, I will not say with the blood of others, but with the very blood of his God. To find himself on the bed of death, to have to present himself before the tribunal of God to give an account of the souls entrusted to him, of the souls for whom he is responsible, and of the sins committed because of him! O my God, what a dreadful, horrible thing! What punishment he must expect from God! What remorse of conscience and what reproaches he will have to experience! And how terrible a sentence he will one day have to hear! Ah, let anyone whom it concerns think well over this! Let us pass on to consider the second kind of scandal, in appearance less grave, but always fatal in its consequences and, what is worse, much more common among ecclesiastics.

Priests who are really scandal-givers are, thank God, very few. But how is it, I ask, that people say so many things against us, and that almost everyone has some complaint to make? I am willing to grant that many of these things are pure invention, and that afterwards, whether in good faith or in bad, they pass through the mouths of many; but at the same time I fear that many times these things arise from the second kind of scandal; from want of reserve, of restraint, from some circumstance which, as I have said, has the appearance of evil, although it really is not so. And here, you will pardon me, if we examine our own case, and go over, step by step, our day as priests.

We have to live with others, whether with relatives or servants, who will be usually persons of the other sex. Now, if we are not careful, how many times will we not find in our houses occasions for giving this kind of scandal! Certain preferences, certain regards, certain imprudent acts of kindness, certain deference and familiarity; speaking too frequently and with excessive praise of certain people, lively resentment at the smallest remark against them, always defending them and with heat, often give rise to suspicions in cases where there is nothing wrong. But I would have you know, says the priest, that this person deserves all that I say, and I do it merely out of good nature. That may be true, but it is not our business to be always eulogizing certain people; and it has to be paid for very dearly, because good-heartedness, when it is out of place, is not prudent, it is excessive, it is a vice and not a virtue.

We priests are commonly accused of being avaricious; I do not believe that the accusation is true of us as a body, but whence does the accusation arise? Very often what gives rise to that scandalous gossip about priests is his complaining about expenses more through habit than anything else; too close inspection about minute details of expense; refusal to give a gratuity or to be generous when occasion demands; always insisting on our rights even in trifles. The priest will reply: my income is small and I must live within it; if I insist, I ask only what is my own, and what is within my rights. I have genuine sympathy with the straitened circumstances of a poor priest which often do not permit him to do what in his heart he would like to do; but with a little care, by adopting a different manner, with a more graceful way of dealing with people, he will obtain the same result or even better. And then we should remember what Moral Theology says about that point: that sometimes we may be obliged to suffer a temporal loss rather than give scandal to weak souls. For instance, can we in conscience insist on what is due to us from poor people in some small matter, when it will give rise to no abuse to relinquish our right; while we know that if we insist on our right, it will cause us to be slandered and will lead to much gossip? I do not intend by that to solve any practical case, for to do so, many things would have to be taken into account; I merely wish to state the theory which can be applied according to individual circumstances.

It is known, for instance, that two priests have had some difference, and that as a result a little coldness has grown up between them, so that the people watch how they will behave towards each other. There is not an open rupture, and they do not refuse to salute one another; but they dexterously keep a little distance from each other, they give only a half salutation, they stay away in certain circumstances, they suddenly find urgent reasons to be somewhere else, such as domestic occupations, and they thereby lose a favorable opportunity to show their sincere affection. Is there scandal in any of these things? The people remark it, some laugh at it, some are grieved over it on account of the bad impression that this kind of conduct makes on all. I know the reply one of the priests will usually make: I bear him no ill will, I give him the common signs of friendship and that is, I think, enough; let people think as they like. But, my dear Father, it is not sufficient to abstain from evil, one must remove even the appearance of evil, and therefore it is not sufficient not to bear ill will, but it is necessary to take away even the suspicion; for we know, and theologians teach, that it is often not sufficient to give the common signs of friendship; that we are bound sometimes to give special signs, when the omission of them would be interpreted badly, or when there is hope of gaining over an adversary. One of the two replies that this does not concern him, but I say that almost always both are bound to show special signs of friendship, the obligation will fall first on whichever of them has the opportunity, because the obligation of not giving scandal arises from the natural law and binds all without exception, and at all times.

A person of the opposite sex comes to the priest's house; there is some reason for the visit and there is no harm whatever in it; but the people outside are not obliged to know these things, and the frequency of the visit of a young person at such an hour without any companion makes people talk, and gives rise to scandal.

The frequent visits of the priest to a house where there are women, where it is commonly known that there is gambling in some form, where the people of the house are accustomed to talk and laugh too freely about everyone and everything, where people know that few, if anyone at all, make their Easter duty, where abstinence is banned, does not get a good name for the priest; the people speak badly about him, they murmur. The priest says: I must keep on good terms with all, I must be a friend of all; well then, why do you not treat others in the same way? Why are your time and your friendly visits all for that house and those people, and not for others? It is one thing to be on friendly terms with all, quite another thing to be intimate and familiar only with certain men and certain women.

(2) *In Avoiding Even the Appearance of Sin*

In all these cases the danger of scandal appears so evident that everyone should see it and guard against it; however, we have to admit that the priest will not recognize it in his own case and that he has always an excuse. In my case, he says, I know that there is no evil and no danger, and besides, I have so many reasons for doing as I do, that I can be easy in conscience. With these reasons, which regard each one in particular, I will not deal here, because it would be impossible to do so without examining the special circumstances of the individual cases. However, I think it will be both instructive and helpful to state the theory which must serve as guide in such cases.

Let us bear in mind that it is undeniable that scandal can be given, and is in fact sometimes given without doing any bad act, but only one bad in appearance: therefore the excuses often heard such as: "I know how I stand in conscience," "let people say what they like," "I am free to reject suggestions; they are valueless." We priests have, on many occasions, fought against such a line of reasoning both in the confessional and in the pulpit; why then should we wish to find a different code of morals for ourselves? Presuming then that material for scandal arises from some act of ours on account of some apparent circumstance even though it be through the weakness or ignorance of others, if it is possible, we should explain what we are doing so as to remove from it that appearance of evil. If we cannot give such an explanation, or if our explanation is not sufficient and, in consequence, the scandal would continue, we should absolutely abstain from doing it unless we have a just and proportionate reason. This holds even though the scandal arises through the malice and malignity of others, since scandal is never licit, and charity never permits us to give an occasion of sin without sufficient reason, even to a person who sins through his own malice. That is the teaching of all moral theologians, even the most benign, although they may vary in the practical application of this teaching to particular cases. To a person who says that he has sufficient motive, I reply: whether you have a motive or not, and whether it is sufficient or not, I leave to yourself to judge. You say that you have a very strong motive for what you are doing and it appears to you that you cannot do otherwise; but suppose in that house that you are visiting, and from those people in the house, you receive an affront, an insult which they cast on your reputation, you will certainly leave the house at once and abandon these people; and even though they beg and pray you, you will not put your foot in that house again. Why this change? Where is now that pressing motive you had to visit that house? As long as theology alone talked, you continued to go, but when self-love entered in, it was a different matter.

(3) *The World Is Watching Us*

Let us, my dear Fathers, open our eyes on this question and not delude ourselves: in proportion as the world is malignant and lax for itself, it is severe and hostile in its judgment towards us; its votaries study us from head to foot, they scrutinize us, you might say, day and night in order to catch us, and if they cannot find anything, they will try to get a pretext to attack us.

Therefore, the priest who wishes to be secure and tranquil in his conscience, and not to expose his honor, mission and character, and religion itself to gossip and insults and sarcasm, should look well around him and remember that he has to live in continuous reserve and caution, always afraid of giving to others the least pretext for suspecting evil. The great Apostle, St. Paul says: "*See therefore, brethren, how you walk circumspectly . . . because the days are evil.*"[5] If that person, that family, my manner of acting, that amusement, etc. gives rise to gossip, gives material for thinking evilly of me as a priest, cost what it may and leaving all considerations aside, let it be stopped, let it be changed, and thus let an end be put to that evil interpretation. This is the example that all the saints have given us. It is the example of the great St. Paul, who said that he would not eat a piece of meat, not even a mouthful, if he feared that anyone would be scandalized by it. He did not stop to distinguish case from case, or to see whether there was a motive or not, but replied frankly: "*Wherefore, if meat scandalize my brother, I will never eat flesh, lest I should scandalize my brother,*"[6] as if he were to say; even if it were to cost me my life, I will never scandalize my brother. This should be the opinion and the mode of action of every priest who wishes to live with an easy conscience that he is not giving any occasion of scandal.

When the priest succeeds in fulfilling this first part of his duty to give good example by taking care not to give the least pretext for blame, he will necessarily fulfill the second part also, to serve for all as an encouragement and a stimulus to do good and to practice virtue. In fact, in order to avoid every danger of scandal, he will be obliged to regulate his hours of repose, his food and drink, and the form of his dress; he will be obliged to use caution and restraint in his amusements, and often he will have to renounce his tastes, his tendencies and inclinations; he will be obliged to live a retired life, to keep far away from the tumult and intrigues of the world; he will be obliged to be most exact in observing gravity and modesty in carrying out his duties, principally those of his ministry; in a word, he will have to exercise all the priestly virtues in a more than ordinary manner, and by that alone his conduct will act as a spur, as a stimulus and incitement for all to encourage them to do good and to practice all the virtues. It is not necessary to delay further on this point; let us go on to consider the necessity and importance of this quality of exemplariness in a priest.

II The Obligation to Give Good Example

"It behoveth therefore a bishop to be blameless": *Oportet episcopum irreprehensibilem esse,*[7] says St. Paul. Note the words he uses: here there is not question of a suggestion, of a counsel, of greater perfection or of fitness, but of absolute obligation and necessity: *Oportet*. Everything calls out for this quality in a priest: the honor of the Church that it is his duty to serve, the salvation of souls that he is bound to take care of, the glory of God which he is bound to procure.

(1) *We Owe it to Our Holy Mother the Church*

The Church may be considered as our mother, and as a mother who regards us priests as her first-born children and most tenderly loved among her sons. And we all know that a virtuous, well-behaved, blameless and holy son is the sweetest consolation, the greatest commendation of a mother. Every virtue, every applause, every praise of that son is considered as a virtue, as a praise of the mother who has brought him up; on the contrary, a wayward, dissipated, ill-mannered son forms the most sensible and acute sorrow of the poor mother, and the dishonor and disgrace of the house and the entire family. Ah, my dear Fathers, we are living in times when, as we know, very many ungrateful, unnatural sons seek to rend the bosom of that mother, and after being nourished by her milk, reject her and repudiate her, and perhaps would even rejoice if they saw her expire, drowned in a sea of sorrows. And could we, priests, have the heart to add sorrow upon sorrow by our conduct, while she, weighed down by such a load of crosses and sorrows, holds out her hand to us priests for a little aid and comfort? *"Thou shalt honour thy mother all the days of her life,"*[8] was the dying injunction of good Tobias to his beloved son; and in order to urge him to do so, he reminded him of all his mother had done and suffered for him. This same injunction, I repeat for myself and for you, venerable Fathers. As long as we have life, let us take care to show every regard for our mother, the Church. The favors that she has conferred on us are immense, almost incalculable, and no pen can describe what she has suffered, and what she suffers every hour for our sake. Oh, let us not add one drop more of bitterness to her cup of sorrows, but rather let it be our solicitude to console her and comfort her, and to be for her a help and succor in the midst of so many conflicts, and this, not only by words, by preaching, by writing, but much more by our deeds, by the manner of our lives, by our exemplary and irreprehensible conduct; so that whoever sees the priest, from seeing the goodness, the virtue and the exemplary conduct of that son, will be forced to argue to the goodness and holiness of the mother who has brought him up, and hence to respect her, to esteem her and to honor her.

(2) *Good Example is Necessary for the Efficacy of Our Ministry*

And what shall we say of the force and efficacy which this good example of the priest exercises on souls? It is a continuous sermon to the people, as the Council of Trent calls it: *"Est velut perpetuum quoddam praedicandi genus"*[9]; since, as the same Council says, there is nothing which urges and incites the people more to virtue and to the service of the Lord than the example of the priest: *Nihil est quod magis ad pietatem, et Dei cultum instruat.*[10]

I shall pass over the many testimonies of the Fathers on this subject and come to reason and experience. We would require no small amount of audacity, said a layman to a priest, to preach to another that he should do what we do not do ourselves. How can a priest in the pulpit, in the confessional, in a private conversation, have the courage to ask a layman to abstain from gambling or from drink, or to lead a retired, laborious life, when he himself is a man of games and sport, and of good eating and drinking? How can he have the courage to teach children that they should respect and obey their parents, if he himself has no respect for the laws and canons of his Church or the orders of his superiors? How will he dare to inculcate the sanctification of feast-days, the attendance at Church functions, when he himself, who has every opportunity to do so, never assists, but prefers to vegetate in domestic idleness and waste his time in trifles and folly rather than edify the people by joining in their devotions? But suppose he does violence to himself and warns, corrects, and preaches, what fruit will his sermons have? Ah! warnings and corrections from such a man excite one's pity; for instead of drawing tears and sighs, they will only draw laughter. What a priest to come to scold us! said a layman, let it be anyone else, but not that man! If he would be only willing to listen to us, we could preach to him! Another priest who was not exemplary said one Sunday to his parishioners that they were not what they formerly had been, and he used the homely expression that "the cart could not go on that way," and that he must see about reforming it. One of the congregation said in a loud whisper to his neighbor: "I am with him about the reform; but before reforming the cart it would be better first to reform the driver." See then what a priest does and what fruit he obtains, when he sets himself to reprove others, while he himself is blameworthy.

Verba movent, exempla trahunt: preach, shout, thunder as much as you like, example is worth more than all the reasons and all the logic in the world. The enemies of the Church know better than anyone else the force of good example in a priest, for when they get to know of an exemplary priest, seeing the great obstacle that their projects find in such a man, they do all in their power to weaken his influence. They deny his virtues as far as they can, and when it is useless to deny them, they enter into his heart and say that they are all pretense and hypocrisy, and that the priest adopts them to gain his ends. "Don't believe that all that is virtue" they say; "in his house, in his private life, who knows what he does?" And when these wicked men wish to bring about the fall of some unfortunate person, when all other means have failed, they use as a lever the example of the priest, whether true or pretended. Oh! they say, what objection can you have to doing it? Don't you know that the priest does so? And if they can succeed in getting what they say half believed, their prey is secure. Such is the force that these magic words have with the people: "The priest does so."

I would never finish, if I were to go fully into a subject so vast and so important; but I cannot finish without saying a word about the delight and gratitude of the people when the Lord grants them the special grace of sending them an exemplary priest. Suppose it happens that in a certain parish the people get a parish priest or assistant or chaplain who lives an altogether exemplary life, attentive to his duties, recollected, keeping away from the intrigues of the world, affable and courteous with all, occupied only with the affairs of the Church and pious practices, and always with decorum, gravity and modesty; who can describe the praise and admiration of the people for him? Ah, what a fine priest! How fortunate we were to get him! Indeed we did not merit such a grace! When they hear the laments and murmurs of other people about their priests they say: Oh, if you were to see our priest, to know him! It was the Lord Himself who chose him for us and sent him to us. Yes, I repeat: Even the most rude and uncultured people cannot fail to recognize that an exemplary priest is a priceless treasure and that nothing can bear comparison to him. So then let us not seek after learning or worldly prudence or riches, for an exemplary life surpasses everything else, for it alone is everything, and all the rest without it is nothing at all.

I will therefore conclude by repeating that if we wish to do good to souls, if it is our heart's desire to be a consolation and an ornament for our afflicted mother, the Church, for the spouse of the Divine Lamb, there is but one sure way: to lead a spotless, irreprehensible life, a life removed not only from every evil, but even from the appearance of evil. This means is, as I have said, safe and infallible and, at the same time, the easiest that we can find, for it suffices to will it. If you want to acquire learning, great skill or experience, the will alone is not enough, but in order to become exemplary, edifying, irreprehensible priests, it is sufficient to will it and we shall become so. I shall finish by quoting for you the ardent desire of that great Doctor of the Church, St. Bernard: "Oh, that I could see in my lifetime the Church of God resting on such pillars! Oh, that I could see the Spouse of my Lord entrusted to men of such faith, given in charge to men of such purity! Oh, if an abundant supply of such men were given to us! What could be better or more delightful!"[11]

---

1 Matt. 5:16.
2 1 Tim. 4:12.
3 Titus 2:7.
4 1 Tim. 3:2.
5 Ephes. 5:15, 16.
6 1 Cor. 8:13.
7 1 Tim. 3:2.
8 Tob. 4:3.
9 Sess. XXV De Reform. cap. 1.
10 Sess. XXH De Reform. cap. 1.
11 De Consid. lib. IV, cap. 5.

Preaching

O NE OF THE most effective means to combat sin, and the principal office of the priest, is that of preaching. Among the various functions which our Divine Redeemer exercised on earth, at the head of all stood preaching: *"The Lord . . . . hath anointed me to preach the gospel to the poor"*[1]; *"I must preach the kingdom of God; for therefore am I sent"*[2]; all the rest served as a help and support to this most important work of preaching. He also assigned it to the Apostles as their principal occupation: *"He sent them to preach the kingdom of God,"*[3] and when about to leave the world He confirmed this by repeating to them: *"Go ye into the whole world and preach the gospel to every creature"*[4] as in fact they did: *"But they, going forth, preached every where."*[5] And that they regarded this as their primary duty is shown by the fact that they selected other ministers to attend to the material wants of the faithful in order that they themselves might be able to give themselves to prayer and preaching without disturbance: *"It is not reason that we should leave the word . . . . and serve tables . . . . But we will give ourselves continually to prayer and to the ministry of the word."*[6] This function of preaching is so inseparable from the apostolate, that apostle and preacher are synonymous terms. Although the offices of a priest are many and varied, such as baptizing, celebrating Mass, administering the other Sacraments, nevertheless, the one that is most proper to him and which particularly distinguishes him is preaching: the great Apostle St. Paul said this of himself: *"For Christ sent me not to baptize, but to preach the gospel."*[7] Accordingly, among the first obligations that he imposed on his disciple, Timothy, was this: *"Preach the word; be instant in season, out of season; reprove, entreat, rebuke in all patience and doctrine."*[8] These words are so clear and forcible that they leave no doubt about our obligations, there is no need therefore to dwell further on the point.

Under this word *preaching* is included every form of announcing the gospel: whether the priest instructs, exhorts or incites the faithful to the service of God, whether he preaches in public or in private, in the church or out of the church, in the confessional or in familiar conversation, all come under the word *preaching*. When this word 'preaching,' is taken in its strict and proper sense, it means that public act, more or less solemn in form, which is exercised in a church when a bishop or a parish priest or other priest delegated teaches or instructs a certain number of people congregated for the purpose of listening to him; it is in this sense that we use the word here. In our times it it not the want of such preaching as much as the sterility of it or the small amount of fruit, that we have to deplore. And does it not appear extraordinary with so much preaching, to see so many sins all the time, and even to see them multiplied every day? Whose fault is it? Is it the fault of the audience or of the preacher? To tell you frankly what I think: there are faults on both sides; in the one and in the other. The whole year long, we are pointing out the faults of the people in this matter; let us today seek to discover our own. To do so, let us see what are the gifts and qualities of an apostolic priest, of a priest who wishes by his preaching to produce fruit in souls; what should be the method, the discernment, the solicitude that he should use in discharging this duty of preaching. The material for this subject is vast, and the subject itself is of supreme importance.

I   REQUISITES FOR EFFECTIVE PREACHING

There are many requisites, the combination of which are required to form a preacher, not so much an eloquent preacher, as one useful and fruitful for the good of souls. Some of these requisites regard the preacher himself, others the material of his sermons, and others, the manner of delivering them to the people. Let us begin with the first, the requisites of the preacher, for the fruit of the sermons will depend on whether he possesses them, and without them the other things would be of no value.

✣   THE QUALITIES WHICH THE PREACHER SHOULD HAVE

The qualities which the priest who preaches should have are the same as those which the first Preacher, Our Divine Redeemer, possessed; they are (1) a right intention in seeking purely the glory of God, like his divine Model and not his own glory, "*I seek not my own glory;*"⁹ (2) to preach first by deed, that is by our own conduct, what we are going to preach to others by word: "*Jesus began to do and to teach;*"¹⁰ (3) to accompany our preaching to the people with the force and aid of our prayers, after the example of our Divine Redeemer, of whom we read so often that He retired alone to pray: "*And, having dismissed the multitude, He went into a mountain alone to pray;*"¹¹ and as His first preachers the Apostles were accustomed to do; "*But we will give ourselves continually to prayer and to the ministry of the word.*"¹²

(1) *Purity of Intention*

The intention or end in every enterprise will provide a good forecast of its outcome, so that if the end is good and right there is every reason to hope that the outcome will be correspondingly good. If this may be said of human affairs, much more is it applicable to divine and spiritual affairs and, in particular, to preaching, both because in it the holiness of the intention forms the marrow and substance of the act of preaching and makes Our Lord recognize it as His own work, and therefore bless it; and because it is the first and, I may say, the only thing that gives force and ascendency over the people, by reason of the spirit and unction with which the priest who speaks with it is endowed. Observe that among the people, the preacher who has this unction, and who shows a right intention in his preaching, is noted and is preferred; both the learned and the unlearned recognize it and relish it, and no one can deny it their respect. And even if other oratorical qualities are lacking, even if what is said appears hardly to make sense, nevertheless, you will notice that these words have a secret hidden force through which you cannot fail to feel their effect. At times, you will not be able to catch the force of certain arguments, and you will find them insufficient to convince you; but in their stead, that unction, that heart which accompanies them will shake you, will move you; and as people say: homage cannot be denied to the heart.

Two laymen were speaking among themselves about a priest; one of them asked the other how he preached. He preaches much the same way as a laborer does his work when you pay him, replied the other simply. What did he mean by the reply? Did he mean that he preached well, or badly, or middling? I don't know, I leave it to you to judge; but one thing appears clear to me in that response, and it is, that in the judgment of this layman, the priest's sermons lacked heart and unction and spirit, the things which a right intention alone can give. If he had preached heresy, or if he had been wanting in voice, or delivery, or eloquence, the layman would have said so; but no; therefore he meant to say that he preached materially all right, but that there was no soul in his sermons; they were therefore like a corpse and hence bore no fruit, and were perhaps heavy and wearisome to those who listened to them.

Do you wish me to say more? When unction and heart are wanting, it even makes those listening doubt whether what is said is true, or whether the preacher himself believes it. It is plain that this priest believes what he is saying, said one of the congregation after hearing a priest who spoke from his heart. Did he mean that other preachers did not believe what they said? He did not say so expressly, but it appears that he feared it. So long as we are all eloquence, all tongue, all style, all far-fetched ideas, all reasoning, worldlings have no fear of us and they can even surpass us; what gives us greater force and renders us far and away superior to them in speaking is unction and heart. It would go hard on us if the world could succeed in possessing this unction. But no, it is a divine spirit, it is like a Heavenly breath which the Lord communicates to His Church, to His minister and his words, and which the world will never be able to acquire either by art or science, or by any force whatever.

(2) *Exemplary Life*

The next quality which should accompany, should in fact precede the priest who presents himself to preach to the people, is example; this implies that he should be a man who practices first, and in presence of all, what he teaches others. What do the people learn from a preacher, even from a very eloquent one, who does not give good example? They learn to speak fair words, but to act badly; they learn to know how to say one thing for themselves, and another thing for others. What is sin? But all the same I am going to commit it! They learn—do you know what? They learn to lose that sentiment of bashfulness, of shame, which even the wicked naturally experience when they inveigh against vices which they know they themselves have, and praise virtues which they do not possess. And, in fact, it is natural that when a person speaks against the voice of his heart which reproves him for vices that he condemns in others, or for being devoid of virtues which he insists others should have, it is natural, I say, that he should feel a certain reluctance of tongue and a blush on his face because of speaking so, unless these sentiments have been lost through the habit of speaking thus. But as the priest in question has lost that sense of shame, he causes the people to lose it also. We would want a face of brass and a forehead of bronze to preach like that, said some laymen after hearing a sermon by a priest who did not give good example: he must not be aware of how he conducts himself, to make a tirade like that against scandal-givers, and then go and give people reason to speak badly about himself. Does he not know how people murmur, and all they say against him on account of that person, on account of his too-frequent visits to that family?

And indeed how will a priest be able to preach with fruit to others that they must wish well to one another, that they must bear with one another, pardon their enemies, pass over offenses, when all know that between himself and a certain other priest there is unfriendliness and that neither will yield, until perhaps some layman intervenes to put an end to it? A priest, for instance, preaches to others about gravity, devotion, and silence in the church; about the terrible thing it is to go to Communion without great preparation and go away without a long thanksgiving; but what fruit will his sermon have if the people see the preacher himself distracted in church; if they see him going up on the altar and leaving the church without saying two words to that God whom he has received in his heart. It happened once that a priest was preaching on the occasion of the Forty Hours, and he was enumerating the sacrileges that are committed in going to Holy Communion, and among them he included that of not making proper preparation and thanksgiving. I don't know whether he said that they were all mortal sins, but as he was declaiming and defining with much facility and in his own manner, in the end someone present said: "Oh! all these sacrileges must be only in his head, but if they are true, the poor man himself will catch it!" And we ourselves experience how easy it is, when listening to a sermon, for our thoughts to be directed to this or that person who has the defect or vice spoken of, and this happens much more easily when it is the preacher himself who has it. The sermons of those who don't practice what they preach move the pious to pity and make the malignant laugh; such sermons in which there is evident contradiction between what the preacher advocates and what he practices were better not given at all, for there would be one scandal less for the people, and the preacher would be spared one additional sin.

(3) *The Spirit of Prayer*

The last quality necessary for the priest who wishes to preach with fruit is that he should be a man of prayer. This is clear in itself; for it is not words, fine phrases, flowers of eloquence, the force of reasoning, the polite manners and gifts of the preacher that are going to conquer and touch men's hearts, but the grace and light and impulse that come from above, and this ordinarily is not obtained except through prayer. If on hearing a sermon, you notice that your heart is touched, you may conclude that the preacher is a man who prays. I shall not delay further on this point, although it is a most interesting one, for we have already spoken of it; the right intention and the unction of which we spoke cannot be had without being men of prayer. Rather, I recommend you to consider this means not only as habitually necessary, but as the proximate disposition for this exercise of our ministry, and to use it as such. Therefore, before showing ourselves in public, and in the act itself of presenting ourselves, let us make fervent aspirations and continue repeating: "O Lord, do Thou come and speak in place of me. How dost Thou expect that an instrument so miserable would be able to speak in a worthy manner of Thee and for Thee? Arise O Lord! Just a little of Thy divine breath, in order that I may not injure Thy cause and the good of souls!"

When the conditions mentioned are found in the preacher, we may be sure that his words will not sound hollow and that his labors will not fail to produce much fruit. However, the fruit will be still greater when other requisites are present: these are the judicious choice of material and proper mode of presentation, and about these we shall now speak.

II THE MATERIAL FOR SERMONS

When speaking about the material for our sermons, I naturally presume that it is the word of God, for there are certain subjects which belong rather to the profane than the sacred, and these would be best dealt with in the lecture hall of an academy, or in the banquet hall, than in a church, where they have no right to enter. There are also certain subjects which, under one aspect, might furnish most suitable matter for the pulpit but which, when treated in a purely human way, and defended and sustained by the pure force of reasoning, can no longer be called the word of God; for the word of God consists in what has been handed down in Scripture and tradition, and recognized as such and proposed for our acceptance by the authority of the Church.

Bearing the above in mind concerning the general matter for our sermons, I make the following three suggestions about the kind of subjects to be chosen: (1) to confine ourselves to doctrine that is certain, whether that defined by the Church or that taught with the unanimous consent of the Fathers and Theologians, and to leave aside controversial points; (2) to select those subjects which are most suitable and useful for our particular congregation, and which they need most frequently; (3) to give preference to those subjects and maxims which serve to enlarge the heart, stir up fervor and make the people eager to walk the path of virtue.

(1) *Preach About What Is Certain: Avoid What Is Doubtful*

In the first place, then, we should confine ourselves to what is accepted by all or almost all as certain doctrine. If we act otherwise we leave ourselves open to great inconveniences; either we explain the state of the question to the people (and tell them that there are various opinions about it), or we select one opinion and, using this opinion, we lay down laws from the pulpit and issue prohibitions. In the first case, the faithful will be more confused than edified and instructed; and either they will not understand at all, or they will only half understand, and will end up by not knowing what they ought to do. We know what embarrassment and how great difficulties such questions about which Theologians disagree cause to the moralist and the confessor. You can argue from that what kind of conclusions will be drawn by rude uneducated people, or by those steeped in the affairs of the world who find it difficult to understand and retain in memory the most evident truths. Add to this the scandal that will arise for the people when they hear that some understand the question in one sense and others in another; it will almost appear to them that our faith and religion is a thing which has been fabricated, and changed according to each one's whim.

In the other case, namely that the preacher mentions one opinion only and gives it as the law on the point, I believe that such a manner of preaching on matters of obligation is reprobated by all; both by those theologians who hold the view that in questions about which there is still controversy each one is free to follow whichever opinion he prefers; and by those who hold that in practice a person is bound to follow, if not the more solid opinion, at least one that is probable. For according to the first, whoever teaches others that they are bound to follow one opinion, and keeps back the information that such an obligation does not exist, evidently contradicts himself, and deceives his hearers. In addition, that manner of preaching only multiplies sins through the erroneous conscience that it forms in those listening. For they, on hearing one opinion only, become persuaded that the obligation based on it is certain, with the result that every time they violate that obligation they will be guilty of formal sin, and this in a matter in which there is doubt whether there is any sin at all; whereas if they had been left in good faith, at least they would not sin formally and would not be condemned by the Lord. This mode of preaching is also reprobated by those other theologians who hold that each one should follow the more probable opinion. This question of probability is a rather subjective affair and varies according to the person, so that what appears to me in one way, may appear to another differently. So therefore, in the given case, if I impose an obligation, I destroy my own system by taking away the right and, in fact the duty, which according to me, a person would have to follow a different opinion, if on account of his own persuasion, or the advice of some expert, it seemed more probable than mine. Therefore, no matter how you consider the question, I believe that it is never expedient to enter into such disputed questions in public.

But what are we to do? Are we to keep completely silent and leave the people without information about such matters because there are different opinions about them? Could it not happen that for some one, and in certain cases for particular reasons, it would be necessary, or at least useful to speak about them. To that question I reply that I would take a middle course.

But first let me make the following preliminary remark: we have very many certain obligations and very many duties to fulfill about which no doubt whatever can be raised, and, what is more serious, duties about which many are ignorant and which many more refuse to fulfill; therefore, very many sins are committed every day. This being so, why waste time in discussing questions, in seeking precepts and imposing obligations about which we do not know whether they exist or not, when there are so many certain obligations that are violated on all sides? For example, why condemn a person who on a day of abstinence takes a certain kind of food, or another who on a feast day does a certain kind of work, if it is not quite certain whether these things are forbidden, when we are living in times when there is open violation by very many of grave precepts regarding the laws governing fasting and abstinence and feast day? Let us attend to the substance, to the most important point, to where there is real certain sin, which is the clear, and I might say, barefaced violation of certain laws; and when we have succeeded in preventing the commission of these true and certain sins, let us thank the Lord that we have accomplished a great work.

This remark being premised, I propose the following suggestion to the preacher with regard to controversial matters: the preacher should first exhaust the portion that is certain and admitted by all, and when he comes to the portion about which authors are divided, he should make up his mind as to whether it is really useful to those to whom he is speaking; if so, he should drop the tone of command, and speak of it as a matter of counsel, and suggest what he believes to be of greatest advantage to the faithful. Having done so he should warn his hearers that in such matters each one should speak to his or her own confessor who, hearing the particular circumstances, and knowing the dispositions of the person, would be able to give directions better than the preacher, as to what in the particular case should be done. For example, when speaking of what should be done on feast days, a great number of pious practices should not be suggested, for if this were done, there would be the danger that the people would not know what was sufficient or what was necessary to satisfy their obligation. It would be better and would produce more fruit, to begin by stating clearly everything that is of obligation, whether from the divine or ecclesiastical law, or from particular circumstances of scandal, ignorance or a person's own danger; and then to limit himself to suggesting as matter of counsel some works likely to be of most benefit, and conclude by telling the listeners that each one should consult his or her confessor about the sanctification of these days. In this way, opinions will be respected, and the faithful will be spared doubtful laws and the danger of sinning by violating them; and at the same time provision will be made for their needs and for their greater good.

(2) *Select the Most Useful Material*

The next suggestion for the preacher is that he should select material that will be of greatest utility to his congregation.

(a)   THE ETERNAL TRUTHS

First of all should come the eternal truths. Ah! my dear Fathers, let us preach often on these truths which are suitable for all and which concern us all without any distinction: the importance of salvation, the great evil of sin, death which awaits us all, and the great subjects of Heaven, Hell and eternity. These are subjects that can never be repeated too often or dwelt on too much, and so I would say: in every kind of sermon, whether it be a catechetical instruction, a set sermon, an explanation of the gospel, whatever be our subject, we should never conclude without touching more or less directly on some of the great truths. A great man has said that they are sauce that suits every dish. Often a reflection on, or a remark about these truths has more effect on the people than the whole sermon. For example; after finishing the instruction and explaining the various obligations arising from it, the preacher might conclude with a reference to the eternal truths saying: What will it avail us, my dear brethren, to know our obligations if we do not carry them out in practice? Who can tell whether this sermon may not serve one day for our greater condemnation and our greater pain in Hell. Think well over it! A few words of that kind will leave a most salutary impression.

(b) SERMONS SHOULD BE PRACTICAL

In addition, our sermons should be practical and should deal with the habits, and doings, not of people in general, but of those listening to us, taking good care however, not to say anything even remotely personal. Lofty, subtle themes, theories, speculative and abstract virtues are fine, edifying subjects to discuss, but for the most part, with rare exceptions, they leave the listeners without anything practical. Either they are not understood, or they rather excite admiration than provide stimulus for action, or show the manner of practicing what was suggested. Let us then keep to ordinary simple subjects, and come down to what is practical, to what can closely interest our people, and let us deal in our sermons as often as possible with the virtues, with sin, with domestic defects, with everyday happenings; in particular, we should preach on prayer, the Sacraments, peace and harmony in families, family sufferings, obedience, respect to those in authority, avoidance of idleness, factions, bad example, self-love, human respect. These subjects should be treated in the practical way and adapted to the congregation so that each one can see reflected in himself the picture being drawn by the preacher, know where harm lies and learn how to remedy it. I know that all this is easily said, but that it is not so easy for all to carry it out in practice; I grant it, but our faults of emptiness and vagueness will be less, and the fruit of our preaching greater when we pay attention to the rules and suggestions given.

(c) THE SERMONS SHOULD PROVIDE ENCOURAGEMENT FOR THE PRACTICE OF VIRTUE

Finally, in our sermons we should touch oftenest on those points, those maxims which can attract people most and stimulate them to serve God, to flee from vice and to practice virtue. And what are these? They are the same as those which in human affairs move people most, namely, what is useful, what is advantageous and what is easy. Succeed in persuading a person that it will be of great benefit to him to apply himself to a given enterprise, and that if he only wishes, he will have little difficulty in accomplishing it, and you will require only another sermon, another talk to induce him to do it; he is already convinced and will begin work of his own accord. On the other hand, beware of being wearisome or discouraging in your sermons. It should always be your object to put before the people in a convincing manner the great advantages, the many blessings that are to be expected from the observance of the law of God; temporal advantages, spiritual advantages, advantages in life, at death, and in eternity; peace of heart, internal consolation, domestic concord, good success in their business, in their crops; and then above all, the great prize which is reserved in Heaven for those who have striven to serve God, who have labored and suffered for God in this world. It is impossible that the heart of man be not moved by the sight of such a picture, by the hope of so many advantages, and not feel itself as it were urged to fly in all haste to share in so many blessings, especially since it has heard it said at the same time that whoever really wants these blessings can easily obtain them.

(d)   THE PREACHER SHOULD NOT EXAGGERATE DIFFICULTIES

For some reason that I cannot explain, we preachers are inclined to speak too often and too willingly of the difficult portions of God's law and to make the difficulty of observing it stand out prominently, instead of smoothing the difficulties that are met with. I do not say that we exaggerate, but from the frequency with which we speak of the difficulties, and the way in which we speak, it would almost appear that it gives us pleasure to do so. For we are constantly saying that it is difficult to make a good Confession, difficult to receive Holy Communion well, difficult even to hear Mass with devotion, difficult to pray as we ought, difficult above all to arrive at salvation, and that the number of those saved is very small. And what is gained by putting so many difficulties before the people? If we do not exaggerate and magnify, at least do we not repeat the same thing too often? The good are left uneasy and are discouraged, while the bad lose hope, and hardly ever think of those things again.

A certain man who had kept away from the Sacraments for a long time, when urged to go to Confession was accustomed to reply that for him it would be useless, that it would be like making a hole in water, which would fill up immediately, and that it would be better to do nothing, and do you know why? He had heard a priest say in a sermon that it was very difficult to go to Heaven, and that those who succeeded in getting there might be compared to the few apples that escape notice when the fruit is being gathered. This man then began to reason as follows: if that be so, those few devout people that I know in this district will find it hard to be saved, and can I have pretentions to be saved, to be one of the few, I who have done so much evil? That is how the devil makes use of these exaggerations to keep people away from the service of God, or at least to disturb their minds. The Sacraments are abandoned, or at least people receive them rarely, for fear of receiving them badly, works of piety are neglected, so also is the gaining of indulgences because people have heard it said that it is next to impossible to gain them in full; people almost despair of going to Heaven, and therefore their efforts to get there are cold and languid, because of their conviction that it will be difficult to get there.

But, in reality, is it difficult to be saved? For if it were truly so, it would be useless, in fact harmful, to pretend that it was not, and to hide the truth.

In the first place, let us refrain from increasing and magnifying the difficulties, even supposing that they really exist, and let us not follow the example of the preacher who, in order to prove that the number of the elect was small (that is in the sense that he understood it), quoted the saying of our Saviour: "*For many are called but few are chosen,*"[13] and who in translating it, perhaps in good faith, exaggerated the meaning, by substituting the superlative, *very very few,* for the positive *few,* and repeating that the number of the elect would be *very very few.* He did not do so through malice, but for the people it amounted to the same thing. These are mistakes that the devil can easily turn to his advantage. In the second place, when we cannot avoid speaking of what is difficult in the service of God, let us act like the doctor who, when he has to give bitter medicine to his patient, puts in something to lessen the bitterness, and then presents it with such reasons and recommendations that the patient does not notice the bitterness. We should do likewise; tell about the difficulty, but at the same time clothe it with such reasons and sentiments that the people will not be disheartened and discouraged.

The road to Heaven can be said to be easy or difficult according to the character and the dispositions of each one; it is easy for all who travel by it with good will, who are determined to live well and to save their souls; it is difficult for those who are wavering and languid in the service of God, and who appear not to be able to make up their minds. When a person has good will, God cooperates with him by being generous with His grace, and so strengthens him, that, instead of finding difficulty in travelling by the road, he runs, and flies without the least feeling of weariness. Let us just ask the multitude of good Catholics who live good lives, and they will reply laughingly and compassionately to the difficulties which the wicked and the tepid imagine for themselves and which fill them with dread; and by their promptness, tranquillity and holy joy, they will convince us that for them there is no difficulty. The difficulty is more in the people than in the thing itself, so that for whoever is really in earnest, everything is easy. The great and continuous helps given by the Lord, the peace and contentment enjoyed by those who live good lives, the spirit and courage which those who are in earnest acquire, the habit of doing good, all combine to make the road of virtue easy and smooth; and if some rough patch is met with, there will be so many corresponding compensations, that it will hardly be noticed. That the difficulty of being saved arises from the want of good will, we see from this same parable in which Our Saviour alluded to the small number of those chosen. Whose fault was it that the number of those invited to the banquet who actually came was so small? Was it the fault of the householder who sent out the invitation? No, for he had prepared everything, even the seats. Was it the difficulty of getting in to the banquet? No, for the doors were open, there was only a small way to go, and the householder had sent his messengers to tell them that all was prepared and to invite them to come. If they did not go, it was therefore because they were unwilling. It is thus that we should speak to the people; let us not he inventing difficulties; it is always the slothful who find pretexts; whoever is really in earnest can do everything required for salvation, and can even experience more pleasure than labor in doing it. The greatest obstacle to salvation, and the one against which we should constantly fight, lies in this: that some people want to serve God and the world at the same time; to be a little of one and a little of the other, and then the work of salvation is not only difficult but impossible. Living in that way satisfies no one; the person in question feels the weight of the yoke of the world and the weight of the yoke of the Lord, and loses the wages and reward from both sides.

III Method of Preaching

Finally, for fruitful preaching we should make sure that our sermons have two qualities; that they are easily understood, and that they be delivered in a pleasing manner.

(1) *Sermons Should Be Clear and Easily Understood*

It is a general lament, common among the people, that they do not understand our sermons, that they cannot grasp what we mean; they therefore become tired of them and cease attending them. This may be due in part to their ignorance, but I fear that it is more our fault because we do not go to sufficient trouble to make ourselves understood, because we go to preach without being prepared. We speak, it is true, but without order, in a confused manner, without applying what we say to the needs of our congregation, or applying it wrongly. And how could you expect that the people would understand what we say when we have difficulty ourselves in understanding it, and would have much greater difficulty in putting together what we had said when the sermon is over? How often preachers are heard to boast: I was not prepared, but I came off all right! Ah, poor Church, poor souls, it would be a bad case for you if you had not other preachers besides these!

(2) *They Should Be Pleasing and Should Not Give Offense*

In addition to this, the preacher should endeavor to make his manner of preaching pleasing to his hearers. I know that certain qualities necessary to win the hearts of men and to make what we say pleasing to our audience do not depend on us, but up to a certain point we can cultivate them. If our sermons are clear, orderly, practical and easily understood, they will by that alone please the listeners in a greater or less degree; but if we wish to be sure that we will not displease or offend any of our listeners, and even to please them, we should be brief in what we say, speak always with respect for the people listening to us, even though they may be rude and uneducated, make common cause with them so that they will know from our manner of preaching that we are speaking as much to ourselves as to them, that if an action is a sin for them it is a sin also for us, and that if there is a Hell for them there is a Hell for us too.

(3) *The Preacher Should Remember that He is Defending the Cause of God*

I shall just make one more remark, and it will form the conclusion: if we wish to have that unction and force indispensable for good preaching, we should keep in our mind while preaching the position that we hold and the affairs we have to deal with in our preaching. A lawyer who comes before a tribunal to defend the property, the liberty, or perhaps the life of his client will do all in his power to come out victorious; we, in that chair of truth, the pulpit, are before a much more important tribunal, and we have a mandate to defend and uphold, not merely the affairs of this miserable earth, but a cause far and away more important, the cause of the Lord, of the Church and of souls. Therefore, my dear Fathers, let us not spare breath, or prayer, or sweat, or study, or labor, so that the words that we deliver from the pulpit may be so many death rays to the powers of Hell, and so many victories that will be gained through us for the good of the Church, for the salvation of souls and for gaining Heaven. Amen.

---

1 Luke 4:18.
2 Ibid. 43.
3 Luke 9:2.
4 Mark 16:15.
5 Ibid. 20.
6 Acts 6:2-4.
7 I Cor. 1:17.
8 I Tim. 4:2.
9 John 8:50.
10 Acts 1:1.
11 Matt. 14:23.
12 Acts 6:4.
13 Matt. 22:14.

The Ministry of Confession

*T*HE OFFICE of preaching is certainly great, it is an office that belongs to the apostle and to the priest; it is the first weapon, the strongest weapon, the most powerful weapon that our Divine Redeemer has put into the hands of us priests: "*Going, therefore, teach ye all nations.*"[1] Fortified with this power, and provided with the words of eternal life, the priest presents himself to the people and like a person come from Heaven, announces the law of God to all without distinction or exception; to rich and poor, to rulers and subjects, to young and old. He pronounces woes on those who transgress it and threatens them with Hell; he guarantees blessings to those who observe it and promises them Heaven. It cannot be denied that the words of the Gospel have tremendous force, especially when they come from the heart of a priest, from a breast truly apostolic. At these words, the wicked and bad-living, if they are not converted, become terrified and tremble, the tepid revive, and the good are filled with joy and become more perfect.

But both the one and the other have need that this word, which shakes them from a distance and in common, be brought nearer to them and, as it were, be applied to each one individually; in other words, it is necessary that the preacher descend and become their director, that is to say, that he speak to each one in particular, that he support him, lead him on, direct him so that he will walk securely on the path pointed out in the sermon. And thus we have the priest changing office, from a preacher he becomes director, and from sitting in the chair of truth, he goes to sit in the tribunal of mercy. The office of confessor is no less great, no less useful, no less important, than that of preacher; and therefore I add: whoever among priests wishes to exercise himself in the performance of great, sublime, noble and glorious actions, let him labor in the confessional; whoever wishes to gain much merit, let him weary himself in the confessional. To put the matter in different words: the office of confessor is great beyond belief; it is of immense, incalculable benefit to our neighbor; it is a most abundant source of merit for the priest who exercises it. These are three thoughts which I shall develop briefly for you, delaying a little sometimes to reply to difficulties brought forward by priests who, either from indolence or excessive fear, withdraw from the exercise of confessor. I shall have to return to this subject of Confession again, for it is too vast and important to be treated in one conference. It is the ministry in which each of us will, more or less, have to spend the greater part of our lives, and therefore it is very necessary for us to study the subject well, and to understand it so that we may be animated with the proper spirit to administer this Sacrament with zeal and constancy.

I   The Power of Absolving is the Greatest and Most Exalted of Powers

In the first place, the power of forgiving sins attached to the office of confessor is the greatest and most exalted among all the powers that can be exercised by man on earth, and I would even say, among all the powers that could be communicated to any creature. It should suffice to say that this power is absolutely divine, and belongs to God alone, just as the power of creating, and that God has never communicated it ever to anyone, not even to the angelic spirits or to the holiest people on earth, outside the priesthood.

Let us examine some of the details of this power of forgiving sins which has been conferred on each one of us.

The first light on this power is got from the following words of the prayer of the Church: "*O God, Who dost manifest Thy omnipotence chiefly by sparing and showing mercy.*"[2] The work of pardoning, of blotting out sin is like the apex, the supreme effort of divine power. We might say in our manner of speaking that God would not have to exercise so great an effort to create another world, or a thousand other worlds, as is required to pardon one sin; St. Augustine says: *The justification of a sinner is a greater work than to create Heaven and earth.*[3] The communication then of this power to us priests means that God has communicated to us what is greatest in Him and what most properly belongs to His omnipotence.

✧ This Power Is Absolute

And to what extent does He give us this power? He gives it to us absolutely so that it can be exercised by us alone without Him; for He gives it to us without limits of time, of sins, of persons, even to the point of binding Himself not to use it without us. Thus, other people obtain extraordinary gifts from God, they work prodigies and miracles, like Moses, Josue, Elias, Eliseus, but what these men have done has been achieved by means of prayer. The priest, on the other hand, does not ask, does not intercede, does not pray, but he acts of himself as if the power were his own; he does not say: "May God pardon you," but "I pardon you, I absolve you."

✧ It is Without Limits

This power, this jurisdiction is without limits: God might have limited it to certain classes of persons, to certain species of sins, or only allowed it to be used at a certain time; but no, He grants it over everything, always, and for every sin, so much so that, as I have said, He has willed, in a manner, to despoil Himself of it and to concentrate it in us alone. St. Hillary indicates this when he says: *Quorum terrestre judicium praejudicata auctoritas sit in coelo;* and the Council of Trent teaches: *Dominus noster Jesus Christus . . . Sacerdotes sui ipsius vicarios reliquit, tamquam praesides et judices, ad quos omnia mortalia crimina deferantur.*[4] No sin is remitted except by Confession or the desire of it: *In re aut in voto,* as the theologians says; so that if a sinner were to refuse to recognize the priest and dared to present himself directly before God, exclaiming: "Have mercy on me, O God . . . . blot out my iniquity,[5] O God, be merciful to me a sinner,[6] Almighty God, as if He could not do so, would say to him: I have handed over that power to others: go show yourself to the priest, open your heart to him, let him know your sorrow, and he will pardon you: *Vade, ostende te sacerdoti.*[7] The above should be sufficient to show the excellence of his office.

✧ The Great Blessings of the Sacrament of Penance

What are we to say about the advantages which the faithful derive from this Sacrament, about its utility to them? I shall abstain from mentioning all the blessings which the proper use of this Sacrament bring to society and to the family; I pass over the peace and tranquility of mind which the sinner gets from this tribunal; I come to the principal gain, which is that of the soul.

The man in sin is a lost man; for him there is no longer Heaven, and in a sense there is no longer God. All creatures are incensed against him and would wish to annihilate him with one blow, and he hangs by a thread over the brink of the terrible abyss of Hell which is ready to swallow him. Suppose that the sinner repents and kneels before a confessor; the confessor, more powerful than Josue when he stopped the sun in its course, commands the elements to be appeased and they obey; he turns to the abyss and closes it, he turns towards Heaven and opens the door; with a word he pardons the poor sinner, restores to him his inheritance and saves him; go in peace, he says, Heaven will be yours. And behold! that sinner has become once more a child of God with all his former merits and rights restored to him, he is in the state of grace and is restored to favor with his God.

It is true that in the Church there are many means to bring back the sinner to the state of grace and salvation: prayer, preaching, exhortation, good advice and such like, but what really saves the man is Confession. As long as the priest continues praying, advising, threatening, preaching, the sinner cannot still be said to be saved; he is saved in the strict sense of the word, when he has made a good Confession. The other means dispose him for salvation, Confession saves him; the other means bring the man to the net, Confession closes it on him and catches him. Confession is like an arena in which priest and sinner come to engage in a contest; after a struggle of patience, charity, and prayer, the confessor, as it were, giving a mortal blow to the devil, finally conquers; the sinner is rescued from Hell and an additional soul gained for Heaven. And what consolation and comfort for the confessor when in a day, and even in a morning, he gains such a victory, and not merely once or twice but many times! Oh, what hours, what moments of Heaven! What compensation for the patience used, for those studies, and prayers with which the confessor prepared himself! And what comparison can those gains, those acquisitions, those conquests of this earth, and even the victories of all the armies of the world, bear with the successes, the victories which the priest gains in this battlefield! So precious and of such immense value are these conquests that in priests of lively faith there are enkindled such ardent desires to administer this Sacrament that they remain almost motionless shut up in the confessional forgetful of everything even of themselves. A great servant of God said that if he had one foot already in Heaven, and was called to hear a Confession, he would return to earth immediately to make this additional conquest. St. Philip Neri was so conscious of the great good that is done through this Sacrament, that he did not even find time to think of himself. In the church, in the sacristy, in his room he was ever ready to hear Confessions, and he continued so without growing weary of it until the end of his life. St. John Chrysostom, as Baronius records, preached and insisted with the people that if any of them should fall into sin, they should come and seek him out immediately, even if they had to arouse him from sleep. *Si quando contigerit ex vobis peccare aliquem, accedite ad me dormientem.*"

❖ THE GREAT MERIT THAT THE CONFESSOR CAN GAIN

However great is the advantage gained by the people from this ministry, the merit, the gain made for himself by the confessor who administers this Sacrament is no less great. How great this merit is and how great the reward of the confessor will be, you can judge from the nature and effects of those acts of charity which the confessor performs for souls in the Sacrament of Penance and from the rewards which God promises for even the smallest act of corporal charity. If God has fulminated such threats against whoever robs Him of a soul by scandal; if, like a furious bear robbed of its cubs, He will fall upon that unfortunate being who has caused another to commit sin, you can argue from the contrary reason, what reward He has reserved for the priest who has come so often to grips with the devil, at the cost of so many inconveniences with such patience, at the peril of his health and even of his life, and saved so many souls for Him. What greater virtue and consequently what greater merit than that of a priest who, burning with zeal for souls, puts himself in so many dangers to save others? Like another Apostle, he can say to the Lord as he enters the confessional: I know that I am going to put myself in many dangers but no matter; my heart will not allow me to see souls lost; for myself, give me whatever Thou wishest, but grant that I succeed in saving them! "*I wished myself to be an anathema from Christ, for my brethren.*"[8] Ah, we may be certain, my dear Fathers, that labors expended in so noble and holy a cause cannot go without being rewarded with the greatest prize.

✧ This Ministry Is Very Necessary

Let us then devote ourselves with alacrity to a ministry so excellent, so noble, so advantageous for our neighbor and so meritorious for ourselves, and I will add, a ministry so necessary. Its necessity is evident, for sins are not wanting; they go on increasing every day; these sins cannot be taken away by any other means. It is therefore necessary that priests set themselves to exercise this ministry in earnest, not merely in a routine manner or at some seasons of the year only, but assiduously and zealously, and at all times and all hours that the good of souls requires it.

II The Principal Difficulties:

Let us now listen to the principal difficulties which those priests raise who keep away from the administration of this Sacrament:

(1) *This Ministry is Wearisome*

I do not hear Confessions, or at least I hear very seldom, because this office is wearisome to me and I suffer from it, and then, to tell the truth, I do not like it, I cannot adapt myself to it, and I see that it does not suit me. Thus some priests reason and they shelter behind such excuses. I shall reply to these various excuses.

It is *wearisome* for you! So far there is no harm; to feel the weight, the burden, the fatigue of an action is not a sin, it is not even a defect in virtue; the fault lies in allowing oneself to be conquered by this fatigue and neglecting the work itself. You *suffer* from it! But I ask you if that priest gives himself to other more congenial and lucrative occupations, or even to heavier and more troublesome works, how is it that he can stand it for whole days? Does he not find weariness in games, amusements, in reading profane books, in transacting temporal affairs? Is it only in the confessional that all pains and aches are found? Are this priest's worries about the confessional real or imaginary? But even suppose he suffers from it, let him have a little courage. How many good priests in poor health, or indeed with infirmities, nevertheless do violence to themselves and labor in the confessional as much as those of robust health! Are you afraid perhaps that the Lord may not intend to pay you for all and that He may wish to defraud you of some of the reward for your sufferings?

Another priest objects, the doctors assure me that I might have a breakdown in health if I continued to hear Confessions. To this, I can give the reply that St. Francis de Sales gave to the person who urged him to lessen his labors, for fear that he might shorten his life: "It is not necessary that I live," replied the Saint, "but while I live it is necessary that I labor." In these cases I do not wish to lay down an obligation, but I do not know whether anyone among us will be able to merit the honor of dying a martyr and a victim of charity.

"I do not *like* it." It makes no matter whether you *like* it or not; have courage, and hear Confessions, it is not taste or inclination or pleasure that should move us to labor. How many things in this world are unpleasant, and yet they are done! The sick man does not like the medicine and yet he takes it. "I cannot *adapt* myself to it." Excuse me, you should rather say, I do not wish to do it. Besides, it is too late to use such language, you should have thought of it before you entered the clerical state and put on the garb. Whether the office of confessor pleases us or not, whether it costs us much or little to perform it, we are now priests and we must attend to it.

(2) *Is there an Obligation for the Priest to Hear Confession?*

But you should know, says another priest, that I have not the care of souls, and that I am not obliged in any way to hear Confessions; and if sometimes I hear them, it is because I wish to do so of my own free will and pleasure. This excuse of which very many wish to avail themselves requires to be examined carefully. Is there an obligation on a priest to hear Confessions when he has no occupation or office which requires the exercise of this ministry? That is a question for Moral Theology. Before replying, I distinguish two points, or rather I consider the question under two aspects: (1) Is the priest bound to render himself fit, or to procure the knowledge necessary to administer this Sacrament? (2) When he has acquired it is he bound to use it?

With regard to the first kind of obligation, I believe that no one can have any doubt about the answer. For what sort of priest would he be who would not be able to reply to the questions of the faithful and to tell them what they must practice or omit in order to be saved? And this is what forms the knowledge necessary for a confessor. If you find a priest who does not know sufficient Moral Theology, how do you think he will be able to decide whether this may be done, or that may not be done?

In the Old Testament we read: "*The lips of the priest shall keep knowledge, and they shall seek the law at his mouth,*"[9] and in the decree of the Council of Trent speaking of priests we find the following: "*For the order of priesthood are accepted those who have been proved capable of teaching the people . . . . and administering the Sacraments.*"[10] Among the Sacraments one of the first and most important to be administered is the Sacrament of Penance. Therefore, if a priest were to ask me whether, being able to obtain for himself sufficient knowledge to enable him to administer this Sacrament, he can be easy in conscience if he should refuse to administer it, I should reply frankly that he cannot.*

Is every priest obliged to hear Confessions, if he has sufficient ability to do so? This is the second question. In reply, I begin by remarking that a priest is bound to labor and to exert himself for the good of souls. Woe to him if he refuses, if he stands idle and wastes his time uselessly! He will have to give a most severe and rigorous account for it. But is there a real obligation for him to labor in this special branch of hearing Confessions? This obligation arises from the needs of the faithful, and the need is present when they reasonably desire or ask to go to Confession and do not find a priest to hear them. Consequently, when at certain times of the year (leaving aside the more urgent cases of sickness or danger of death, in which it is evident that all priests are bound to administer that Sacrament), the faithful desire to receive the Sacraments, and the parish priest and his assistant are not able to hear them all, so that many people would be deprived of the Sacraments, any priest available able to hear Confessions has the obligation to present himself, and if he should refuse, he would sin against charity, which requires that we should go to the help of our neighbor, when he is in any necessity, especially spiritual necessity.

* See Code No. 129.

(3) *We Should Not Ask What Do Others Do, but What is the Law*

There is the further excuse given for not hearing Confessions, that many priests never hear, or very rarely. I am not going to enquire about what others do, or about what you do, or to weigh the reasons that some priest in particular might have for not hearing Confessions; I will tell what is the law for all, what every priest ought to do, including myself and all of you. And since the example of others is put forward as a reason, I shall make the following reflection on this point. It is a great misfortune for us priests to consider so often what others do, and bring it forward as a reason to excuse ourselves. We condemn this mode of action in lay people and we do not hesitate to say frankly to them that this is not the law that a Catholic should follow; that whoever goes through life following after others is bound to end badly like others; and why should we ourselves want to do the same? Every priest should close his eyes to what others are doing. Let others do as they will, the priest should study his duties solely from the example of our Divine Redeemer and regulate his conduct exactly according to the sayings of that great Master. A time will come when all priests will wish that they had regulated their conduct in that manner. This being premised, we can say that a time will come when those others who could have heard Confessions but would not, will wish that they had done so. I ask you: when death comes for you, what would you have wished to have done in this matter? To have heard Confessions or to have avoided doing so? I have never heard or read that on this point any priest was sorry or discontented because he had administered that Sacrament, while I could tell of the anguish and remorse of not a few who died with that thorn in their conscience.

(4) *Is Time Spent Hearing Confessions Ever Wasted?*

We have heard, my dear Fathers, the excuses and pretexts usually put forward by those who have little will to labor; let us pass on now to other excuses, in appearance more plausible and reasonable, but which in reality are not valid excuses. They come from those priests who are good, if you will, but who in practice have a repugnance to administering this Sacrament; they will occupy themselves willingly with other works of the ministry, but they do not want even to hear of work in the confessional; they never hear Confessions, or very rarely, and when they do, it is with a bad will, as if they were forced. And why all this aversion and repugnance? Their reasons can be reduced to two: the time spent in the confessional is time wasted, because the penitents are always the same and have always the same defects and sins, and no sign of fruit can be seen. Hence, these priests say that it is better to spend the time at something else, and to allow some better qualified and more willing priest to fulfill the office of confessor. That is the first excuse. Another, of much the same nature, is that the office of confessor is a very delicate one, that the confessor is liable to make many mistakes; that it is dangerous for his own soul, especially when he is subject to certain temptations and weaknesses. These priests come to the conclusion that it is better to refrain from hearing Confessions, and to apply themselves to other easier and safer kinds of work. To answer these questions it will be necessary for us to review the whole case and to examine all these reasons to see whether they are valid or not, and if valid, up to what point, for the devil is only too eager to take the priest out of the confessional or only allow him to enter it as rarely as possible.

I shall commence by remarking that if these reasons were valid, they should hold good for one as well as for another; and if this were so, who would be got to hear Confessions? But let us examine the reasons in detail. These priests say that they reap little or no fruit from their work in the confessional; that they are always hearing the same sins and the same failings. Even if that were so, it would not mean that the priest is losing his time and that his labor will be devoid of merit and reward. God will pay according to the good will, and the reward will be greater if the priest has to do violence to himself on account of the little or no satisfaction that he finds in the work.

(5) *No: It Is Time Spent Most Profitably*

But, dear Fathers, beware of paying attention to the fear that a priest may lose his time in the confessional. I need not speak of those penitents who, having confessed with all the signs of true sorrow die suddenly and are saved, nor of those—and they are not few—who being truly penitent, have been pardoned in Confession, and continue constant and firm afterwards without ever falling again, nor even of those who, having fallen again into grave sin, return penitent and rise anew; for it is evident that in these cases the work of the confessor has not been useless. I believe, however, that those who give the above excuses are alluding to certain penitents who are always relapsing into the same sins, and who, on account of obstinacy and hardness of heart, will not consent to do what the Church requires for absolution. But do you think that even with these the priest is losing his time? No, Fathers, I repeat that he is not; even if he had no other penitents but these I would always say to him: Stay in the confessional, remain in it as long as you can, and you may be sure that you are spending your time excellently. In fact, if you examine carefully these persons who, you say, are gaining no fruit from their Confessions but who are always falling in the same manner, if you examine them in thought, word, and deed, it is impossible that you will not find that at least one sin less has been committed after the penitent was with you. Even though he would not go as far as to deserve absolution, and even though he has fallen again, you can be sure that in a day, in a week, or in a month he will have abstained from some sin. And is this abstention from sin nothing? Who will have the merit for it? And who will reward it? Suppose a priest only confessed twenty or thirty persons in a month; well, there would be twenty or thirty sins less in a month. Are you sure that you could prevent as many if you spent your time at any other form of ministry?

But let us take worse cases, even the very worst; the cases of those who come indisposed and whom there is no means of disposing, or hope of reducing the number of their sins; even from these, I say some fruit can be obtained. The sweetness and charity that these hardened sinners have found in the confessor, those words of salvation and repentance spoken into their ears and hearts, will certainly not be without effect. On the day of Confession they will make a greater effort to resist evil, on the following days, many times, in spite of themselves, those words of the priest, those loving pleadings will return to their minds with the result that some day or other they will truly repent. We ourselves often have proofs of these effects in this Sacrament. Suppose one of these who left us the last time after refusing to give up sin returns to us. If we ask him how he has got on since, whether he has been tranquil and contented during the time and what was the motive that caused him to make up his mind to return, you will hear him reply, that he had experienced greater remorse and uneasiness, that he was not able to put out of his head what we had told him, that he could no longer live, that he felt constantly remorse of conscience, and that he wanted to put an end to it if possible. Thus more or less, even the most obstinate sinners speak. And is all this lost time? Ah, believe me the confessor makes a very great mistake who leaves off the administration of this Sacrament because of the fear that he is losing his time and laboring without profit. Let us learn a lesson from the devil, who, in his hunt after souls, *"as a roaring lion, goeth about seeking whom he may devour"*[11]; he goes about seeking, he goes about tempting, and if he does not succeed today, he returns tomorrow, and many times more until, if possible, he succeeds. And are we going to cease our efforts and give up because we cannot bring all the souls we want to Heaven?

❖ THE OFFICE OF THE CONFESSOR IS DELICATE AND DIFFICULT

Finally, it is said that the office of confessor is a very delicate one, and that the confessor's own soul is exposed to many dangers in the confessional. That the office is a delicate one, I grant, but that it is dangerous, that there is a risk for the soul of the confessor who discharges it with due caution, I deny outright. Yes, the office is a delicate one, and therefore should be approached and exercised with a certain fear; with a fear, be it well understood, that will make the confessor alert and attentive to what he is doing, but not with an excessive fear that will unnerve and dishearten him, and render him useless in such a ministry. Those confessors who fear such a ministry please me very much, because their fears drive away my fears for them, but those other confessors who have no fears, and who go to sit in the confessional as if they were going to sit at table, fill me with fear and dread. With all that, I would never approve of any confessor retiring from the office, or growing cold in the exercise of it on account of that fear.

❖ PRECAUTIONS TO BE ADOPTED

We have only too many reasons to make us have some fear: we are dealing with immortal souls, the loss of even one of which is a calamity; especially since a word too may, or a word too few may be the cause of

192 THE PRIEST THE MAN OF GOD

saving or losing a soul. Besides other considerations, we have to deal with deep wounds most difficult to heal, and we therefore need knowledge, experience, and skill in no ordinary degree. We have to deal with so many characters, so different from one another, and how are we to be able to find the proper way suited to each one of them? There are so many sins, of so many kinds that you would say that they were epidemics, contagious diseases; the poor confessor is to be pitied, if he is not on his guard! Yes this is true, but it is also true that there are means to guarantee him safety, to render him immune from every danger. If in our ministry we find difficulties and special dangers, you may be sure that there are also special graces for us. And do you think that the Lord is that kind of master who would allow one of His servants to perish, who, with good intentions, with proper safeguards, and for the sole purpose of saving souls, willingly puts himself in that danger? But how are we to know, these priests ask, whether we have done all possible on our part, whether we may not have made mistakes, whether we have used all the necessary safeguards? No one has ever said or claimed that the confessor is infallible, that he is not liable to err. A confessor may make a mistake but he does not sin by making a mistake, and as long as the opinion of his superiors, obedience or the advice of his director tells him to continue, he should not fear. Why stand hesitating, losing hours, days and perhaps even months with such fears? Remember that while you are hesitating, contrary to the opinion of your director, sins are being committed in the world, and people are falling into Hell without interruption. Reflect that the devil does not sleep: he goes, comes, returns, seeks every way, intent only on gaining a victory. Even though the confessor may be subject to temptations and human weaknesses in this ministry, let him not be afraid or alarmed; these things will be for him but a cause for additional merit and reward. But if I fall, if I consent? This will not happen: if you yourself had to judge another in such circumstances, you would pronounce him free from sin, and rightly; in your own case you do not dare to pronounce, and you do well, but your confessor will pronounce you free, and until he does, I for him pronounce you free.

Let us therefore conclude, my dear Fathers, by vying in our encouragement of each other to administer this Sacrament. Being convinced of the great good that we are doing to our neighbor, to families, to

Christianity and, comforted by the great merits which we go on acquiring, let us make it our duty to administer it continually until our death without distinction of persons to all who present themselves and to as many as we can. The penitents that we have confessed will be all so many persons who one day in Heaven will be under special obligations to us; or, to express it better, will be so many obligations that God will have towards us. Yes, every soul that we have helped to save by absolving it after Confession will be like a document of acknowledgement that the Lord puts in our hands, in which He protests His obligation towards us, because we have carried out His work. This was the opinion of St. Mary Magdalen de Pazzi, who was accustomed to say that she preferred to help a soul to be saved than to go into an ecstasy or to perform a miracle. Let us then encourage each other to become good, capable ministers, as worthy, or rather, as little unworthy as possible to sit in that great tribunal and take the place of God.

We shall see what are the means that will help us to succeed in becoming so; for the present, let us excite in ourselves a firm, unwavering resolution to give ourselves to this office and, by doing so, to render ourselves true ministers of the Lord; so that at the end of our days we may be able to merit for ourselves from our common Master that beautiful eulogy, that sweet and precious invitation promised to the faithful servant: "*Well done, good and faithful servant, because thou hast been faithful over a few things, I will place thee over many things, enter thou into the joy of thy Lord.*" [12]

---

1 Matt. 28:19.
2 Dom. X post Pent.
3 Lib. retr.
4 Sess. XIV, cap. 5.
5 Psalm. 50:3-4.
6 Luke 18:13.
7 Matt. 8:4.
8 Ad Rom. IX, 3.
9 Malach. 2:7.
10 Sess. XXIII, cap. 14.
11 I Pet. 5:8.
12 Matt. 25:21.

The Qualities of a Confessor

*H*EARING the Confessions of the faithful is, as I have said, among our ministrations the most sublime in its greatness, the most meritorious for us, and the most profitable for Christianity and for the Church of God. It would therefore be desire-able that all priests should not only ardently desire to exercise it, but should make it their earnest endeavor to acquire for themselves a good store of those gifts and qualities which are indispensable for the fruitful administration of this ministry. Since if, on the one hand, this office is most sublime and most useful and, as such, excites the desire to exercise it, on the other hand, it is perhaps among all others the most difficult and dangerous, and so the priest should approach it with a certain amount of fear.

Desire and fear are two affections very different, in fact contradictory. Desire urges a person towards the desired object; fear, on the contrary, stops him, holds him back and, in a certain way, keeps him far away from it. How then are we to reconcile these two affections in the same person at the same time and towards the same object? Let us act like the doctor who is called to minister to a person infected with plague. The doctor wishes to treat the patient and cure him, and therefore he is all anxiety to set about restoring him to health as soon as possible; but at the same time he fears, he fears for himself on account of the infectious nature of the disease, he fears for the sick man and is almost sorry that he has been called to attend such a case. But meantime what does he do? Will he, perhaps, abandon the sick man? Certainly not; if he has any spark of charity in him or of attachment to his profession, he will at once make the necessary preparations to deal with the case, and at the same time render himself immune from the disease by the recognized precautions; he will adopt every means to protect himself from danger. When the excessive fear has vanished and his first good desire has revived, he will begin the treatment of the sick man. Well, let the priest do likewise; let him in the first place provide himself with everything necessary to administer this Sacrament properly, that is to say, let him acquire the gifts and qualities that are required; in the discharge of the office, let him make use of all those means that will protect him against danger and insure the good of the penitent, and if he does so, everything will be equally provided for. Filled with this salutary fear which makes the confessor cautious and having laid aside the excessive fear which he may have had in the beginning, he sets himself to work, labors, and hears the Confessions with alacrity.

We shall dwell today on the remote dispositions necessary for a good confessor, that is, on the qualities which the priest should cultivate before entering the confessional. These qualities I reduce to two: more than ordinary goodness of life and sufficient knowledge for this special work. This is the indispensable equipment for a good confessor, and it will be the theme of the present conference. On the next occasion we shall speak of the principal means to be employed in the administration of this Sacrament. I trust, dear Fathers, that you will not consider three conferences on this subject of Confession too much. Certain subjects that have been treated during these days might perhaps have been omitted, and others put in their place with equal spiritual advantage for you, but I do not think that the same can be said of the present subject, such is the importance I see in it. I therefore ask you to be patient and to make a sacrifice to God, if you find these conferences wearisome.

I   Goodness Is Required in the Confessor

That goodness is required in a confessor appears to be so evident that it does not require proof; however, it will be beneficial for us to stop for a short time to examine the necessity of this quality. Now, I say that goodness is necessary in a confessor, in order that such a ministry may be entrusted to him; it is necessary, in order that he may have confidence in himself; and it is necessary in order that the penitents may have confidence in him.

(1) *Because of the Nature of this Ministry*

Observe, in the first place, how such a delicate and confidential ministry as that of hearing Confessions is entrusted only to the care of the priest. He exercises it without dependency, and without anyone on earth examining his accounts with regard to it; no confessor was ever called to render an account for what he had done. There is no appeal from the sentence which he pronounces; the penitent can indeed go to another confessor and remake his Confession, but not properly by way of appeal from the first judgment, because in that act the confessor has no superior on earth. In addition to this, he works in secret, without any other witness but the penitent; he has not therefore those incitements of shame and fear which working under the eye of the public provide, and which usually influence people to do their work well. The confessor must work all alone; accordingly, in so great and so varied needs he cannot have the advice or help of any other, all which circumstances should make superiors and Bishops use all reasonable caution before entrusting so great a ministry to a priest. It is true that to have this confidence, many conditions are required, but the chief of these conditions is the goodness of which we speak, for it is the foundation of all the others.

(2) *In Order that the Confessor May Trust in Himself*

In addition, goodness is required in order that the confessor may trust in himself. Woe to the priest that is not good who puts himself in such danger! Woe to that weak and inexperienced soldier who rushes into the thick of the fray without the necessary training! I shall not here go over the whole series of dangers which the priest who is devoid of the necessary equipment of goodness and virtue is going to encounter; I shall confine myself to noting that these dangers are many, continuous, varied, unforeseeable, formidable, whether we consider the nature of the material, the quality of the persons or the variety of the sins. Add to this, the rage, the hatred which the devil certainly entertains against this Sacrament and against the priest who administers it. He will avail himself of every occasion, he will make use of every means to make the penitents prevaricate and the minister not do his duty; he will make use of sloth, ill-temper, impatience, curiosity, human sympathy, geniality, delicacy, sensibility, to pass over the worst; he will leave nothing untried in order to gain his end. And what will the priest who is not good do? How will he get out of these difficulties? Oh! May God grant that a tribunal of mercy and salvation be not transformed into a tribunal of sin and ruin!

(3) *In Order that the Penitents May Have Confidence in Him*

Finally, goodness in the confessor is necessary in order that the penitents may have confidence in him and may approach this Sacrament with open hearts. What confidence could a sick person have in a doctor, if he knew that he was infected with the same disease and was unable to cure himself? With what security could a traveller have recourse to another for information about the right road to a certain place if he knew that this man was travelling by a wrong road not leading to his own destination? Such is the pitiable lot of the poor faithful who have to go to Confession to a confessor who is not good; they have to present their ailments for treatment to a person who is sicker than themselves, they have to ask the road to Heaven from a man who is travelling on the road to eternal perdition. Yes, my dear Fathers, if you take away this quality of goodness, there will be reason for all to fear and lament; reason to fear for the person who has entrusted so holy a ministry to unworthy hands; reason to weep and deplore the misfortune of those faithful who have to confide in such a confessor; and most of all, reason to tremble for that rash man who, without being in the possession of true and solid virtue, has the hardihood to sit in such a tribunal. And who can tell what mysteries of iniquity will one day be brought to light which, through want of goodness in a confessor, have been operated in that very place from which every kind of evil should be banished? Goodness therefore is essential in confessors if all those blessings that we have spoken of are to he obtained: the honor of the Sacrament, the tranquility of the faithful, the safety of the confessor himself all demand this goodness; all preach that the confessor should be good.

(4) *Natural Goodness is Not Sufficient*

But what kind of goodness? It is not natural goodness of character that I mean; that goodness that makes people pleasing, courteous, civil, affable, compassionate; the goodness that I mean is something very different. I mean a foundation, a provision, an equipment of more than ordinary virtue, of virtue capable of producing the following three effects in the priest: (1) It should make him firm and secure in the face of sin, so that instead of sin overcoming him, it may be conquered and destroyed; (2) it should give him an air of authority which will make him respected by the people, because they have to listen to what he says; (3) it should make him experienced and practiced in virtue in order that he may teach others virtue. To express myself in other terms: the goodness of the confessor should consist in true virtue; it should be positive virtue that will not only keep him immune and far away from all sin, but will make him practiced in virtue; in addition, it should be conspicuous, visible, well-known virtue. Let us not delude ourselves; we shall never have good confessors without such goodness; and in order to convince ourselves of this, let us examine the inconveniences, the consequences, and the dangers that result when this quality is wanting.

(5) *Dangers that Arise if This Goodness is Lacking*

Suppose the priest is in sin who enters that tribunal to combat and destroy the very sin that is in his heart: I do not know whether to call such a situation ridiculous or lamentable. A sinner contends with a sinner, a devil with a devil; what kind of struggle or battle is that? Is it a real battle or is it mere mockery? "But what are you coming to do, and why do you molest me?" I seem to hear the devil exclaiming in anger and amazement: "Anyone else but you!" I know that this Sacrament can operate by its own innate virtue without the concurrence of the virtue of the minister, but you all know how few in practice are those who come penetrated with sorrow for their sins and truly penitent, and how much they need the help of the confessor. Suppose then that they come to a confessor of this kind. How do you expect that he will be able to make others penetrated with what he himself does not feel; that he will be able to make others conceive that repentance and horror for sin that he himself has not; that he will be able to reason with, persuade, convince, lead the penitent to such a horror for sin, that he will be ready to die rather than sin again, when he himself at every shock, at every wind that blows, falls into it and keeps the sin all the time in his heart? I do not wish to say that this priest will approve of, or keep silent completely about the sins he hears; he will talk, he will declaim against them, but what he says will be mere words, mere sound and nothing more. The penitent is cold, the confessor, still more so; the penitent does not know the great evil that sin is, and therefore he does not detest it, and the confessor is not capable of making him know it. The Confession will be sincere, long, perhaps longer than it need be, but languid, cold and in no way sorrowful; thus it begins, and thus it ends. The Confession will not be sacrilegious, but who can be sure that they are not invalid and without fruit through want of true sorrow? Thus it will happen once, a second time, and who knows how many times more; and why? Most often it will be through want of goodness in the confessor.

On the contrary, how many times a sentence, a single word, a groan, a sigh from a good confessor will be enough to penetrate the heart. St. Paulinus relates of St. Ambrose that every time a penitent came to him confess, he showed himself so penetrated with sorrow that he groaned and sighed and wept, with the result that the penitent, however obdurate he might be, was constrained to weep also: *Quotiescumque aliquis ob percipiendam poenitentiam lapsus suos confessus esset, ita flebat, ut et illum flere compelleret.*[1] "O Father, leave the sighing and weeping to me," said one penitent who was moved to sorrow by his confessor, "it is I who have sinned." "Oh! if only I too could have for a moment the sentiments that you have, Father, the horror, the hatred that you have for sins," repeated another. Behold the effects, the resolutions, which true goodness in a confessor generates in the heart of the penitent! It is not the long discourses, the studied words, the declamations, the severe corrections that are going to touch and move the heart of the penitent, but the unction, the spirit which accompanies our words and which the good priest alone possesses. This effect is much greater when the goodness of the confessor is, as I have said, palpable and well known. Then it is that our words have authority, and fall like a thunderbolt on the heart of the penitent since every word that we say is supported by facts, and the penitent, whoever he may be, cannot help thinking and saying to himself: "This man is right, he is telling the truth, he speaks as he does himself." Take away this recognized goodness in the confessor, and make a case in which the contrary is even suspected, then the penitents, when confessing to such a man, will be provoked to laughter, if not in the act of confessing itself, at least afterwards.

So far, we have spoken of the greater evil that occurs when the confessor is not in the state of grace and carries sin in his heart; let us pass on to that which, under a certain aspect, is lesser, but not less serious for the confessor himself, that is, when he is not firm in virtue and falls easily when he is tempted. Who is going to keep him on his feet when he has to treat certain wounds, if he has not a more than ordinary horror for sin, if he is not ready to protest frankly and at a moment's notice that he is ready to die rather than commit sin; if he is not sustained by an already acquired habit of turning his eyes towards God in time of difficulties, and recalling to mind immediately the great eternal truths, and if he has not this habit so firmly rooted that it has become part of his being and defends him and saves him? And if it happens that he falls, how many sins are sometimes committed in a morning! And when and how is it going to stop? This is the reason why, as I have said, mere ordinary goodness is not sufficient; for it is one thing to be good enough to administer the Sacrament in grace, another to be so good as to be able to administer it with fruit and without danger to ourselves.

Furthermore, the confessor sits in that tribunal not merely to liberate souls from sin, but at the same time to put them on the road to and guide them in the practice of virtue. Now what kind of master or director would that man make who does not know how to make one step on the road on which he is to guide others, and whose highest ambition is not to fall into sin? What answer will such a confessor give to questions very often asked by pious penitents, such as what is the best way to celebrate a novena or to prepare for a feast day; how would he advise them to spend their days so as to advance in virtue, what advice would he give about certain acts of mortification and penance etc.? Either he keeps silent or he will make a few dry remarks which show that these questions do not belong to his sphere or, at best, if he is clever he will give an evasive reply which means nothing. In the meantime, good simple souls capable of making great progress in virtue will remain stationary, because they have as guide a confessor who is not good or at least who has not that goodness of which I have spoken.

But someone will say: If it is true that all this virtue is required in order to hear Confessions with fruit for the penitent, and without danger for the confessor, we would be obliged to say that whoever has not these virtues sins in hearing Confessions and should therefore cease doing so and retire. To this I reply that I make no such pronouncement, nor do I express an opinion so easily on a general question. Where there is question of sins and obligations one must be slow in defining. I say merely, and I repeat, that in order to succeed in being a good confessor and in doing great good to others without danger to himself, as a first requisite, the priest must have goodness of life beyond the common and ordinary. But if this goodness is wanting even in part, or goes on diminishing, I add, that in proportion as virtue is wanting in the confessor, or diminishes, in the same proportion the good done to others will diminish, and the danger to himself will increase. And how will the matter end? I leave that to you to decide.

II THE CONFESSOR SHOULD BE A LEARNED MAN

The other quality that the priest should bring to the confessional is a knowledge of theology which is sufficient, and which is proportioned to the work. That a priest should be learned is undeniable; without learning, one can be a good, quiet, calm, retired, charitable and pious man, but he can never be a good priest, because to be so, he must be capable of fulfilling his obligations, and this he cannot do without being learned. Thus, strictly speaking and keeping within the limits of reason, we should say that among those who are learned, the confessor should hold the first place; the titles which he bears and the roles that he has to occupy as judge, physician, and teacher evidently demand this.

✢ BECAUSE HE IS JUDGE, PHYSICIAN AND TEACHER

In the first place, he is a judge, and of what questions? Of all causes and of all cases into which sin in any form, or even the suspicion of sin can enter. Judge of whom? Of all, without distinction or exception: of kings, of magistrates, and even of the confessors themselves. He is a physician; of how many diseases and of what kinds? Imagine to yourselves, all the diseases and maladies of the soul! Well, for all these ailments there is no other physician but the confessor; and there can be no kind of new malady for him; he must know them all and must be able to cure every kind of wound or ulcer, even the most complicated and difficult. He is also a master and teacher, and we can say, in every art and profession, because all classes of people come to him: to him come the artist and the peasant, the merchant and the soldier, the rich man and the poor man, the layman and the priest, the lawyer and the functionary, in fine, to him come every kind and class of people, and they all want to know from him clearly what they may do, and what they may not do, what they ought to do, and what they ought not to do. These remarks should be sufficient to convince us completely of how fitting and necessary it is that the priest be a learned man.

✢   What Kind of Learning Should the Confessor Possess?

But what kind of learning should he possess, and in what degree? I shall leave aside every other branch of knowledge and restrict myself to speaking about what directly concerns our subject. I shall not even mention those branches of knowledge which could be most useful to a confessor and could help him to do good, such as history, particularly Church history, Canon Law and Sacred Scripture; I shall not even include Dogmatic Theology but shall concentrate on Moral Theology alone.

(1) *Knowledge of Moral Theology*

The necessity and importance of an expert knowledge of Moral Theology in a confessor appears clearly from the consideration that it may be called the key of his ministry. Of what advantage would it be for a penitent that his confessor should be the most distinguished linguist in the world, or the greatest historian or writer, or that he should have the most expert knowledge of politics or geography, if he is weak or deficient in the knowledge of Moral Theology? It is not knowledge about profane subjects that the penitent is looking for; what he wants to know for certain is, whether he is in sin or not; whether or not he is bound to do this thing or that; and whether he can, with all confidence, rely on the replies that he receives from the confessor. Which of you would go to consult a doctor or a lawyer, about an infirmity, or a lawsuit if you knew that they were indeed men distinguished in other branches of knowledge, but that they knew very little of medicine or law? I will even say: of what use would it be to the penitent if the confessor was a great dogmatic theologian but knew very little about Moral [Theology]? He is able to confound and convince the incredulous and the heretics, but he is not able to decide with equal clearness and skill what is a sin and what is not.

(2) *This Knowledge Should Be Accurate and Extensive*

There is no need to dwell at further length on this point, because I am convinced that you all agree with me about the necessity of this knowledge in a confessor; but are we all in agreement in the ideas that each of us has about the amount of Moral Theology required? What do those priests think and say about this science who have studied it merely for a few terms, and once for life? And what about those others who boast that in so many years in the ministry they had never need to study, and that they had never found a case that gave them the least difficulty to solve. If you ask these men, they will tell you that the study of Moral Theology is not of great importance, that with a little critical ability and common sense a priest can easily solve any case; that as long as he remembers the general principles, he can go ahead without fear; and that it is not so much the study of theology as the practice that will help him in his ministry. Fine practice that is, to go ahead always, no matter what might be the difficulty of the question at issue! I too know something about what helps a priest in the ministry. But let us leave all such men there, for in order to disillusion them it would not suffice to bring forward reasons; it would be necessary to come to actual facts and make them touch their ignorance with their hand. Speaking among ourselves, I say what those who have made a deep study of Moral Theology— especially those who have continued that study for their whole lives— have always thought and said; I say that the study of Moral Theology is very different from what many priests think it is; I say that it is more vast and extensive than it is believed to be; that a good knowledge of all its branches is most difficult to obtain, and that this study is interminable; and therefore that there is need of more than ordinary time and labor and patience in order to acquire it.

I shall not stop to give you a list of all the volumes and treatises on the subject; I shall merely quote for you the words of the Roman Ritual for the direction of confessors:

"*The priest shall make sure to acquire an accurate knowledge of all the doctrine concerning this Sacrament of Penance; and all other things necessary for its proper administration.*"[2] The confessor must therefore have a knowledge of two things, and not any kind of knowledge, but an accurate knowledge: of all that directly forms the material with which this Sacrament is concerned, and you all know what this is: the nature and necessity; the minister and the subject; integrity, contrition, purpose of amendment, satisfaction; reservation, the sigillum; the qualities and defects of confessors: and then the Roman Ritual adds: "*All other things necessary for its proper administration.*" And what are these "*other things*"? They embrace the whole of Moral Theology as found in these books for the use of priests. And remark that in all these volumes, which are so numerous as to frighten anyone, we have only compendiums of Moral Theology giving the principles and the theory, and that these have to be amplified by the confessor and applied to the individual cases. If therefore you consider Moral Theology in its application, you can say that it is almost inexhaustible, that it is infinite, just as adjuncts and circumstances that can modify individual actions and the judgment to be given on them are infinite; and therefore under this aspect Moral Theology becomes vast, ample, extensive, and limitless, just as the heart and thoughts of man are varied, extensive and limitless. And after all this, who will say that Moral Theology is easy, that it is merely a trifle, a subject of little consequence? To prove the contrary, it should be sufficient to state the fact that moral theologians of indefatigable and continuous study, men of keen intellect and experience, in spite of all their study, find great difficulty in many cases of conscience and have still to spend time in studying and examining them before giving a solution and assuming the responsibility for a reply.

(3) *This Knowledge Must Be Ready for Use*

The confessor must possess all this knowledge, so vast in its principles and so varied in its application, and must have it ready for use at a moment's notice; at most times, the pressure of work on him is so great that he has not the opportunity of thinking calmly, but has to decide and reply on the spur of the moment. A lawyer who has to defend a difficult case or a theologian who has to expound an abstruse and subtle proposition is not in such an embarrassing position as a confessor. These men can study the case, arm themselves as much as they like with information about it, and defend themselves by bringing forward proofs. The confessor, on the contrary, enters the confessional like a soldier on an open battlefield, not knowing from what direction he may be attacked. How often it will happen that in a single morning and even in a single case he will be obliged to run over the vast sea of Moral Theology, as it were, in a flash. The most varied demands will be made on him, the most intricate questions will be put to him on matters both difficult and delicate, and he must grasp them sufficiently, give the necessary solutions, know the principles to be applied and, in the application, must take into account the circumstances of time and place and especially of person; and all this he must do carefully, conscientiously, and with due regard for the consequences. And will this be easy? Will a superficial study hurriedly made, once and never more, suffice? No, it is evident that it will not suffice.

(4) *Necessity of Constant Study*

And here it may be remarked that insufficiency of knowledge in the confessor will become more evident as time goes on than in the beginning of his ministry, for in order that a priest be approved for hearing Confession, he must have done considerable study of Moral Theology, so that at the beginning there will still be a certain fund of knowledge, but once the examinations are passed, he may think no more about Moral Theology. Moral Theology is like a passport for men of this kind: once it is presented, and the frontier crossed, it is regarded as no longer any use, and is either thrown away or kept as a souvenir. They had got a few books on Moral Theology and had studied them hastily; the passport is made out and appears to be in order; for good or evil, they are approved for hearing Confessions, and the frontier is crossed. What further use is there for these troublesome documents? If they do not get lost, they are kept for souvenirs. If you ask one of these men whether he studies Moral Theology he will answer: What Moral Theology? I have been approved for Confessions long ago, and I do not think any more about it. And there are priests who speak thus. Tell me, is there any hope that confessors of this kind will possess the "sufficient and proportionate" knowledge which is both necessary and indispensable? Certainly it is not required that all priests should be equally learned in this matter; the grades of knowledge necessary are measured according to the places where Confessions are heard, for you remember that I said, "sufficient and proportionate knowledge"; I did not say eminent knowledge. But believe me, in order to acquire and preserve that grade of knowledge which is sufficient for the places and persons where the priest is to hear [Confessions], long, serious, and patient study is necessary.

If we wish our studies to yield knowledge that will edify and not puff up, that will help to work out our own salvation and that of others, we should, in the first place, see that they be done with a right intention and that they should tend towards the only end to which all our actions ought to be directed, which is the honor and glory of God. In addition, let us make sure to unite prayer to study, for prayer is the book that can teach us more than all authors. I do not mean by this that we should neglect the human means of which we are bound in duty to make use. These are two: to study the authors, and to consult with priests of knowledge and experience. From the one we shall learn the theory, from the other, the practice; the one and the other are equally necessary. Theory without practice is like a house for which the plans are drawn and nothing more; practice without theory is like a house without foundation or plan, and which will therefore be more of a danger than a shelter.

❖ WHICH AUTHORS ARE TO BE PREFERRED?

And here the question arises: among the many authors and the many different opinions, which authors are to be preferred, and which opinions are to be followed in order to succeed in being good confessors? It is hardly necessary for me to reply to this question, for either the confessor is furnished with that goodness of which I spoke, and in that case he will obtain benefit from any approved author that he consults, because the virtue he possesses will season everything; or he has not this goodness, and in that case it would be useless to speak to him, for whichever author he selects, if he does not do great harm from the use of his books, he certainly will do little good. But if we must speak on the question, I shall give my own opinion and let each one do what he believes to be the best before God: (1) The confessor should respect all good authors: (2) he should make use of all for the good of the penitent. In this way, charity is observed, and the greatest good possible is obtained. It is only the ignorant and the proud who despise the opinions of others. The priest who is learned, humble and good knows what respect he should have for them and what esteem they merit and, when he thinks it right to follow one rather than another, he does not cease to respect all equally.

In the second place, we should be ready to make use of all the authors. The various opinions of theologians—I speak of opinions held in the schools, and not of particular opinions commonly rejected by authors—these various opinions should be for us what the various tools, each put in its own place around a great workshop, are for the craftsman: the craftsman takes this or that tool, according as he needs it for his work and without troubling about who is the maker of it or whether he likes him, he examines and takes the tool which he considers most suitable for the particular work that he is doing. Thus should we do in the great workshop of souls, which is the confessional. We go there to save souls; before us is a great series of theological opinions, like so many instruments to be used in our great work; in making our selection we do not mind who the author is who teaches it or which author pleases us most; we look at and select that opinion which we believe to be most suited to the penitent, when all circumstances are taken into account, and which we think will do him the most good. We hear Confessions in order to prevent the commission of sin; well, let us select that opinion which, in the particular case, seems to us to be most likely to keep our penitent from sin. This is the true way to safeguard the interests of our Master and to show the greatest charity possible to the soul of our neighbor.

But perhaps you will say, are there not some who could not in conscience use such an opinion? I have no intention of entering into controversy or of giving the reasons to convince you, I will merely state: if, in the case, there was any evil in that probable opinion you used, who is to blame for it? The authorities of the Church, who knowing of it, tolerate it, the author who teaches it, or the poor confessor who, with a good intention and in order to save souls, follows it? Let each one pray, and if that does not suffice let him pray again, and he will see that God too will look after his conscience.

---

1 Vita S. Ambros.
2 Rit. Rom. De Sacr. Poenit.

The Way to Hear Confessions

GOODNESS AND KNOWLEDGE are two gifts, two qualities indispensable for the confessor who is to act as judge in the tribunal of Penance, and to administer this Sacrament with fruit. Woe to the imprudent, the presumptuous and the rash who, without the proper equipment of virtue and knowledge, go forward and assume a responsibility so terrible and so dreaded! It is not lawful or permitted to men here below to enter into that mysterious tribunal; the judgment pronounced cannot be touched on earth; a most profound secret, a most sacred and inviolable seal covers and hides everything. But a day will come when all will be made known to the glory of the good confessor and the ignominy and condemnation of the indolent and perverse. I believe that all creation will be amazed at the amount of good done by the good confessor in this ministry; this man who never appeared, whom but few appreciated, perhaps because he disliked doing things that attract applause, and yet such a man was able to do immense good in secret and unknown to the world. How many offenses were spared to the Lord! Oh! how many persons, how many families and perhaps how many countries will speak of him! Who knows how many are indebted to this good man for having saved their honor, and their property and perhaps their life: masters served faithfully, servants treated humanly and with charity, poor relieved, creditors satisfied; and not to make the list too long, it is incredible, I repeat, the good that will come to light, which has been done by a good confessor. But if I speak of the good, I must not be silent about the bad; and I fear that it will also be incredible the amount of good missed as well as the evil caused by a priest who, without the required qualities, intruded himself into so great a ministry.

I   Precautions Necessary

But it is not my intention today to dwell on these reflections; I shall pass on to point out to you the means and the precautions that a confessor should use when he wishes to discharge the duties of so great an office without loss to himself. These means and precautions are many and varied, but I shall restrict myself to recommending two, which are: vigilance over himself, and charity towards the penitents: vigilance over his intentions, vigilance over his senses, vigilance over his conduct; charity towards the penitents, charity in receiving them, charity in disposing them for absolution. This shall form the subject matter for the present conference; it is no less important for us confessors, than for the faithful. Give me good confessors, said a great Pope, and I will give you the whole Church reformed. And I repeat: put a good confessor into a district, and even if he does not convert it all, much time will not pass until you see a great change.

(1) *Vigilance Over Ourselves and Our Motives*

Severe, continuous and never to be omitted vigilance over our motives, over our senses, and over our manner of acting is an absolute requirement in confessors. The motives that should bring us to that sacred tribunal, which should direct our every word, our every act, should be the glory of God above, and the salvation of souls. Everything merely human, everything not upright, everything that does not conduce to these ends must therefore be put aside; all useless conversations, all sensible affections, all show of geniality or sympathy, all human motives such as striving after esteem or temporal advantages must be suppressed. In the confessional, we are Gods and not men; the affairs of God are the only things to be transacted in that place and at that time; every other affair, every other interest must be banished from it, both in order to gain for ourselves the necessary graces and blessings from God—for God does not give His blessings to a work which He sees is not done for Him—and in order that we ourselves may not succumb to the dangers which we have to fear, when we expose ourselves for our own ends and not for the cause of God. For me, it would be sufficient to know that a confessor is motivated by pure zeal, to be tranquil in mind for both himself and his ministry, while, on the contrary, I would fear for him if I saw him go to the confessional only through habit, taste, or the fear of losing his office or of being reproved. This point, my dear Fathers, is of such extreme importance, it is so essential, that we should not be satisfied with forming that right intention on a few rare occasions, but should renew it as often as possible. Every time that we go to the confessional and at the time we are actually engaged in hearing Confessions, let us remember to renew our pact with God and say to Him: "O Lord, for Thee I go, for Thee I speak, for Thee I remain, for Thee I labor; if other motives present themselves to my mind I will not be swayed by them; either I labor for Thee and only for Thee or I leave this place." Oh, what merits, what happy days, what hidden treasures when one labors for the Lord with this intention!

(2) *Vigilance Over Our Senses:*

(a) OVER THE EYES

In the second place, vigilance over our senses means custody of our eyes, of our ears and of our tongue. How unbecoming it is to see a priest on entering the confessional looking from right to left, fixing his eyes on the people as if to know who they are. This is dangerous for ourselves, uncomfortable for the penitents and a cause of scandal for all. And in the confessional itself when the Confessions are being heard, is there not perhaps still need to keep a guard on our eyes, so as not to place an occasion for levity and curiosity and, what is worse, expose ourselves to ruin while we are offering medicine of salvation to others? God grant that priests may not learn to their cost and pay very dearly for want of vigilance in the confessional.

(b) OVER THE HEARING

With regard to vigilance over our hearing, there is need of much continuous care in order to see that the penitents do not bring in useless, extraneous matter that does not belong to the object of Confession, and especially in order not to allow them to open wounds in a way that is inconvenient and dangerous for the confessor. Many times, penitents do not know how to express themselves decorously in accusing themselves of certain sins of the flesh or in asking advice about these matters, and, either through ignorance or want of modesty, they use terms and adopt language not in keeping either with the Church or the confessional, to their own danger and confusion, as well as that of the confessor. Should a confessor keep silent and listen in such cases? Certainly not. We must be careful about this point for we hear penitents reply too often when corrected; I have always expressed myself in this manner, and no one has ever corrected me. Perhaps the confessor in order to understand the matter clearly may listen to penitents expressing themselves in this way? Far from it; for it is one thing to find out, and to find out clearly, what we must know in order to give our judgment, quite another thing is the manner of procuring this information. As soon as we notice that the penitent does not know how to express himself without making use of the unbecoming expressions referred to, we should stop him and tell him to confine himself to replying to the questions we put him; by a few dexterous questions we will be able to get all information necessary to form our judgment. Let us be careful therefore about this point. I have always found the manner I suggest to be a great help and a great relief to penitents; besides, the holiness of the place and of the Sacrament that we are administering requires this reserve.

(c) VIGILANCE OVER THE TONGUE

After vigilance over our hearing, comes vigilance and restraint over our tongue, so as to speak only when and in what form the good of souls requires. And here I remark that to say that such a confessor is one who knows how to restrain and guard his tongue is the same as to say that he is a cautious and prudent confessor.

❖ GREAT PRUDENCE IS REQUIRED

Now to be convinced that prudence is required in a confessor, it is sufficient to consider what Confession is, and what are the acts that a confessor must exercise in the confessional.

(1) *Because the Tribunal of Penance is a Species of Government*

Confession, on the part of the priest, is a kind of government; a spiritual and internal government of souls. This government is both particular and universal: it applies to every individual, and extends to all the faithful: its function is to conduct them to eternal salvation. It is an office therefore that requires in the priest a prudence almost divine. It has always been the opinion of the sages that the government of others is a most difficult office; more difficult still is the government of souls, and in the government of souls, the most difficult part is that which regards the interior. The exterior government of souls which is exercised by religious superiors has its limits and its regulations, the observance of which certainly presents its difficulties. The interior government extends to the whole man, and is concerned with laying down regulations for all his powers, his passions, his inclinations, his affections, all of which can be so many and so varied as to border on the infinite. It therefore requires in the confessor a prudence equal to the difficulties, if he is to discharge the duties of his office with fruit. Now would that priest be considered prudent, with a prudence equal to the difficulties of a confessor, who does not possess an absolute mastery over his tongue and who is not accustomed to watch attentively over his speech.

(2) *A Most Difficult Form of Government*

Let us consider for a moment the duties that the confessor must perform. Placed, as he is, at the head of that government, many are the acts he must perform and the parts he must play in the discharge of his office: he must listen, interrogate, reply, instruct, arouse, calm, absolve or refuse absolution. A word too many or a word too few, one term used rather than another in all these roles, in the series of these actions, may lose or win the case, may alienate or gain a soul, may move to compunction or irritate a penitent; all which things we know from experience. And to talk only of the interrogations, what vigilance and attention must we not use in order not to expose ourselves and the penitents to the danger of scandal, and the Sacrament and the holy place to profanation! How necessary it is to measure our terms, to balance our words, to use every care in interrogating certain persons, especially in the more difficult and delicate matters! These are things on which there is no need to dwell, for they are evident and have been confirmed by experience everywhere.

✣ THE OBLIGATION OF THE SIGILLUM

I shall add just one recommendation on this question of control of the tongue, and it is to be very careful never to speak of what one has heard in Confession. At first sight, it might appear that this recommendation to a Confessor about secrecy is superfluous, because everything is buried beneath the sacred sigillum. However, without perhaps knowing or thinking of it, priests more than once have left themselves open to blame in this matter. There are three cases in which, according to the teaching of all theologians, a confessor may not speak of what has been matter for Confession: (1) when there is danger of direct or indirect revelation; (2) when the penitent, even though there is no danger of discovery, will not consent to allow it. So far I am sure that the secrets of the confessional are kept by all. But there is a *third* case (3) in which we are bound to keep silent about things heard in the confessional, and it is: that if in speaking of these things there may be some scandal given, and this is the point in which confessors may more easily fail. The danger of scandal is present on every single occasion that lay people become aware that we confessors, whether we are talking among ourselves or with them, whenever we speak of anything that we have heard in the confessional, even though it be so long before, or the place be so distant that there is no danger of revealing. We should be therefore most careful about this point which is so very delicate and important.

✣ VIGILANCE OVER OUR MANNER OF
HEARING CONFESSIONS

Finally, we should exercise vigilance over our conduct, that is over the manner in which we behave when hearing Confessions. This vigilance, extends to every part of this ministry, to every duty that concerns a confessor. It consists in thinking over often and examining in our own minds the omissions, the defects, the faults to which even a good confessor is subject in the administration of this Sacrament, in order that a defect in connection with one Confession may not pass on to the next. To obviate this, I would suggest that when thanking the Lord after hearing Confessions we make a brief examination. I do not say that we should go over the things heard, for such would at times be more harmful than useful, but rather that we should make a review of the manner of dealing with, correcting and instructing the penitents. The effects obtained or the difficulties encountered may serve to guide us in other cases. Such a passing examination can even be made between one Confession and another without the penitents noticing it; a thought, a hurried reflection may be sufficient to put us on our guard for the subsequent Confessions.

II Charity Towards Penitents

The most extensive field, the immense space, in which the confessor must excel and shine is charity. This virtue is so closely connected with a confessor that his office is properly called the office of charity. The charity displayed in the fulfillment of this office has always been compared by the Fathers to the help which the Good Samaritan gave to the man travelling from Jericho who was attacked by robbers, despoiled of his clothes, wounded, and left half dead on the road; the traveller being a figure of the poor sinner. If many qualities are needed in a confessor in order to deal successfully with penitents, he needs charity above all. This is so true that the penitents themselves when they present themselves for Confession have the habit of saying: Father, do me the charity of hearing me, of helping me! And they are not mistaken, for if they find charity, they will find all that they can have need of, just as the wounded traveller on the road from Jericho found in the charity of the Good Samaritan all that he had need of. He found wine, bandages for his wounds, oil, a horse to carry him, and an inn; in a word, he found complete hospital treatment. The other two, the Priest and the Levite, although they were in all probability more cultured, more learned, more esteemed and richer, yet, because they had not charity, they were for that wretched man just as if they did not exist. The same thing may be said of every confessor who has not charity. The priest who is devoid of this beautiful virtue will do little good in whatever branch of the ministry he may select and, least of all, in the confessional.

There are three principal points in which the charity of the confessor makes itself known and shines forth: in receiving the penitents, in hearing them, and in disposing them for absolution.

(1) *Charity in Receiving Penitents*

In the first place, charity will make him always disposed to welcome the penitents, always ready to go to hear them when he is requested, just as the eager and solicitous servant goes where the voice of his master calls him; no time whether day or night, no place however distant being excepted. He is ready in the church, in his house, everywhere, he is ever at the beck and call of those who need him. How those poor penitents are to be pitied who wait there hour after hour, who ask, ask again, and yet the priest does not appear! They might be expected to have patience if he was occupied in some other work for the Lord, but it sometimes happens that the reason why he does not go is just some whim; to have a sleep, to talk and jest with others, or to occupy himself with some business that does not belong to his ministry. And what can be expected from such a confessor who shows so little charity before he begins at all? Will he know how to bear with the penitents, to be compassionate, to use patience and good temper in reasoning with them and persuading them? Will he be willing to make every effort to satisfy them, to gain their hearts by his charitable manner, to influence them to the point of gaining them over then and there, or at least of having hopes of gaining them later on? It is impossible, my dear Fathers, and unfortunate are the penitents who meet a confessor of that kind. "Oh, if I had had better fortune," said a penitent, lamenting on his deathbed, "I would not have committed so many sins, I would not have led the life which alas, I have led!" He was alluding to the harsh words used by a confessor to him many years previously.

The first and principal way of manifesting our charity to the penitent who presents himself is to show the most benign manner and use the kindest words in order to lighten the burden on his heart. This may appear to be a very easy thing to practice; but to do it always, without distinction, with every kind of person, when the confessor is already tired, annoyed, with his head occupied with many troubles, when he is in poor health, with headaches, it is not so easy as one might think. And how often on such occasions, a hasty word or a sign of irritation that escapes from the poor confessor, may have fatal consequences, as is alas, seen from experience! The penitent knows nothing about our state of exhaustion, about our ailments, our likes and dislikes; accordingly, a slip of the confessor in such circumstances may convey a bad, or at least an unfavorable idea of the confessor and even of Confession itself. In addition to this, the devil, who wages relentless warfare against this Sacrament because it snatches so many souls from his grasp, is ingenious to use every occasion to drive as many souls as he can away from it. The charity about which we speak will therefore be a remedy against such dangers, for through it those who approach the sacred tribunal will find it to be what it is in reality, a tribunal of mercy and charity. "Courage," the charitable confessor will say to the penitent, "this time we will finish with the devil! What a grand opportunity! With a word you will be able to purchase Heaven! Oh, if you had only come a little sooner! However, if you come a few times, you will see what tranquil days you will have, and how light-heartedly you will live. So then, courage! I repeat, if you do just a little, I will do the rest, and the Lord will do most of all. Look around at all that is best in Heaven and on earth; all that will be yours, if you only give up sin: quiet and peace of mind, the blessing of the Lord, His grace, a holy life and a happy death, and in the end, Heaven, provided you abandon sin." With such sentiments, zealous and charitable confessors are accustomed to welcome poor sinners. Such has always been the practice of the Saints, and of apostolic men who have done so much good by means of this Sacrament. St. Francis de Sales was accustomed to say to most perverse sinners: "Do not make any distinction between me and you." St. Francis Xavier embraced his penitents tenderly and bathed them with tears. St. Philip Neri could not contain his delight and joy when he saw certain penitents before him that he had not seen for some time.

I know that in welcoming certain penitents we must abstain from expressing friendship, and that we must measure our words, but charity will find a means of fulfilling one duty without transgressing against a greater one. It may well happen that a confessor has not time or strength to hear an additional person; but in that case we must be well on our guard not to incur a loss that would be very painful for us, because very often when we are finishing at a late hour a person will come along who has just had a long struggle with the devil in order to come. In these circumstances let us receive the person in a friendly manner, to do which, neither much time nor energy will be required. When we cannot hear him immediately, in order to make sure of him, let us fix a time for him to return. If we show ourselves friendly and charitable at the first meeting, we can be sure that he will return.

The following then are ways in which our charity will be shown in welcoming penitents: (1) by giving our services to hear them with great promptness and good will; (2) by welcoming all equally without any distinction. I would however give permission to make an exception in favor of one class, and it is that he should confess the men before the women. A lady was complaining much because a certain confessor gave the preference to men. When asked by the confessor whether he was doing right, and whether she would advise him to do otherwise, she replied that he was doing right and excused her complaint as being due to irritation; (3) by making sure to use some words of encouragement, when the penitents present themselves, gravely indeed, but sweetly and benignly so that the penitent will know that we take their case to heart.

(2) *Charity in Hearing the Penitents*

The second act in which the charity of the confessor is to be shown is in the hearing of the penitents. Among these, some are ignorant, rude, coarse-mannered, dull penitents who do not understand; others want to show off all they know and appear to have come rather to dictate the law than receive it, while perhaps they know less than the first class. There are others who are oppressed with fear or uneasiness; who are suffering and are unwilling to be calmed; others are hardened, obstinate, tenacious, who are reluctant to yield; others are prolix, wearisome, minute in their explanations, who would weary a person to death; others are so sparing of their words that it is difficult to get anything out of them; others contradict themselves, or repeat; others are eager, vivacious, ready to get heated over a word; others, on the contrary, are languid, phlegmatic, cold, and it would take an earthquake to move them. How will the confessor manage to deal with all these? Charity will provide the means of being all things to all men, in order to gain them all for the Lord. *I became all things to all men, that I might save all,*[1] said St. Paul. The confessor will be able to find in his charity means to appease and to satisfy all, because he will speak or keep silent, evade or reply, be eager or slow, yielding or firm according to the circumstances, the dispositions and the characters; but the confessor will not succeed in doing all this unless he has a great fund of charity. Even to insults in the confessional, the confessor must not oppose any other defense but charity.

But you will ask me, cannot a confessor sometimes speak with a tone of authority, and even with a little asperity? I reply: he must speak always with gravity, and as briefly as possible, many times with immovable firmness, but never with asperity or harshness. Rough manners in dealing with and speaking to the penitent must be discarded completely by the confessor. He must be long-suffering and charitable with all, even in circumstances naturally disgusting, as when he has to attend sick people in the midst of dirt and fetid odors. A rough word or gesture is sometimes enough to close the door, to take away confidence and cause perhaps an irreparable loss. One day a confessor was called to attend a dying man; when he came to the bedside the sick man tried to take his hand and press it in sign of confidence (note that it was a man, not a woman, for with a woman he might have acted differently). The confessor took the hand reluctantly, and immediately afterwards tried dexterously to wipe his own hands in the sheets of the bed. The sick man noticed it, and that alone was sufficient to make him refuse to go to Confession. You will ask me, is a confessor bound to show extraordinary signs of friendship? And is there not sometimes danger? I do not raise the question whether there is an obligation: I say simply that a confessor who had a proper fund of charity, rather than alienate a penitent by displeasing him, would have acted with good nature and courtesy, and would have allowed the Lord to dispose of his life as He wishes, for it is the business of the Lord to preserve the life of His priests who act with this spirit.

How irksome then it must be for penitents to see a confessor who gets impatient, who is pained, who suffers in hearing, and hardly allows himself to breathe, such is the haste and eagerness with which he tries to finish the case. Indeed, it is so great that sometimes the penitents themselves are forced to say to the confessor: "Have patience, the Lord will repay you, but just give me a little time to open my heart and unburden my conscience." Thus pupil and master exchange places, and the patience and charity which the confessor does not possess, are found in the penitent. Naturally, I am speaking of these cases in which there is a need, an advantage to allow the penitents to speak, otherwise it might be misplaced charity to permit it.

Charity is also required in the confessor in order not to allow his penitents to be aware that he sees the defects in their manner of confessing. There are many who jump from one thing to another, and introduce details and stories that have nothing to do with Confession. Well, even in these cases in which most of the penitents will act thus through ignorance, instead of reproving them and shouting at them, as if they did not know how to make their Confession—as indeed may be true—the confessor should act as if he did not see the defects and, with charity and dexterity, show them the proper way to make their Confession by instructing them, taking care, however, not to offend them. Our charity therefore in hearing Confession should be shown by adapting our method to the needs and capabilities of each penitent, so that each of them will find in his Confession a motive, an incitement to return again.

(3) *Charity in Disposing Penitents for Absolution*

The last exercise of charity and zeal in the confessor consists in disposing the penitents for absolution; and because it is the last it should be the most conspicuous. I distinguish four kinds of penitents in connection with the object about which we are speaking. The first are the good who present themselves already penitent and fully disposed; the second are those who are not disposed, but who will allow themselves to be disposed; the third are those who cannot be disposed immediately, but who give hope that they will be disposed the next time; the last are those with whom we can do nothing and for whom we have little hope of doing anything afterwards. I do not intend to make this a conference in Moral Theology to consider whether these can be absolved, when they can, what rules and methods are to be prescribed for dealing with them, and what we must insist on to make sure that they are disposed. I leave all that aside, and I shall consider solely what is the office of charity that the confessor must fulfill with each of these four classes.

With the first class the question is easily dealt with; we have only to rejoice with them, animate them to greater efforts, and secure that these not only leave sin but that they strive to cultivate virtue and reach perfection; we should show them the way to sanctify themselves in their state of life, a question that we have already considered, and it will be seen in how many cases this class of penitent provides a fruitful soil for whatever hand cultivates it.

Let us pass on to those who present themselves indisposed: how are we to deal with them? Are we to tell them to go away and dispose themselves and then return another time? That appears to be what is done by a number of confessors; but will these penitents return? And if they do return, will time have given them the dispositions that they had not on the first occasion? It is doubtful, and in that case, must the confessor tell them to go away and return a third time? And then will we be at the end of it? But what should be done? Is there not an obligation on the confessor when dealing with such penitents to try every means to dispose them and to convert them before sending them away? I believe that there is. For how could it be that charity would not oblige a person to speak, to succor his neighbor when he finds him on the brink of ruin and perdition, if he could easily do so? If a person may keep silent in such cases I do not know in what other case he would be bound to speak. But a person may object: the necessity of these penitents is voluntary, therefore they should be able to get themselves out of it and repent of themselves. Even though that be true, I say that it does not take away the obligation in charity according to which a person is bound to correct one's neighbor in sin; and sin is, as you know, always voluntary in the person. The objection may be urged that the confessor does not know whether the penitent will listen to him. Well, he should make the experiment, all the more so, because the fact that the penitent comes of his own accord is a good indication; and in any case, it is the best opportunity that could be found to try to gain our brother. But what means are we to use, how are we to proceed in our effort to dispose him? When the confessor has the requisite qualities, when he is good, learned and, above all, filled with charity, he will find the appropriate means to assist him in the attempt to save the penitent. It will not be necessary to deliver a long discourse, which might only have the effect of irritating the penitent. Instead, his remarks should be like sparks of fire; brief remarks on the unhappy life that the penitent is leading, the monster of evil that sin is, the uncertainty of life, the remorse and sorrow he will one day experience if he loses this chance, on how easy it is to amend one's life, on the peace and happiness he will acquire in this life, and the glory in Heaven that he can regard as his if he repents. One or other of these thoughts may easily induce him to make up his mind.

But if the penitent cannot get so far as to be disposed here and now but gives us hopes of coming to better sentiments later on, and if he makes known his willingness to present himself again, either to us or to some other confessor, it only remains for us to do all in our power to ensure that he will return by making the most attracting and alluring promises: by assuring him that we are always at his service; that we will give him the choice of any time he prefers, and that we will do everything possible for him, almost even to making ourselves responsible for him. There should be no threats, but we should make the obligations and penances imposed as light as possible; and we should do all this with the greatest kindness possible, showing that we are sorry that we cannot on the present occasion gratify his desire and our own of putting him in the grace of God.

But what are we to say, what are we to do, when we have at our feet that class of penitent who on no account will consent to listen to reason, and who remain hard and obdurate against the most extreme efforts of charity even to the extent of saying that they are resigned to go to Hell rather than abandon sin, for the pleasure of enjoying what they want in this world? It would appear that the reason of this obduracy is that these penitents regard their case as desperate; if this be not the reason, then it may be that they presumptuously rely on that great Mercy which wishes all men to be saved, and which exercises so much patience and waits so long because it does not wish to punish. Let the priest who is appointed to be the representative, to act the part of this great Mercy, make a last effort, and seek in his charity a thought to give these penitents a last thread of hope. Let him say: My son, we shall perhaps never see one another again in this world, but we shall meet in the next. If you are satisfied, I shall always pray for you, whether I am alive or dead. You are unhappy, my son, because you have had bad luck today; if you had met a better confessor, you would now have been penitent, you would have been pardoned and would be safe; whereas you are on the brink of Hell. And how do you know what may happen to you tomorrow? Pray to God that He may pardon me, and that I may not soon have to render an account for you. I shall die soon. Pray for me that I may be saved, so that when I get to Heaven, I may do as much for you, and that one day I may see you also arrive there. Sometimes a reflection of this kind will suffice without anything else to dispose a penitent, and to conquer a fortress that appeared to be impregnable. But let us suppose the worst; that the penitent goes away without leaving us hope of any sort. We do not know what the Lord may work in him later on through one of such thoughts; perhaps He may deign to crown so pious an outburst of charity of His minister by granting salvation to that soul for which he has labored so much! If it does nothing else it will always serve as an additional proof to justify that Infinite Mercy which, together with Its minister, wished to save that man, and if he is lost, he alone is the cause; by himself he has caused his own ruin.

These are then, my dear Fathers, the characteristics of a true minister of God in the confessional: he should be good with no ordinary or common goodness; he should be equipped with sufficient knowledge and doctrine; he should be attentive and vigilant over himself and his ministry, but above all, he should be filled with patience and charity: charity in welcoming the penitent, charity in hearing them, charity in disposing them; charity in fine, that is benign, solicitous, industrious, which seeks and tries by every means to prevent offenses against God and, if possible, save all sinners. Oh, would that God might send many of these workmen into this mystical vineyard! Let us pray that He may send them to all those countries and peoples that are groaning under the weight of innumerable needs and dangers, and let us, my dear Fathers, do all in our power to correspond with so lofty a vocation, so that, as worthy ministers of the Sanctuary, we may be able to save many souls in the exercise of our ministry, and may one day enter along with them to share in those festivities, in those triumphs, which await us in the eternal kingdom of Heaven. Amen.

---

1 1 Cor. 9:22.

The Priest Devoted to Mary

*I*T would be a great omission and at the same time a grave want of duty in a family, if the sons, when about to leave and separate did not invite their mother to be present among them and if each one, filled with that affection that is proper in a son, did not vie with the others in showing his most ardent love, his most lively gratitude and his acknowledgment of his obligations towards her. Forgetfulness to do so on the part of the sons would be regarded as hardness of heart, ingratitude, or at very least, inexplicable thoughtlessness. I leave you to imagine what sorrow, what a painful wound, such an unexpected parting, such a want of delicacy and affection would cause in the mother's heart. Such it would be for us, sons, and in a certain manner for our good Mother, around whom we have been gathered as one family during these holy days, if we departed today without saying a word to her, without bidding her adieu, without saluting her and thanking her for all that she has done for us. In order then to fulfill so sacred and sweet a duty, I call her this evening, I invite her in the name of us all, to descend and remain among us, in order that she may deign to accept our most respectful salutation and to strengthen us with the assurance of her efficacious protection, so that we may one day be able to pay her our homage in person in the dear land of Paradise.

It is impossible to imagine a good, docile, obedient and respectful son, a son who is a consolation and help in a house, without being at the same time truly affectionate towards his own mother, because this may be said to be what characterizes a good son and gives the clearest indication of all his virtues. If you see that a son is all heart, all love for his mother, ready to make any sacrifice to please her, and resolved not to give her the least displeasure for all the gold in the world, I am sure that without any further inquiry or investigation you will conclude immediately that he is a rare and virtuous son. The same can, it appears to me, be said in our case; and it has been said repeatedly by many others. Not only would it be a rare and difficult thing, but it would be almost impossible to imagine a good, virtuous, devoted priest, a priest who serves God, the Church and souls, without a tender affection for this beloved Mother; a priest who, according as this love goes on increasing in him, will at the same time make progress in the whole series of the other virtues, becoming more detached from the world, more zealous, patient, humble and pure. Therefore, whenever you happen to hear of a priest who is devoted to Mary, you need not enquire further, you may be sure then he cannot be otherwise than good, and perhaps of rare goodness too; but if, on the contrary, you come to know that a priest is cold and insensible in affection towards this Mother and to the sound of her name, you need not hope for much from him, for if he has not much affection for the Mother, he will not have much love for the Son, or much zeal for His glory, or for the salvation of souls. From this each one can see the obligation, the propriety, the importance and the necessity of speaking on this subject.

We shall therefore dwell this evening on this most sweet and consoling subject: on Mary, the most tender of mothers, the friend, the companion, the guide and confidant of the priest. And in order to know better and to savor with you this sweet and important material, I shall divide it into two parts: in the first, we shall seek to find out who among priests are those who are devoted to Mary; and in the second, we shall see how happy and blessed the priest is who is truly devoted to Mary. It gives me great pleasure to speak of this great Lady; for what son does not take pleasure in, does not delight in speaking of his mother? My only grief is that my words are not equal to the merits and the heart of this Mother. Do you, my dear Fathers, supply for my want by adding your love and pious devotion, so that when concluding this retreat, I may not have to reproach myself with having rather obscured than exalted and amplified the honor and glory of a Mother to whom I protest myself a debtor for all that I have received, or hope to receive from the Lord in time or eternity.

✣ First Condition for True Devotion to Mary: An Exalted Idea of Her Greatness

An essential condition which is required, and which forms the first step the priest must take in order to become truly devoted to Mary is that he should seek and endeavor to conceive and form for himself the most sublime and exalted idea possible of this great Mother, for it is impossible for a person to have a truly great affection for another without having also a great esteem.

✣ The Devotion of the Laity to Mary

Among the simple faithful are found many times good souls who have such an exalted idea of Mary that they experience towards her the greatest possible transport of devotion and fervor imaginable. For them, Mary is an object to which nothing can stand comparison, to which everything in creation is inferior. They know well that God is above everything, but as if not daring to treat with Him about domestic matters they turn their eyes to Mary and they attribute to her all that is great, beautiful, amiable and holy that they are able to express or imagine; from this comes the transport of lively warmhearted affections towards her, the promptness and confidence with which they have recourse to her in every trouble and difficulty; from this source comes the eagerness and joy to celebrate all her feasts, to take part in all the practices that redound to her honor and glory.

✣ The Priest's Devotion to Mary Should Exceed that of the Laity

If such is the case with the simple faithful, what should be the esteem and veneration of Mary by the priest who is the first and most beloved of her children? Is the disciple to be superior to the master, will the priest have to learn from the laity, the first born from the youngest children? That must not be, my dear Fathers; it would be too humiliating a position, too opprobrious for a son of honor and character, such as the priest should be towards Mary, to be thus outdone by the laity. But what in the simple faithful is the fruit of pure faith and filial affection, must be in us priests something more; it must be the effect and the fruit of intimate and sincere conviction, so that our appreciation and esteem of Mary will not only make ourselves devoted and affectionate to her, but will put us in a position to confirm and strengthen in that devotion those who have it already, to inspire with it those who do not possess it; and, if occasion should arise, to uphold it and defend it against the ignorant and the proud who may scorn it or hold it up to ridicule or mockery. We have in the prayer of the great servant of Mary, St. Alphonsus Liguori, the first requisite of true devotion to Mary: "*I pray Thee my Lady, that I may have true knowledge worthy of Thee.*" This is the first step the priest must take towards acquiring this devotion: to conceive lofty sentiments worthy of her, *De te vera et digna sapiam*, and to make his words and deeds conformable to his sentiments: *Vera et digna loquar, vera et digna diligam.*[1]

✣ The Exalted Dignity of Mary

It is not given to us to grasp here below who Mary is or to comprehend the loftiness of her vocation, the sublimity of her state, the eminent degree of her virtue, the greatness of her glory, the power of her arm. It would be necessary to know who God is, in order to know what God has operated in Mary. This great Lady is a mystery, and God alone who was the Author of her can comprehend her and praise her in a worthy manner: *Deus solus potest illam pro meritis laudare, qui mira . . . . fecit in illa.* Let it suffice to say that, outside God Himself, there is not either on earth, or in Heaven, either among men, or among Saints, either among the Angels or the Seraphim, a being who, in greatness, power, prerogatives, virtue and merit, I will not say surpasses her, but even equals her or comes near her. She is so great that the great Doctor, St. Bonaventure, goes as far as to say that not even God could go further and make her greater: *Majorem mundum, facere potest Deus, majus coelum, majorem matrem quam Matrem Dei non posset facere.*[2] He gives the following reason for this: the position of Mother is relative to the quality of son, and hence to have a greater mother we should have a greater son, which in the case of Mary is not only impossible, but intrinsically repugnant: *Sicut nec major inter filios nasci potuit, sic nec major inter matres esse potest* (ibid). The Angelic Doctor, the most severe critic of all inaccurate expressions, confirms this when he says: "The Blessed Virgin, from the fact that she is Mother of God, has a certain infinite dignity from the Infinite Good which God is; and from this aspect nothing greater can be made." *B. Virgo ex hoc quod est Mater Dei, habet quamdam dignitatem infinitam ex bono infinito quod est Deus; et ex hoc parte non potest aliquid fieri melius.*[3]

This quality of Mother of God it was that inspired those prophecies and figures by which she was foreshadowed and delineated by the Prophets; this was what inspired the praises and eulogies with which the Fathers and Doctors of all ages exalted and magnified her; this was the origin of all those eminent and glorious titles and names with which the Church invokes her and proposes her for the devotion of the faithful; this, in fine, is the foundation for all the manifestations of honor and homage which peoples of all countries and all ages have vied with one another in offering to this great Mother. And will the priest, the first born among her children, be the only one to stand idle and unconcerned in the midst of such manifestations of heartfelt affection? Will the priest be the only one to stand looking an coldly and indifferently to this rivalry of the people without doing anything himself? Such an attitude, my dear Fathers, would be too opprobrious for a son, and too painful for a mother. The name, the sight, the thought of this Mother should be for us, after God, the object of all our esteem and veneration, the focus of all our attention. So long as we are here below, it will not be given to us to arrive at understanding the greatness of Mary; only when we go to Heaven, shall we see and study and admire this wonder of divine power, this mystical ark of infinite wisdom. But in the meantime, till we get there, let us raise our voices in unison with that of our Mother to praise and glorify God who has been pleased to exalt her so much: *Magnificat anima mea Dominum . . . . Quia fecit mihi magna qui potens est.*[4]

✤ The Portrait of a Priest Devoted to Mary

When the priest has succeeded in forming for himself this kind of idea, this concept of Mary, it will be easy for him to become devoted to her. Oh, what great things I promise myself, I hope for and expect from the priest whose heart is full of love for this great Mother! How happy and fruitful his life will be when it is spent under the care and affection of this tender Mother! There will be no one more content than this son, no one more joyous, more confident, more generous, more loving than he. Have you not often observed how a child behaves with its mother? When the mother is present, and especially when she has the child in her arms, it is brave and confident, it laughs and plays; whom could you find more joyful, more talkative, more courageous than it? But suppose the mother goes away and is hidden from its view; as soon as it notices it and looking round is no longer able to see her, it suddenly stops its childish prattle and becomes sad, melancholic, timid, afraid; everything alarms it, everything terrifies it; by its whole appearance, but more by its cries and tears, it will tell you how unhappy it is, that nothing will satisfy it, that everything makes it sad. And why? Because its mother cannot be seen. But if you pass from that contentment and courage which the presence of the mother gives the child to the way that it behaves towards her, you will be witness of the most tender caresses which, though childish, are most expressive and significant. What looks, what impetuous attempts to leap for joy, what embraces! Everything speaks eloquently of a loving and affectionate heart; if anyone else speaks, the child will give no sign that it gives it any pleasure, but if the mother speaks you will see, if not by its words, at least by its gestures and smiles, the pleasure it takes in it. You have, my dear Fathers, in these few reflections the portrait of the priest devoted to Mary; for the priest devoted to this tender Mother becomes simple and innocent like a little child. Mary, after God, is everything for him, and there is nothing else that consoles him, contents him, restrains him, sustains him so much as the thought of and affection for this good Mother.

The first priests, the Apostles, were very fortunate, and we cannot help experiencing a certain praiseworthy envy at their happy lot of being able to see Mary, to speak to her, to live with her and to pray with her. Now, the priest who is devoted to this good Mother, and, like another Jesus, lives subject to her, obedient and affectionate, in strict truth is not far away from the happy lot of the Apostles. He can be said to live with her, he shares his fears and his hopes with her; with her he makes his plans for his undertakings and his labors; in fine, this son belongs to Mary entirely, and appears to have no other life outside of her: whether he thinks or speaks or works, all is for her.

✧ THE PRIEST DEVOTED TO MARY WILL SPEAK AND
THINK OFTEN OF HER

When a person loves it is natural that he should think of the object loved, that he should speak often of it and with pleasure; that he should study the way to see it and to enjoy its presence as much as possible. It is a kind of love unheard of, to love a person and at the same time to avoid that person's company and conversation: *Inaudita dilectio qua amicum diligit et praesentiam eius non amat.* Language is the most ordinary way of expressing the sentiments of the heart. Observe a person who is passionately fond of riches, of hunting, of certain games, of travelling etc. The way and the frequency with which he speaks of what he prefers, the knowledge and skill that he displays in speaking of it reveal to us at once the passion that dominates him. Do you wish then to know whether a certain priest is much or little devoted to Mary? Observe his manner, observe the sensations he expresses when he looks at an image of Mary, when he speaks of her, or hears others speak of her; penetrate, if you can, into his mind and heart to perceive the tenderness of his affection towards her. If in the course of the day, he turns often to Mary; if in the difficulties and vicissitudes of this life he puts his trust in her help; if in the exercise of his ministry, in the pulpit, in the confessional, in his familiar discourses, he is ingenious in seizing the least occasion, and is most dexterous in speaking of her, and if it is evident that this is not done artfully or by an effort, but naturally and joyfully, and even with transports of delight; if, I say, such effects result, then you may conclude that he is a true son of Mary. On the other hand, a dry cold manner of speaking of her is not a good sign; a priest may say nice things and even amazing things, but the most necessary thing is wanting: there is wanting that warmth, that heartfelt affection which is the characteristic of the lover; in a word, he does not speak as a son. Imagine to yourselves a son full of affection for his mother and imagine what he says about her; put these same words on the lips of anyone else; materially, there will be no difference; the same terms will be used in praising and extolling her, but you will see a great difference; in the language of the first you will see a different force, a different unction, and you will experience a different impression; the reason for the difference is that one is a son, the other is not; one loves, the other is cold and indifferent.

Consider the writings and the lives of the Saints of all times, such as St. John Damascene, St. Cyril, St. Bernard, St. Thomas, and in later times St. Alphonsus; ponder over the way they wrote and spoke of Mary; what words inflamed with love they used, what beautiful ideas they expressed, what eagerness and joy they showed in praising and exalting her; is there any need to ask whether these Saints loved Mary and were devoted to her? Anyone will be persuaded and convinced that such language could only come from a heart that feels, from a soul that loves. All over the world innumerable good and holy souls, even among the simple and unlettered, have given proof of the same devotion to Mary. If you ask them are you fond of Mary? Do you love this good Mother? You may be sure that they will be all eagerness to satisfy you, and that they will say with emotion: And why not be fond of her? How would it be possible not to love her? Ah! I only wish to know what I could do to love her more; if I knew it, I would do it at any cost. Thus those who are truly devoted to Mary feel, and thus they speak; can we say as much of the priest, this beloved eldest son nearest to the heart of this Mother?

✥ He Will Take Care Not to Offend Her

Other indications of devotion to Mary, which are at the same time indispensable conditions that the priest can be truly said to belong to her, are these: that he take care not to offend her, and that he endeavor to imitate her Divine Son. In the first place he must take good care not to offend her, not to displease her, and that not only in matters amounting to grave sin which, as all can see, is incompatible with even an ordinary or common love, but also in small light matters. Between two people who love one another in such a way that they only stop short of not hating each other, of being outright enemies, small offenses, slight displeasures are not noticed very much. But between two hearts that love each other truly, between two persons who profess to love each other, even small acts of discourtesy are regarded as a great evil: an inopportune joke, a hasty word, a careless act, a want in showing esteem, may sometimes give rise to trouble, to unpleasantness, to coldness and suspicion. What would you say of a son who, in his conduct towards his own mother, just stopped short of not offending her gravely, but was completely indifferent about smaller offenses because they did not make her weep or die of sorrow? If you were to say to such a son: Look here, my dear man, don't you know that what you are doing displeases your mother, disturbs her mind and makes her uneasy, afflicts her and makes her spend her days in sadness and gloom? And if you were to get the reply: what does that matter to me? As long as what I am doing does not afflict her so far as to cause her death, it is sufficient for me, and I don't want any more. What would I say of such a man? Well, that is a picture of a priest who cares little about offending Mary in small matters: he knows that these jests, that light conduct, that want of guard in looking and speaking, although they do not amount to mortal sin, nevertheless cannot be pleasing to this Mother of purity and candor; he knows that they disgust her, that they afflict her, all the more because they come from the priest, her son of predilection; nevertheless, he will not abstain from doing them, he even beguiles himself and soothes his conscience by saying: it is not serious, it does not amount to a mortal sin. Ah, my dear Fathers, if that were true of any of us, it would be useless for us to pretend; we would be very far from being true and devoted sons of Mary.

O priest who aspires to become a true son of Mary, I give you as a rule to guide you that you have this thought ever present in your mind: never do anything that your heart tells you is displeasing to Mary; and in addition, never deny her anything that you know she would welcome and desire from you. Sleep protracted in the mornings to the detriment of pious exercises and the works of the ministry, haste in celebrating Mass and in Church functions, eagerness to gain from the exercise of the ministry, hours lost in useless secular affairs, frequent visits to certain persons, looking at and losing time with everything that presents itself, are not things that a good priest will do, and certainly cannot be pleasing to Mary; I must therefore abstain from them. And then, in order to please this Mother, I will make some act of mortification: I will cast down my eyes, suppress that word, deny myself that amusement; I will make a visit to the church, practice some devotion, some act of virtue. I know that there is no harm in this, that there is no obligation to do that, but I know also that they provide an occasion to please Mary, I will therefore give her the pleasure. Give me a priest who allows himself to be guided by this thought during the day, and without seeking any other indication, I will give you a true and devoted son of Mary.

✣ He Will Model His Life on that of Her Divine Son

The second means, no less essential, by which we can become pleasing to Mary is to make ourselves true copies, true portraits of our great Exemplar, her Divine Son. Our Divine Redeemer on the Cross, with His own lips, entrusted us to the care of the tender heart of His Blessed Mother. He left us to her to have instead of Himself, to occupy His place in her heart, so that in looking after us, loving us, working for us, she regards us as holding the place of her Son. Mary, as was natural, knew to its depths the spirit and the Heart of her Divine Son: she held Him in her arms, she had the care of Him for thirty years, she was constantly present at His discourses during the three years of His public life, she was present at the end when He hung on the Cross. All that, besides what she knew by other extraordinary means, rendered her conscious of the wishes and even identified her with the designs of her Divine Son, for she saw His objects, His wishes, His desires, His designs; she knew the importance, the nature and the scope of His mission; the ways and means He used; the eagerness, patience and charity with which He labored to attain His objects; she knew the standard, the regulations, the lessons and example that He left His priests to whom He gave the charge of continuing His mission. Bearing this in mind, I ask you how can you expect that Mary will be satisfied and content with a priest whom, having been left to her and put in her charge as another son, she sees different from, and out of tone and harmony with her Divine Son; different in his tendencies, discordant in his affections, in his ends and his mode of working? Fine consolation that for a poor mother who having lost a respectful, obedient and affectionate Son, sees substituted another, indocile, cold, and disrespectful. Every look and every word of his would only serve to render more bitter the loss of the first, and more painful the exchange.

Who then among priests can be regarded as truly devoted sons of Mary? That priest, and that priest alone who renders himself conformable to the original, that priest who forms in himself a copy, a portrait of the great Son of Mary; that is to say, a priest who is hardworking and zealous, a priest who keeps himself aloof from the tumult and intrigues of the world, who watches carefully over himself and seeks no other end but the honor and glory of his God and the salvation of souls; so that, to use our earthly way of expressing it, every time that Mary looks down from Heaven and sees him, she will be able to hear reechoed and repeated to her: *"Woman, behold thy son."*[5] Mother look at your son, study him carefully; you will see that he is a real son because he has a real resemblance to your Divine Son: he thinks and works like your Son. Like Him, he is retired, attentive, obedient and affectionate to you; like Him, he works solely for the interest of the Eternal Father and does not occupy himself or lose his time with the wretched things of this earth. Conscious of and persuaded of the importance of his Heavenly mission, he goes on repeating the words of your Divine Son. *"I must be about my Father's business,"*[6] and like Him, goes wherever the glory and the will of his Heavenly Father demands. Ah! yes, I repeat, he is truly your son, reborn, risen again, a true copy; take him, embrace him, love him: *Woman, behold thy Son!* He, the true son of Mary, alone has the right to expect the special graces and favors of this Mother; to him deservedly will come direct the beautiful words: *"Behold thy Mother."*[7] Son, look and be consoled, I entrust you to My Mother, I place you in her arms. Oh, what a moment! What happy embrace of Mother and Son! In some danger, in some trouble, in some crisis of life and death, Mary will say: "Be of good heart, son, I am your Mother," and the priest will exclaim: "Save me, I am your son."

✤ FRUITS OF DEVOTION TO OUR BLESSED LADY

What shall I say to you about the happiness of a priest who is devoted to Mary? I do not intend to draw a picture of all that is reserved on earth for a son devoted to Mary, for it is impossible to conceive here below what things the maternal heart of Mary is capable of doing for her sons; only in Heaven will it be given to us to see and to measure her goodness and power. I shall merely recall to you that the help and intercession of Mary is not merely a pious belief, the effect of excessive, ill-directed piety, but is, as you know, a dogma of faith. The authority of the Church, the unanimous consent of the Fathers, the voice of all the ages leaves not the slightest doubt on this point; those mighty helps of Mary can therefore not only be hoped for but can be counted upon, specially by us priests, as a thing that is certain and unfailing, so long as we do nothing to deprive ourselves of them. This being certain, I shall mention for our consolation and comfort three special favors that we priests should expect from Mary, which are: the spirit of our ministry, a blessing on our labors and a great crown in Heaven proportioned to the love and zeal which we have had for her on earth.

(1) *The True Spirit of the Priestly Vocation*

It happens often that a priest is assailed and troubled by the fear of having been mistaken about his vocation, especially when his ministry, whether through his own fault or the fault of others, has been useless and sterile. There is no denying that this is a terrible thought. I shall therefore speak more willingly on the point and say that we may banish every kind of uneasiness and lay aside all fear, if we are truly devoted to Mary, for we may be certain that we have not made a mistake, since devotion to Mary is one of the first and essential signs of a sacerdotal vocation. The spirit of Mary is the same as that of her Divine Son; whoever belongs to her cannot therefore be far from Him. Even if it should happen that a priest entered the ministry without a vocation, if he sets himself to become a true child of Mary and succeeds in doing so, you may be certain that this good Mother of mercy will obtain from her Divine Son that which he had not; that spirit, those gifts, in a word, that combination of graces which will makes him a true minister of the Lord, just as if he had been really called from the beginning. Although he may have lost his way, although he may have been tossed about on a stormy sea, if he has recourse to Mary, he will reach the port and be saved: *He that shall find me shall find life;*[8] *I love them that love me.*[9] And what has a good priest to fear or dread when in every difficulty, in every trouble, in every embarrassment, he can say and repeat to himself: I am a son of Mary, it is God who has placed me in her hands, she has made me secure and I am certain that I shall be saved.

(2) *Assistance and Blessing in All Our Labors*

The second special fruit of our devotion to Mary is her assistance and blessing in all our labors in our ministry.

What heart was there ever in the world more zealous than the heart of Mary which cooperated in everything that her Divine Son wrought for the good of souls, and which itself felt at the foot of the Cross that ardor, that thirst with which He burned as he died. Ah, with what heart, with what promptness she will give her assistance to her son who demands it! You know better that I do the wonders and miracles of zeal that so many holy priests have wrought with the aid of Mary. The best fishers of souls have been always devoted to Mary, and it can be said frankly that the fruit of their sweat and labor increased in proportion to their devotion to Mary. How many accounts of conversions of sinners do we not find recorded in history to have been operated through Mary! And if we ourselves have sometimes done a little good, if we have gained some souls for her Son, if we only reflect a little, we will see the hand of Mary in it. A feast, a sermon on Mary, some pious practice in her honor, a grace received, sometimes just a look at her image may have been what enticed her and won her assistance. It has happened to ourselves more than once in the ministry that we expended both energy and time in vain to snatch from the hands of persons objects either evil or dangerous; that we found their hearts impervious to every reason and adamant against every loving attempt; but when the help of Mary was invoked and they were asked to give the object as a gift to her and not to refuse it to their good Mother, that they immediately yielded and surrendered. Let the priest therefore take Mary as his inseparable companion in his whole ministry; in the confessional with Mary, with her in the church and out of the church, in the house and out of the house, with people in health and with the sick; in fine, let him never give the signal of battle without invoking the aid of Mary. Let an *Ave Maria*, an aspiration, or even a look with faith towards an image of Mary, be the signal of combat, the first shot of the battle, and then let him not fear. She who has already conquered so many times, who already counts nineteen centuries of victories and triumphs, will never allow anyone who trusts in her to lose the battle.

(3) *A Special Crown in Heaven*

Finally, the priest devoted to Mary will have a special crown in Heaven proportioned to what he has done for her on earth: *"He that honoureth his mother is as one that layeth up a treasure."*[10] If such is the merit of a son who honors his earthly mother that he is compared by the Holy Spirit to a person who accumulates riches and treasures, what are we to say of a priest, of that son of Mary who spends and consumes his own life for her honor and glory? What treasures, what riches, what joys in Heaven! Every word said, every step taken, every labor endured for this good Mother will be remunerated, everything will get its reward in Heaven: *"They that explain me shall have life everlasting."*[11]

My dear Fathers and brothers in Christ, I shall conclude with this consoling thought: If you wish to walk securely and be certain of your salvation, if you aspire to a great crown in Heaven that will never fade, love and honor Mary, and strive to make her known, loved and honored by others. A son who has honored Mary will never perish. Let us cherish all those pious practices, those ways of paying her homage, which the Church approves and recommends in her honor. Let us speak often of her and from our hearts; let us show all the way to honor her, so that every heart on earth and every tongue will have an affection, a word of praise to offer to this Mother. Happy the priest and happy the people who are devoted to Mary. I shall finish with the beautiful words of the devout author of *Vita Sacerdotalis: Beatus ille sacerdos qui servus est Mariae, ipsique servos congregat! Beatus Populus qui illam colit! O Maria, serviant tibi populi; honorant te tribus . . . . Det mihi Dominus ut cultum tuum quocunque dilatare possim et hostes tuos debellare.*[12] Amen.

---

1 Serm. I, De Assumpt.
2 Spec. B. V. lect. 10.
3 I P. Q. XXV, A. 6 ad 4. m.
4 Luke 1:46, 49.
5 John 19:26.
6 Luke 2:49.
7 John 19:27.
8 Prov. 8:35.
9 Ibid. 17.
10 Ecclus. 3:5.
11 Ecclus. 24:31.
12 Arvisenet cap. XXI, 4, 6.

The Comforts and Consolations of a Priest

W E HAVE SEEN in the course of these exercises what the priest is and what he should be in the Church of the Lord; the sublimity of the office that he occupies, the virtues which correspond with it, the obstacles, dangers and difficulties which he has to overcome in the exercise of his ministry, and finally the great and manifold obligations which lie upon him. It is possible that all this may have the effect of exciting in us feelings of dismay, fear, alarm, uneasiness. Some of us may have thought or said to ourselves during these days: perhaps it might have been better if I had not become a priest, for who knows how I shall finish up? I see that it will be very difficult for me to be saved, but what am I to do? I am a priest and I cannot turn back; I must go ahead, and let what comes, come: and from this thought there arises melancholy, sadness and pusillanimity, and the priest falls into a kind of nonchalance, slackening of effort, and dissipation, as if in order to forget, if possible, an uncertain and doubtful future which terrifies him. And our enemy is too crafty and knows his trade too well not to come along and assail us in this manner; and at times it happens that a priest who has been able to keep his feet and successfully overcome all the fury of passion, shows signs of yielding in this kind of battle especially if, unhappily, he may have fallen into sin more than once. Ah, it is impossible, the devil goes on suggesting, that a man like you with all these sins to answer for should succeed in saving your soul! This kind of temptation, my dear Fathers, is too dangerous, the question is too important; we must therefore take away every doubt, clear away every difficulty and endeavor to guard ourselves against it at any cost.

God has called us to these Exercises in order to speak to us as a friend and a Father, and He has spoken clearly to us. He has spoken to us in many ways, now simply, now a little more severely; He has spoken to us by means of warnings, remorse, reproofs, examples, threats and promises. *God calls us in various and wonderful ways,* says St. Augustine. *He calls us by granting time for meditation,* and that was the voice with which God has spoken to us in the solitude of retreat; *He calls us by divine knowledge,* and how many new and vivid thoughts He has suggested to our minds! *He calls us by the rod of correction:* many times we have heard in the meditations of the scourges, the chastisements that God will one day be constrained to inflict on the priest who remains obdurate. But He calls us also *by the mercy of consolation,* and this is the voice He uses most frequently because, being more tender and appealing, it is more in accordance with His nature and therefore stronger and more efficacious for us. It is with this language of goodness and consolation that I wish to end my considerations and suggestions. I shall go over with you the motives of comfort which should animate and sustain a good priest in his apostolic career. The comforts and consolations of our priestly career will be the last subject to be considered, and I wish it to be my parting handshake with you, my salute, my adieu on leaving you, but an adieu of peace, consolation and comfort; an adieu of strength and courage to animate us to bear invincibly and unwaveringly the burden of those days which still remain for each of us to suffer and to labor in the vineyard of the Lord.

✧ MOTIVES FOR CONSOLATION:

(1) *The Apostolate of the Priest Is a Divine Work*

There are three principal thoughts which should animate and sustain the priest in the exercise of his ministry and be a source of great comfort to him. The first is that our apostolate is not a human institution, a work of man, but a work of God, and that accordingly it will remain firm and unshakable in the midst of all the shocks and assaults of the world. The second is that God, having called us to that great apostolate, has at the same time strengthened us and furnished us with all the gifts and qualities that are necessary for us to fulfill and exercise this apostolate. The third is that God, not content with furnishing us with these lights and graces, has pledged His word and promised us very special assistance reserved for us alone.

"*Ye men of Israel,*" said Gamaliel to the Council of the Jews, "*take heed to yourselves what you intend to do, as touching these men . . . . For, if this counsel or this work be of men, it will come to nought. But, if it be of God, you cannot overthrow it, lest perhaps you be found even to fight against God.*"[1] The work of the Apostles is still our work, the cause of those times is the cause of our days, and will be so until the consummation of the world. What comfort, my dear Fathers, should not this be for a priest when, in his endeavor to animate his faith, he thinks that the work for which he labors suffers and exhausts himself is the work of God, and that it rests securely under the shadow of its Founder and under the shield of His word that can never fail! Let the world and the powers of Hell do as they will; they will never make that great work one iota more or less than what has been determined.

Perhaps someone will say: this is true when we speak of the Church or of the apostolate in general, but not of each one of us priests. It is true of each of us in a certain sense. We know that when we speak of the Church we mean the congregation of all the Faithful scattered over the world under the rule of their respective pastors, who themselves are united together and subject to one visible and supreme Head. The apostolate then or ministry of the Church is nothing else than that operated by each of these pastors and their assistants, each in his proper sphere, for the good of the Faithful, through the means established by God Himself, or by the Church in His name. Therefore, when each of us works as a priest, whether we celebrate Mass or preach or administer the Sacraments or occupy ourselves in any other way for the good of souls, this ministry divided and scattered among the individual members forms a united whole which the forces of the world and the powers of Hell will never be able to overthrow.

✣ THE PRIEST WILL HOWEVER, HAVE TO
SUFFER PERSECUTION

The protection, however, will not prevent the world from molesting us and making us suffer; we must therefore expect it and be prepared. When Gamaliel gave expression to that statement in the Council of the Jews, the Acts of the Apostles tell us that all approved of his opinion and acquiesced, but in what sense? They did not put the Apostles to death immediately as they had decided to do, but with all that, they molested them and they even had them scourged and charged them not to speak any more of the name of Jesus: "*They consented to him. And, calling in the apostles, after they had scourged them, they charged them that they should not speak at all in the name of Jesus.*"[2] The world was always so and will always be so: whether it rages or revenges because it cannot succeed in overcoming us, or whether it beguiles us in order to succeed in another way, it will not let us alone. That is its determined policy; we are an object of reproof and confusion to the world and an obstacle to its designs, and therefore the spirit of the world can never accommodate itself to the spirit of the Gospel, and for this reason it makes war on us; but great good results from the struggle: the triumph, namely, of our work. The ministers will suffer, it is true; they will be harassed, afflicted, oppressed, persecuted; but no matter, Religion, the Church, Christ will triumph. But how will they be able to stand firm in that struggle? How will they be able to endure it? God will assist them. That is the second comfort for a priest.

✠ The Lord Will Assist Us

The Lord has called us to this great apostolate; He has laid upon us immense and formidable responsibilities, and with this vocation He has placed us in the world as a target for attack and contradiction. Let us console ourselves however, for God has thought in good time of providing us with the necessary equipment. When God had decided to send Moses to Pharao, He appeared to him and ordered him to go to him. Moses was afraid and sought to decline the task. Courage! said the Almighty; why these fears? I shall be with you; if Pharao is firm and obstinate, I shall be firmer and more obstinate. And to Jeremias likewise he said, Courage! O Prophet Jeremias, unloose your tongue, cast in the face of the King and the people their villainy, and warn them of My anger and My chastisement. Jeremias hesitated and said: I am but a child and I hardly know how to speak: "Be quiet," repeated the Lord: "Say *not: I am a child: for thou shalt go to all that I shall send thee . . . . Be not afraid at their presence: for I am with thee to deliver thee, saith the Lord.*"[3] If you read the history of the prophets you will see the same truth constantly asserted and verified.

✧ God Has Special Graces and Helps Prepared for Us

God has acted in like manner with us; with less external display such as would flatter our pride, if you will, but with no less security to us. God has called each one of us to the priesthood, and in calling us He has fixed the road for us, He has foreseen the dangers, the obstacles and the difficulties that we were to encounter, and in consequence He knows that we need knowledge, prudence, fortitude and other virtues. He has provided for all this with both ordinary and extraordinary helps; with lights, inspirations, protection and assistance. All has been, as it were, put aside for us, and it is as if the Lord had said to us: Look, I have thought of you, and I wish that you be My priest on earth, My minister, My co-operator in the saving of souls. I know all that is going to happen to you: I know that it will be impossible to go on without many obstacles and threats of various kinds; but do not be afraid, I have thought for you. You will need fortitude, fortitude you shall have; you will need prudence, wisdom, patience; you can count on them that they will be given you, each at the proper time. On certain occasions you will have to be greater than yourself, to go beyond what you are; do not fear, I tell you, I have accomplished that for others, I will renew it for you. It will suffice to read the lives and the doings of the many workers in the ministry in order to assure yourself of this truth. What obstacles and difficulties they encountered! What an uproar was raised against them and yet they succeeded! We ourselves in our state, in our own little endeavors, have been able to see how God has given His hand and guided us in the direction of certain affairs; what lights, what means, what counsels, what inspirations, that we may have perhaps thought were mere accidents! But they all came from above, and in fact the case could not have been otherwise.

✧ The Sacramental Grace of Holy Orders

The Fathers of the Church and all theologians are agreed in saying that in the very act in which God destines a person for a certain state, He puts at his disposal all the graces, lights and supernatural helps that will be necessary for him in each single circumstance during his life, and this is specially true when, as in our case, that state is initiated with a Sacrament. For we know that the Sacraments, besides conferring sanctifying grace, confer also another grace which is called sacramental, which consists in the totality of special helps which serve to make us carry out well the obligations we assume with the reception of the particular Sacrament. And reason itself is sufficient to convince us of this truth; for though our vocation is gratuitous and without any merit on our part, since it has been God's will to raise us so high, we have a corresponding right that He should help us and give us all the graces necessary to sustain us in the state to which He has called us. Accordingly, whatever be the distress in which we may find ourselves, whatever be the necessity or the want, I am sure that God will sustain us even though it be necessary to work a miracle; I speak of difficulty or distress in which my ministry, and not my caprice or passion, places me. And now tell me, should not that reflection be a great comfort for a priest? Come what may, let people conspire against me as much as they like, I am certain that God will help me and that I shall always conquer. It is not my own worthless person that will conquer, but God, and His honor and glory; I am certain that I shall come off victorious in this sense, and that everything will end in such a way that God will gain by it, and this suffices for me, for it is the best, and indeed the only victory for a priest.

✛ THE SPECIAL PROMISES MADE BY JESUS TO HIS APOSTLES

Add to this the special promises made to the Apostles for us, the following three of which we shall consider here: "*I will not leave you orphans*"[4]; "*I am with you all days, even to the consummation of the world*"[5]; and "*A hair of your head shall not perish.*"[6]

I will not leave you orphans. Do not believe that I could have the heart to leave you alone; *I am with you all days.* Here it is evident that He is speaking of us, and for what purpose has He remained with us? *A hair of your head shall not perish:* truly, if it was a mere man who had made these statements, we would say that he allowed himself to be carried away, and that he was using exaggerated language when He said that He had taken account of even the hairs of our head, and yet there is no exaggeration. It is God who speaks, and it is not lawful for us to restrict or limit His promises; if you have difficulty in believing, I will add still more: Whoever touches you; I do not say ill-treats you, but even touches you, touches Me to the quick, as if he touched the apple of My eye: "He *that despiseth you, despiseth me."*[7] *He that toucheth you toucheth the apple of my eye.*[8] Go forward therefore courageously, fear not this world that will make so many efforts to scare you, I have already beaten it to the ground, I have conquered it for you; "*Have confidence. I have overcome the world.*"[9] I do not know what more any priest who has a spark of faith could ask for; for which of us would have dared to carry our hopes so far if God Himself had not said it. Suppose a father had used such language with his son, tell me could he demand or desire any more?

But here doubts will be raised, which are never wanting, because it is too much in the devil's interest to raise them. If I do not cooperate, what use is it that so many helps have been prepared? I will have to yield all the same, and succumb to the weight of difficulties. Ah! my dear Fathers, that is understood; I am speaking to priests of good will who are disposed to cooperate and to contribute all they can on their part. If I say that a healthy, robust, young man will travel the road securely, I do not at all mean that in order to walk securely it is enough to have good legs; he will walk if he puts his will to it, but he is master of himself and can refuse to walk if he likes. Thus it is with the priest who has all the helps given for a good priest to help him on his way, and who refuses to use them. We, I hope, are not among such.

✣ THE QUESTION OF A VOCATION

That is all very fine so far, someone will say, but how is a priest to get out of his difficulties who has entered the priesthood without a vocation? That consideration is more grave, so we must make a few reflections on it. In the first place, I am speaking to an assembly of priests, each one of whom has, I hope, in his heart the comforting testimony that he has been called, and with that, the difficulty vanishes. But since the case is too important to pass over, we shall speak of the worst supposition; that someone should find himself in the clerical state without a vocation.

✣ ALL MISTAKES CAN BE REMEDIED

I shall begin by stating in advance two points which are absolutely certain: (1) It is certain that a person who has not been called to this state cannot find prepared for himself the corresponding helps, all the more so, when many extraordinary helps are required, as is the case in the state of the priesthood; (2) such a person certainly commits a grave sin, and if he dies impenitent, it is evident that he is in a state of damnation.* But it is also certain that such a man can repent, and that when he repents he will be pardoned, since there is no sin that is irremissible, and when the sin is remitted, he can become a good priest and live in such a way as to be saved, since no one is damned by necessity. This, according to the teaching of good theologians, cannot be denied, but how are we to reply to the question and solve the difficulty? The following is in a few words the solution. This man by prayer can obtain from the mercy of God what in right and justice is not due to him, and this is nothing more than a corollary or consequence of what has been said about prayer, namely that, provided the requisite conditions are fulfilled, it is of infallible efficacy. The most essential among these conditions is that what is asked for must have reference to salvation, and this is so in the case I make. Therefore, an ecclesiastic who is in doubt, or even who is fully certain that he has entered the clerical state without a vocation; can pray for forgiveness in some such terms as the following: O Lord, I know and confess my sin. I am unworthy, I am an intruder who have entered the ministry as a robber; this place was not for me. If I had not actually entered, I would take good care not to profane it; if I could withdraw, I would do so at once for my sin is great, but it is not possible for me to withdraw, and for this I grieve exceedingly. O Lord, I know that Thou willest not the death or the loss of a sinner, this I know and believe. I therefore throw myself into the arms of Thy mercy and I ask pardon and help. Grant me Thy divine assistance to carry the burden that is crushing me, and to the multitude of Thy great mercies add this new triumph by saving this poor sinner. Can we suppose that language of this kind, that a heart so penetrated with compunction, will be repulsed, and find a refusal in the Heart of God?

But someone may say: It will be difficult for one to repent who has become a priest without a vocation, and more difficult still to persevere in repentance and in a good life. In this case I repeat what I have already said: any person who has sinned, not merely a priest, but any sinner who can but does not repent or does not persevere, certainly cannot be saved,

---

*See Second Conference, p. 19. By a person without a vocation the Saint means one who has entered the priesthood purely and solely for material gain.

but it will be through his own fault, and he could have been saved if he had had the true will. So then to conclude I say: give me a priest who leads a good life, works as a priest, is a priest both in name and deed, and I will not go enquiring whether he has been called or not, I will say only and will say always: let him persevere to the end and he will be saved.

✤ God Rewards the Good Will

Another priest will say: I have little ability, little aptitude, very poor health, what I undertake is very little, and even that little I find it difficult to do successfully; all are doing something, all are laboring, but I do not even know what to do. It must be either that I was not called, or that I have not the requisite gifts, or that I do not know how to correspond with the graces of the Lord; consequently, I am very far from having that comfort and consolation in my state; I find it rather a bed of thorns, and a wellspring of troubles and fears. I shall reply briefly by saying: it may be all that you say, you do little, or even you do nothing, but I ask: is there fault or not on your part? If there is fault, why do you not correct it? Why do you not live a more retired life, give yourself to study, deprive yourself of some of your amusements, spend more time at prayer, in a word, live as a good priest? If you are not willing to do so, I also know that you cannot have that consolation of which I spoke, and not even I, with all my eagerness to send you home quiet and tranquil in conscience, can procure it for you. But if it is not your fault, and you can be sure of that from an examination of your life, from the advice and light given by your confessor, and much more from the retreat that you have just made, then I tell you frankly: cast away all fear and alarm; if you cannot apply yourself, or succeed in anything at all, that does not matter, it is a sign that God does not demand success from you. He will see your good will, He will see that you are trying, that you are making an effort and that nothing comes from your effort. By these efforts, you have already conquered, the glory of God has been safeguarded and, in addition, you have the merit that comes from the pain and sorrow you experience from seeing yourself incapable and powerless to labor for God, from being aware that your efforts are useless and vain, since the Lord knows how much a zealous priest suffers and grieves in these circumstances.

✥ THE MINISTRY OF THE PRIEST ABOUNDS IN CONSOLATIONS

For the rest, my dear Fathers, all of us here must not omit to thank the Lord with all our heart for having called us to a ministry which abounds in so many consolations and which is capable of making of this earth a kind of Paradise; this is a new motive for our common comfort and encouragement.

I do not wish to deny, for I have already stated it, that many crosses and contradictions are met with in our state, but the consolations which this ministry gives to the heart are so many and so great that it can be boldly affirmed that what we suffer bears no proportion to what we enjoy. St. Augustine has said: *There is nothing more difficult or more laborious than the office of the priesthood, but with God, there is nothing more blessed.*[10] And the great Apostle, St. Paul, exclaimed: "*Who then shall separate us from the love of Christ? Shall tribulation? Or distress? Or famine? Or nakedness? Or danger? Or persecution? Or the sword?*"[11] "*I am filled with comfort; I exceedingly abound with joy in all our tribulation.*"[12]

It suffices to read the lives of the innumerable workers in the vineyard of the Lord to see and touch with the hand the joy, the satisfaction, the consolation that they found in their ministry, and in our own days how many good priests, in spite of the contempt cast on our character, would not change the priestly garb for all the delights and riches in the world.

✥ THE CONSOLATION OF LABORING FOR THE GLORY OF GOD

I do not wish on the present occasion to speak to you of the reward that awaits God's minister in Heaven, of that chalice of delights that he will drink forever in that kingdom of happiness; neither shall I dwell on that peace and calm and tranquillity which the testimony of a good conscience gives. I leave aside also the sweetness and the holy and joyful affections with which the good priest who has labored for the Lord will terminate his days, and I shall confine myself to the consideration of these consolations which belong exclusively to us, because they are the effect of our ministry. What does the priest do during the day?

Observe him in the course of his day in everything he does: he thinks, he prays, he studies, he preaches, he labors. Observe him again and study him closely; you will notice that he is a man of deep thought, that he must have some very important business on hand, something very great to get done, and you are not mistaken. His whole thought, his whole occupation, the great affair on hand is this: to procure, increase, expand the glory of God upon earth, to snatch souls from Hell and increase the number of the blessed in Heaven; to strive continuously to spare His Lord some offense and to diminish the number of sins in the world. O holy and divine occupation! Oh, my dear Fathers, if we only have a little faith, we have a Heaven on earth! All around me people are laboring in this world, they are studying, they are exhausting themselves, they are wearing themselves out till they can do no more; but they labor for the mud and dirt of this world, for empty, useless folly, while I labor for God and for His glory! People in other walks of life labor and are often ill requited; their labors often displease people and produce no result whatever; while, on the contrary, when I work and labor I am certain to please, certain to obtain a reward, certain to be well paid. The whole world is working and striving, and in a short time all the fruit of its labors will disappear as if it had never existed; I work and labor too, but the fruit of my labors will be eternal, as that God is eternal to whose service I am consecrated.

✣ Grandeur and Nobility of the Ministry of the Priesthood

And what shall we say of the nobility and grandeur of this ineffable occupation? I labor, I exhaust myself for God! Who is that man, however holy, learned, or fervent he may be, or who is that angel who can estimate, comprehend and esteem as they should these terms and these words? A God who entrusts Himself to a man and hands over to him the care of His honor and glory; a man who consecrates himself to God to guard and extend that glory! Ah, priests of the Lord and my dear companions, I prefer to be silent than to speak of this at the risk of expressing myself badly, of speaking on a subject that is beyond my understanding and yours. At the feet of the crucifix, in the presence of our Eucharistic Lord, let us meditate on and turn over in our minds this truly great and consoling thought: I live, I work, I labor for God, and under this aspect, I am greater, more fortunate, more blessed than any man in the world even the inhabitants of Heaven, since the blessed in Heaven gain in God because they delight in Him, while on earth God gains in the priest who expands and extends His honor and glory.

If all priests understood the beauty, the sweetness, the grandeur of this occupation, what added zeal they would have to use well the time destined for such an exalted enterprise! Is it not pitiful to see how so many priests allow to pass badly, or idly and uselessly, those days which are the envy of Heaven itself? I think that ever so many priests who are now in Heaven would be ready to descend to the earth again and to accept as many days as God would allow them in this vale of tears and misery in exchange for an equal number of days in Heaven, just to be able to have the satisfaction of increasing even a little the glory of their Lord. And shall we who have these days, who possess them though they are escaping from our hands so swiftly, devote them to the foolish and empty things of this world, thus bartering the glory of God for a little of the slime of this earth?

✥ To Obtain this Consolation We Must Labor With a Right Intention

But in order to be able to relish and enjoy these comforts and consolations of our ministry it is necessary first of all to labor, and to labor unweariedly without losing a moment, for every second of it is a treasure which if lost can never be recovered. And this is not enough: it is necessary above all that in laboring we do not seek or look for anything else but purely and solely the glory of God. Purity of intention is so necessary and important that I cannot refrain from saying a word about it which I shall leave you as a summary and memento of what I have said to you during these days.

Believe me, my dear Fathers, the want in us priests is usually more in the heart than in the hands. What I mean to say is that, with the exception of a few, the general body of priests labor hard, but what value have mere external, apparent, superficial works, if the marrow and substance, which are a right end and a pure intention of pleasing God and seeking only His glory, be wanting? It is true of nearly all priests that they labor; but some labor for gain and temporal interests; others labor for ambition and for a little human glory; others, who are talented, labor according to their natural bent; others in fine, labor through custom and habit. These are usually the motive causes impelling very many priests to work, even those who are occupied from morning till night in works more or less directly concerned with their ministry. It is true that in that Mass, in that sermon, in that other function, the object aimed at is not just material gain, but at the same time is it not true that certain calculations and schemes are based on the external occupation of the ministry? That there are intrigues, that differences and quarrels arise, not indeed for the glory of God, but for some human motive such as gain that someone will not relinquish? I will not here speak of these matters or of those who might find themselves involved in them; you can recall to your minds what I said on them when treating of the subject of scandal; I allude only to what has relation to the motive of our actions.

And in the first place, speaking of intentions, someone might ask me: Is is wrong, is it a sin, is it a grave sin, to have our temporal interest as our end in the exercise of the ministry, or to do some act that is proper to our state for the temporal gain annexed to it? To answer that question it will be necessary to make a distinction. If the ecclesiastic totally excludes the glory of God, and much more, if his affection for gain is so great that it causes him to do the action without caring how he does it, or whether he has the requisite dispositions, it is certainly a sin, and sometimes even a grave sin. Oh! I would not dream of doing the like of that, I seem to hear someone say, no doubt, I have a useful end in view, but I always have at least the implicit intention of the glory of God. Well then I say; when the action is done well and with proper dispositions, and there is only question of uniting to it, or mixing up different intentions, the priest loses or gains in proportion. He loses in proportion as he allows earthly and human motives to enter in; and he gains according as the eye, or the intention, is pure and holy. But let us observe what kind of loss he suffers: it is the loss of what is most precious in Heaven or on earth, which is a degree of merit here below and a corresponding degree of glory in Heaven. The losses are irreparable, for they can never be made good in all eternity, and they are all the more painful because with very little care which would cost us no labor, merely by changing our motive, we could have avoided them. This holds good for motives of gain, as well as for the other motives that I have mentioned.

✧ FOR WHOM OR FOR WHAT DO WE LABOR?

For whom or for what do we labor and fatigue ourselves? This we can deduce from what can be seen and known. If there be question of doing something striking, something which is appreciated in the world, we readily grasp at the opportunity and do it with all possible solicitude and even exert ourselves to the utmost; but if it be something common and ordinary, such as teaching catechism, visiting the sick, assisting the dying, we either seek pretexts for evading it or we accept it with reluctance and do it with bad grace and bad will. If our actions do not succeed in gaining a little approval and applause, we are sad, melancholic, and feel a void within ourselves, and it appears that we have lost our time. What does all this signify? That our hearts are more warmed by the smoke of vanity than on fire for the glory of God. Ask another who is constantly occupied and labors at his work why he attends to this rather than to that, why he selects a place, a duty, an occupation rather of one kind than another, and you will get the reply: because that study, that place, that life pleases him, is to his taste, contents him, satisfies him; it is therefore the satisfaction, the gratification of his will and inclination that is in question. And where does the glory of God come in? Oh! that is not excluded; but in the meantime we suffer losses, and if it is nothing else, we gain little in proportion to our labor as I have already remarked. Oh! What a life you lead! You are always alone, living apart from the world, always engaged in reading or at your favorite occupation! You are living the life of a priest! Oh! don't be surprised; that is my custom, my habit; if I were to do otherwise, I could not stand it, I would suffer. Here we have another mistress who commands, custom; we live, we work by custom, and may God grant that through it we may not suffer great losses of merit for our actions.

✧ WE SHOULD RENEW OUR GOOD INTENTION
    FREQUENTLY

How are we to prevent such frequent and notable robbery as wrong motives for our actions may cause us? There is one means only, but it is certain and infallible and at the same time very easy; it requires neither time, nor effort, nor labor to adopt it; it is to take a most firm resolution, and to renew it as often as possible, to act always completely and solely from the motive of pleasing God and for His honor and glory. Let us put far away from our actions every idea of gain, of glory, of the applause of the world. It would be the greatest folly on our part to seek to please and serve a world which, as we can see, everywhere despises us, scoffs at us, makes little of us and seeks by every means to humiliate us. This thought of the ingratitude of the world in our regard should serve to make us resolve to direct all our intentions, all our affections, all our desires to labor for God. But other very strong incitements are not wanting to urge us to make this resolution.

✢ Purity of Intention is Necessary in Order to Enjoy Consolation

In the first place, if we wish to feel and, as it were, touch with our hands, the consolations and sweetness of our state, purity of intention is indispensable. Take away the pure intention from the exercise of our ministry, and you have a most irksome, tedious, burdensome state. What greater annoyance, what more insupportable life for a priest who does not act for God than to have to recite daily a quantity of prayers for which he has no taste! To spend hours in the confessional listening to nothing else but misery and wretchedness; to be called, night or day, now to a sick person, now to one dying; now to be occupied in studies that weary and annoy him, now to be disturbed by a thousand vexatious problems that crop up daily. Thus it is one day and the next and the next; always the same things, the same annoyances without ever having time completely free to spend according to his own pleasure. Hence it comes that things are done with such bad grace, with such displeasure and repugnance that everyone notices it. A priest who does not work for God easily gets impatient; he complains, and sometimes he even goes so far as to say, to the scandal of the good, that if he had known before his Ordination that he would have such annoyances as a priest, he would have thought twice. And why all this noisy complaining? The reason is clear; because he does not act for God, because he does not work for Him. Take on the other hand a priest far more heavily burdened with troubles of all kinds but animated with a different spirit, who in all his actions seeks only the will of God and His honor and glory, and you will see immediately a very different spirit, very different manners and methods. Observe with what hilarity and joy, that shows itself even in his exterior, he comports himself in the midst of the most vexatious and annoying circumstances. And what would we say if we could enter into his heart! Whatever that priest is engaged in, he has always the consolation of Heaven within him.

✤ Purity of Intention Stimulates Activity

In addition, purity of intention is of great help and provides a strong stimulus to do our actions well and to render them useful and fruitful to our neighbor. What a motive, what an incitement have I not, to do my actions with promptness, gravity and devotion, if I am fully convinced that what I am doing, the Sacrament I am administering, the Mass I am celebrating, the carrying out of that function, the works for my neighbor, are not for myself, are not for any man, but for God, and that He sees these things, that He approves of them, that He takes pleasure in them and is satisfied with them!

✤ It Draws Down the Blessings of God

Finally, purity of intention will draw down the blessings of God on all our labors. It is vain to hope that God will bless our actions when He sees that we make use of the aids which He gives us for ends beside those for which they were intended and that, instead of seeking His honor and glory, we are looking only to our own interests. God will condemn, He will curse those actions in the performance of which we abuse His help as He threatened the priest of the Old Law that He would do: "*I will curse your blessings: yea I will curse them, because you have not laid it to heart.*"[13] Furthermore, if we rob Him of His glory He will not allow us to find ours, and the ambitious priest will find his humiliation and shame where he expected his triumph and honor: "*Therefore have I made you contemptible and base before all people, as you have not kept my ways.*"[14] But if, on the contrary, we really have at heart to do a little good in our ministry so as not to find ourselves one day weary and exhausted with empty hands, let us renounce personal ambition, let us set ourselves decisively to labor for God and, turning to Him, let us

say to Him and repeat it often: O Lord, this is for Thee, I do this for
Thee. Be it understood between us that nothing comes to me, that it is
completely and entirely for Thee, for by every right it belongs to Thee.
Let the world say and think what it likes; let it praise me, let it exalt
me, I pay no heed to its gossip; the world is blind and ignorant, and
does not know what it is saying. The world had no part in making me a
priest, it should have no part in my ministry. It was for Thee alone that
I entered into this state, for Thee alone I wish to labor, to me belong the
confusion and the shame and the blame for not doing Thy work in a
worthy fashion. And if there should be any fruit from my labors, know
that I absolutely wish, desire and maintain that it is all Thine, because
Thou alone meritest it. Give me a priest of this spirit, and you will see
how much good he will be able to do, and what great consolations he
will have in thinking of those souls that he is helping every day, and of
those sins and offenses that he is sparing his Lord. What it means to
save a soul or help a soul to be saved, what it means to prevent a sin and
spare an offense to the Lord, we shall understand only when we are in
Heaven. The whole world combined would not he able to estimate or
recompense the work that a priest does when he prevents a sin or when
he saves a soul. It is a work so great that all the Saints together could do
nothing nobler or greater; this work the priest accomplishes and often
obtains with a groan or sigh, with a word or a prayer.

---

1 Acts 5:35, 39.
2 Acts 5:39, 40.
3 Jerem. 1:7.
4 John 14:18.
5 Matt. 28:20.
6 Luke 21:18.
7 Luke 10:16.
8 Zacc. 2:8.
9 John 16:33.
10 Epist. 148, ad Valer.
11 Romans 8:35.
12 2 Corinth. 7:4.
13 Malach. 2:2.
14 Malach. 2:9.

CONCLUSION

Labor to Gain Souls for Heaven and to Prevent Sins

O my dear Fathers, if I were to say all that should be said on these topics I would never finish, however, the time has come to finish. Souls and sins, that is the conclusion, that is the end of my talks; souls and sins are like two rings in which I enclose all that I have been saying these days. Give me O Lord, let us say with the great apostle of charity, St. Francis de Sales, give me souls to save; give me sins to combat and destroy. Let us leave the vanities and the foolish things of this world to whoever wants them and let us apply ourselves to the task of recruiting souls for Heaven. I hope and pray that there may be much fruit from our retreat, but if I could hope for nothing more than that each of us here present would prevent a single sin in his life, I would die too content, for I am certain that there would be many voices calling out for mercy for both me and you.

Courage then, my dear Fathers, every day let us work to help some soul, to save some soul, to prevent some sin by preaching and talking with those in health and those sick, in the confessional and in the pulpit. If it is only given us to prevent one sin, the day will be for us too grand and too happy. And when we cannot do otherwise than we are doing, when we have not the convenience or the opportunity, let us turn to God and say to Him sincerely: O Lord, I wish to have something to offer to Thee today, I am Thy workman, I am a soldier who is fighting for Thee, I do not wish to leave the field without having the fruit of my day's work in my hands. I do not ask Thee for riches, health, comfort or honors. I ask for what my compeers have the right to wish for, souls and sins; grant that through my prayer one sin less be committed today and that one soul more be saved. Give me this recompense, O Lord, and

255

Thou shalt have the happiest and most contented priest in the world. Oh, how many more people there would be in Heaven, how many disorders would be spared this vale of misery, if every priest had a little of this zeal, of this faith! Courage, my dear Fathers, I repeat for the last time, the struggle will perhaps be a little hard and the labor a little long, but let us think of the end of the work, of the recompense. Let us think that the Lord delays not but that the day is approaching when He will reckon up the accounts of our labors and give us our recompense: *Non tardat Dominus . . . . Properantes in die iudicii . . . . satagite, fratres, ... ut per bona opera certam vestram vocationem faciatis . . . . molesta est lucta, sed fructuosa: quod resistentem fatigat, vincentem coronat: hic contendimus ut alibi coronemur.*

Let such be our ardour and our zeal on earth, and such will be the glorious lot for me and for you in Heaven!

LaVergne, TN USA
04 February 2011
215344LV00001B/4/P